Forensics of Capital

Forensics of Capital

MICHAEL RALPH

The University of Chicago Press
Chicago and London

Michael Ralph is assistant professor of social and cultural analysis at New York University.

The University of Chicago Press, Chicago 60637
The University of Chicago Press, Ltd., London
© 2015 by The University of Chicago
All rights reserved. Published 2015.
Printed in the United States of America

24 23 22 21 20 19 18 17 16 15   1 2 3 4 5

ISBN-13: 978-0-226-19843-9 (cloth)
ISBN-13: 978-0-226-19857-6 (paper)
ISBN-13: 978-0-226-19860-6 (e-book)
DOI: 10.7208/chicago/9780226198606.001.0001

Library of Congress Cataloging-in-Publication Data
Ralph, Michael (Anthropologist), author.
    Forensics of capital / Michael Ralph.
        pages cm
    Includes bibliographical references and index.
    ISBN 978-0-226-19843-9 (cloth : alkaline paper)—
ISBN 978-0-226-19857-6 (paperback : alkaline paper)—
ISBN 978-0-226-19860-6 (e-book)   1. Senegal—Foreign economic
relations—History. 2. Senegal—Politics and government. 3. Senegal—Social
conditions. 4. Senegal—Economic conditions. 5. Capital—Social aspects—
Senegal.   I. Title.
    DT549.62.R35 2015
    332'.04109663—dc23

                                                              2014045145

CONTENTS

PROLOGUE

"People always think that we are here to get oil. But Senegal doesn't even have any oil." Lieutenant Colonel Matt Sousa is the senior defense officer, defense attaché, and chief of the Office of Security Cooperation for the US Army at the US embassy in Dakar. He is eager to set my mind at ease as we chat in his office on what we later discover is the final day of the January 25 uprising in Cairo's Tahrir Square.

It's true that Senegal does not even rank in the top ten of Africa's largest oil producers.[1] But it's strange that he didn't acknowledge growing interest in foraging for oil along Africa's Atlantic coast and throughout the continent.

More than a decade ago, *Le Monde Diplomatique* published an article titled "The New Gulf Oil States," where it discussed telling shifts in the geopolitics of oil post–9/11. "The United States used to attach little importance to Africa," the French publication observed in 2003, "but now it is reviewing its oil sources strategy." "Sub-Saharan Africa, with its good quality oil reserves, could account for 25% of all US crude oil imports by 2015."[2]

Sousa's comments are even more curious in the context of a 2006 book he wrote with James Forest, then an assistant dean and professor at the US Military Academy: *Oil and Terrorism in the New Gulf: Framing U.S. Energy and Security Policies for the Gulf of Guinea*. In a section titled "Oil and Security in West Africa: A Chance to Get It Right," Forest and Sousa note, "The Gulf of Guinea presents some unique opportunities, quite distinct from the Middle East. Oil is plentiful, the people are incredibly poor, and state infrastructures are weak." Sousa and Forest are keen to identify the political virtues of this region where "oil is plentiful": "[R]adical Islam has only a limited influence in the region, and the US has good relations with many African nations." Hence, a proposal presented as a scholarly conclusion: "This analysis suggests that [the United States] must adopt a long-term, integrated approach to protecting our energy and national security interests in West Africa."[3] Of course, by the time I met Sousa, a Nigerian group that went by the name Boko Haram (meaning "Western education is forbidden") had gained notoriety for launching intermittent, yet fatal, assaults against civilians in the effort to destabilize the Nigerian government and to curb US influence. By the time of my visit to the Office of Security Cooperation in 2011, affiliates of al-Qaeda were making their way into West Africa via conduits in Mali. In other words, the forensic calculus involving Africa's oil-rich countries had been transformed, with implications for Senegal's diplomatic standing.

In subsequent conversations when I reminded Sousa about his prognosis for US foreign policy in Africa some years before, he noted that his 2003 publication with Forest carried a disclaimer that it was written from the perspective of a civilian and not with strategic interests in mind. Still, I wondered what to make of the fact that a US military officer had helped to write a book emphasizing the strategic advantages of pursuing oil in Africa but would actively discount this possibility in conversation with scholars interested in these issues. Sousa's stated position was especially odd given the way Senegal has attempted to position itself in recent years.

On August 1, 2011, the World Trade Center of New Orleans, together with the Republic of Senegal Consulate of Louisiana, hosted a visit by Her Excellency Fatou Danielle Diagne, Senegal's ambassador to the United States, as part of an Oil and Gas, Maritime, and Investment Roundtable.

An Associated Press news blast discussing the roundtable noted that Senegal had already "recorded promising geological surveys that are ramping up interest in onshore and offshore petroleum exploration." The article further noted that "the Port of Dakar is the first major port-of-call from Europe" and that it is "served by several major shipping lines." The panel discussion featured "geologists making presentations on oil, natural gas and mining projects in the Senegal Basin." In this connection, it's worth noting that President Macky Sall of Senegal—who in March 2012 secured his bid for the nation's highest office amid widespread protests and public consternation concerning suspected corruption by the incumbent president Abdoulaye Wade—is a petroleum engineer.

Does becoming an oil-rich country mean adopting a particular political profile? The presence of oil reserves creates political complications that articulate with the potential for acts of extralegal violence deemed "terrorism" but are not reducible to them. Nigeria's oil complex has caused widespread environmental devastation for all the billions it has generated. Intellectuals and activists attempting to critique the way US oil executives dictate federal policy are routinely intimidated. An alarming number have died under mysterious circumstances.[4]

The question of mortality surfaces in other ways. While African states boast that oil engenders economic opportunities for their citizens, oil firms routinely contract with desperate workers from diverse nations of the global South to reduce the liability engendered by a workplace injury or fatal accident.[5] Given this, what are we to make of the fact that the present period of US interest in African oil coincides with efforts to construct an expansive military infrastructure in Africa—stretching from Dakar to Djibouti?[6] What does it mean that Dakar is pivotal to this elaborate operation? My interview with Sousa took place amid widespread discontent with the national government in Senegal—including what many human rights organizations cited as excessive force by police and military personnel—even as US military and embassy officials lavished praise on Senegal as a model democracy.

Should Senegalese people be heartened or concerned that some of the primary architects of this massive plan to develop a security apparatus that benefits economic "development" seem oblivious to the burgeoning relationship between governance and petropolitics emerging in Senegal? Is this an aberrant event in the landscape of Senegalese politics? Or might it be evidence that there is more to Senegal's favorable diplomatic standing than is readily apparent?

One of Africa's few democracies, Senegal has long been considered a leader of moral, political, and economic development on the continent. We tend to assume that any such nation has achieved favorable international standing on its own merits. In what follows, I interrogate this conventional thinking, demonstrating that Senegal's diplomatic standing was strategically forged at key historical junctures and is today entirely contingent on the consensus of wealthy and influential nations and international lending agencies.

Pragmatic decisions have historically structured Senegal's economic and political trajectory, such as its opposition to Soviet involvement in African liberation—despite itself being a socialist state—and its support for the United States–led war on terror, despite its population's being predominantly Muslim. In what follows, I show how these decisions have helped Senegal to secure diplomatic standing as a democratic exemplar and a highly credit-worthy nation even as its dedication to due process has faltered and its domestic economy has suffered. Exploring these and many other aspects of Senegal's interface with the international community, I demonstrate how the effort to establish a profile for any given country or demographic is fraught with contradictions that are illuminating once we begin to grapple with rather than ignore them.

INTRODUCTION

In July 1895, a team of French soldiers was dispatched to arrest Amadu Bamba. Once colonial authorities had him in their custody, they brought him before the Privy Council of the governor-general, which found him guilty of waging jihad against the French. Bamba was swiftly deported to the colony of French Equatorial Africa.

Although Amadu Bamba claimed to be a mere scholar of Islam and a mentor to followers in his faith, the French found it suspicious that the ranks of his devotees had grown exponentially during the past few years. As evidence that he had been conspiring against them, colonial officials noted that some of their long-standing enemies had recently joined his flock.

To combat this perceived threat, French authorities commissioned regional leaders to prepare intelligence reports on Amadu Bamba's activities. Colonial officials were tasked with reporting on his conduct. On July 10, 1895, a colonial administrator known as Monsieur Leclerc collaborated with an intelligence agent in a report that claimed the religious leader had secretly acquired a massive cache of weapons. They accused Bamba of trying to turn regional chiefs who had been hired by colonial officials to spy on him. Leclerc conceded that none of his spies had yet found any proof that a jihad was under way, although they "had been monitoring" Bamba "and his disciples' activities for some time." Yet instead of encouraging the French to revise their stated position, Leclerc argued that the absence of evidence affirmed that Bamba was a formidable adversary.[1]

France's network of spies included people with ties to area kings and high-ranking bureaucrats who resented the influence Bamba had managed to acquire during the decades following the formal abolition of slavery in 1848. Consequently, there were plenty of people willing to collect intelligence data about him and about his disciples, known as Murids.

Though the peoples and kingdoms of the Senegal River valley have historically been grouped under the ethnic designation Wolof, this distinction derives from a complex political geography. The kingdoms that dominated the Senegal River valley from the sixteenth to the nineteenth century shared many customs and rituals, linguistic patterns, and ways of being in the world, since they had a common ancestor in a bygone kingdom. The Murids were Wolof as well, but their dedication to an unprecedented genre of Islamic piety involved rejecting ties to the aristocracy. Indignant spies commissioned by Wolof monarchs routinely embellished reports about Amadu Bamba and his disciples, carefully tailoring reports to confirm French suspicions.

On the rare occasions when such information was in short supply, colonial officials embellished with gusto. Picking up where Leclerc's report left off, Martial Merlin, director of political affairs for the colony of Senegal, reached similar conclusions in his report on Amadu Bamba and the burgeoning Murid movement. Like Leclerc, Merlin granted that there was little "material evidence" to substantiate a formal legal indictment. Yet he deemed Bamba a sophisticated adversary and encouraged the French to take "preemptive measures."

Merlin carefully reconstructed the details of Bamba's life, suggesting that whereas he claimed to be a devout scholar and student of Islam, it was possible to discern the work of a crafty insurgent who had systematically established alliances with displaced Wolof monarchs, most notably Lat Joor, the famous king[2] of Kajoor. Where Amadu Bamba and his disciples had claimed the hinterlands of the Senegal River valley in the explicit effort to establish settlements and sites of worship, Merlin saw a strategy of territorial acquisition "consciously designed to elude French control."[3]

These reports had the desired effect. The French government swiftly dispatched troops to arrest Amadu Bamba. Yet within a couple of decades the colonial government reversed its position. By the twentieth century, Senegal was the world's leading groundnut producer, owing in large measure to an economic framework designed by the same Murid marabouts the French had previously viewed with great suspicion.

Murids were hardly France's first choice of allies. When Louis Faidherbe became governor-general of Senegal in 1854, promoting territorial acquisition as a chief objective, he aspired to secure the support of Wolof monarchs he hoped would help him defeat local protest movements before he polished them off in turn. But the model of slaveholding aristocracy that had long dominated the region fell apart amid a dramatic change in the international landscape of labor. Legally sanctioned slavery not only had become unpalatable as a model of political organization but had become increasingly difficult to sustain. Systems of economic organization that treated labor as homogeneous, calculating productivity using interchangeable units of time—systems that enabled merchants to price one commodity against any other in the marketplace—seemed to deliver profits at higher rates. These forms of commerce suddenly appeared more lucrative and generated profits that seemed easier to predict than those based on circumstantial strategies for extracting productivity from bonded workers. Systems of exchange that depended on harvest yields valued through subjective estimates had become increasingly untenable.

As the legally sanctioned forms of coercive labor that had defined the transatlantic slave trade fell into disuse, the French had hoped they might compel wealthy merchants to forge enduring partnerships. After all, these individuals had managed to control much of the choice land, were politically influential, and boasted lucrative international trade networks.

But in the aftermath of emancipation, the Senegal River valley was home to scores of newly freed persons, some arriving from neighboring polities. They were disenchanted with both slaveholding monarchs and French colonial officials. And they did not share the cultural mores or political priorities of the merchant elites. They found solace in the hinterlands of Kajoor and Bawol and gravitated toward the message of piety promoted by Amadu Bamba, a dynamic young marabout who promoted an idea of mutual aid and a model of social organization that spoke to their interests.

Thus, although much of the intelligence the French and their allies collected about Bamba was steeped in exaggeration, the sense that Murids had organized a movement that threatened to destabilize their hold on the region and its peoples was empirically sound. In this connection, it is crucial to consider the techniques of governance the French used to reach this conclusion. By the end of the nineteenth century, the primary apparatus of French power in the region had shifted from commerce to conquest to forensic analysis and surveillance. In this moment the French were concerned to identify and monitor populations as never before. The colonial government evolved discrete protocols for producing and managing distinct demographics. Thus, while at one moment Murids were viewed as a threat to French governance, later they were seen as powerful allies. In either case the forensic profile the French assigned them shaped their access to resources. In the century to follow, the style of Islam that Murids helped to pioneer has consistently been characterized as distinctly Senegalese and uniquely cosmopolitan. Accordingly, it has helped Senegal secure favorable standing in the realm of international governance.

From the latter part of the nineteenth century through the middle of the twentieth, members of the Murid *tariqaa* (Arabic for way) amassed capital through revenues from groundnut production. When the years following independence met with agricultural crisis, Murids translated that capital into commercial trading ventures all over the globe. From Turin to Tokyo, Murids have steadily built a peaceful army of traders.[4] "Entering legally, working furtively," then "leaving harmlessly" is how anthropologist Paul Stoller characterizes the activity of Senegal's model merchants.[5] And this idea of Senegalese people as models of comportment is associated not merely with diasporic trade but with the overriding historical disposition of the Senegalese state. During his 2003 visit to Gorée Island, US president George W. Bush lavished praise on Senegal for founding and spearheading an African coalition against the "global war on terror." Bush emphasized the significance of Senegal's being an Islamic country that condemned an alleged jihad waged by Muslims elsewhere. He then promptly committed hundreds of millions of dollars in donor aid to Senegal, a shining example of democracy in action.

These dynamics indicate that the forensic profile assigned to a person or polity shapes access to resources. They also suggest that a forensic profile fosters unintended consequences: if the forensic profile is a kind of diplomatic profile, it is also a kind of credit profile. That is, whether someone enjoys favorable social standing determines whether that person will enjoy political and economic participation along legal channels: whether a polity enjoys favorable standing in a diplomatic arena shapes whether firms see that polity as worthy of investment.

The favorable standing of people and polities is often taken as a transparent reflection of their adherence to well-established laws and norms. The history of Senegal undermines that facile assumption.

In 2000, Abdoulaye Wade became president of Senegal by persuading youth to vote in unprecedented numbers. Desperate to overcome a thirty-year labor crisis, young people identified with a man who had spent decades as part of the main opposition party, dubbing Wade the "youth president" although he was nearly eighty years old at the time. A nation racked by 48 percent unemployed—40 percent of them "urban youth"—had been transformed.

The 2000 election was a watershed, for it broke the Socialist Party's forty-year hold on the nation's highest office. Léopold Sedar Senghor led Senegal from 1960 until 1981, when he stepped down in midterm, which meant that his prime minister, Abdou Diouf, automatically became president. Now Abdoulaye Wade, a four-time candidate for the nation's highest office, finally prevailed. And, as observers noted, it is rare for a party to capture the presidency peacefully after another party has dominated it for decades. In reporting on these events, the British Broadcast Corporation (BBC) News gushed: "The peaceful and democratic change of power in Senegal was a highly unusual event for an Africa dominated by military or otherwise authoritarian regimes. The result is not only important for Senegal, but could have a profound influence on democracy elsewhere in Africa by encouraging voters to realise that other long-term leaders are not invincible."[6] Forging a new political course for the nation, Wade appeared ready to empower a young electorate, the demographic largely responsible for his newfound success.

In 2002 Wade selected as his prime minister Idrissa Seck, who had engineered Wade's unsuccessful bid for the presidency in 1988. Then the young campaign manager, not yet thirty years of age, had distinguished himself as one of Senegal's most promising politicians. On the eve of his appointment, Seck declared he "knew the president so well" that it would take very little for him to translate "Wade's vision" into a political program. Seck, in fact, claimed to be "an embodiment of the president's vision."[7] Yet in the early months of 2005 rumors began circulating that Seck was plotting to displace Wade from the presidency and then to gain control over Parliament in the elections of 2006 before running for president himself in 2007. Faced with this prospect, President Wade had the man he once called his "son" taken into police custody on "corruption allegations" stemming from his alleged mismanagement of state funds. As Senegal prepared for national elections, Seck was imprisoned under the charge of "undermining state security."[8]

Wade delayed the elections scheduled for 2005 for an additional two years, citing fiscal instability. By the time the elections were finally held in 2007, the nation's young people were utterly disenchanted. Young musicians and artists—who had galvanized an unprecedented youth contingent for the millennial elections—rallied against Wade, believing he had systematically ignored his most cherished constituency.

But in 2007 Abdoulaye Wade was reelected. Amid protests that he had somehow "stolen the election," scholars and pundits highlighted Wade's strategic shift in constituency. He no longer needed votes from the group he had hailed as the nation's "most precious resource" during his inaugural address. Instead, Wade had spent his presidency courting leaders in Senegal's most powerful Islamic brotherhoods, who used their political influence and wealth to fortify his base of support.

By the election cycle of 2011, the situation was even more dire. Newspapers in Senegal and elsewhere were thick with rumors that President Wade was hatching a scheme to transfer power to his biological son, cabinet member Karim Wade. In the waning months of the second term of a disappointing presidency, people worried that Wade was not yet ready to vacate the nation's highest office, even though the national constitution specifies a two-term limit.

Speculation forced Abdoulaye Wade to make a public announcement where he assured the people of Senegal that he had no plans to support Karim Wade for the presidency. As it turns out, Wade had already picked a candidate he liked even more.

Himself.

Public outrage erupted in widespread protests. Scores of people took to the streets to express their discontent. "On what grounds could Wade justify a third term?" they wondered aloud. "Isn't that prohibited by the constitution?" Wade meanwhile argued that since a new version of the national constitution had been ratified during his time in office, and since the new constitution stipulated that a president can serve two terms, he was entitled to two terms *from the new date of ratification*. Senegal's national judiciary agreed.

Meanwhile the people of Senegal viewed this development as a naked power grab. Students, activists, journalists, and scholars made a concerted effort to share what was happening with the wider world. After four people died during a demonstration in January 2012, the United Nations high commissioner for human rights issued a statement expressing concern that law enforcement officials were using "excessive force" against protestors. Undaunted, Wade dismissed his opposition as "a light wind which rustles the leaves of a tree but never becomes a hurricane."[9]

Articles in the French and British media started to ask if Senegal might no longer be a beacon of democracy in Africa. Might Abdoulaye Wade be guilty of political malfeasance? Was Senegal witnessing a plague of corruption? US officials have raised these concerns in confidential meetings with Senegalese diplomats,[10] marking a dramatic departure from historical perceptions of Senegalese governance, and the credibility of Wade more specifically.

Thus people within and outside Senegal were excited when former prime minister and president of the National Assembly Macky Sall received 26.5 percent of the vote in the elections held on February 25 to Wade's 36.8 percent. Rivals turned into allies as supporters for the twelve initial candidates joined forces to defeat the incumbent in a runoff election. Still, with an almost endless tally of overseas votes and what appeared to many election monitors to be a concerted effort by the government in power to derail democracy, people wondered whether there was any chance that Wade could be voted out of office.

So on March 25, when Abdoulaye Wade conceded and Macky Sall abruptly ascended to the presidency of Senegal, many people were elated. The BBC News quoted citizens of neighboring countries who now viewed Senegal with "envy" for having managed such a peaceful transition of power. *Al Jazeera* newspaper quoted president-elect Sall, who bragged, "We have shown to the world that our democracy is mature,"[11] though the *New York Times* perhaps best captured international opinion when it suggested that the elections marked "a rare example of a prompt and peaceful political turnover in a region tormented by coups and leaders who refuse to give up power."[12]

Still, the news came as something of a surprise. Not all the votes had been counted. And many people had expected Wade to contest the outcome had it not been in his favor. What accounted for his sudden change of heart?

International news agencies and analysts quickly settled on the position that Senegal's democratic tradition had prevailed. Despite years of half-hearted commitment to democracy, Wade retained the mantle of one of Africa's democratic leaders. And yet there bubbled to the surface a story—one few news agencies bothered to remark on—that in fact a coup had been brewing in Senegal. Apparently some Senegalese, alarmed by Wade's authoritarian leanings, had explored the prospect of mounting an armed resistance. From this perspective it was the threat that a recent coup in Mali might incite similar dynamics in Senegal, not some overweening commitment to democracy, that finally persuaded Wade to leave office and prevented Senegal from following the authoritarian trajectory it is frequently commended for having avoided.

So which is it? Was political malfeasance so much at odds with Senegal's governing principles that it could not gain traction? Or did criticism of Senegalese democracy point to a more fundamental problem that had been camouflaged until that moment—that Senegal's standing as an exemplary polity had enabled it to avoid sanctions for an array of injustices that had plagued the country for some time?

We tend to think of forensics in relation to policing—as a set of protocols concerned with adjudicating the social standing of an alleged criminal. But the tendency to privilege specific kinds of evidence, and to use that evidence as the basis for moral judgments about people and polities, has broader applications. We use a similar protocol to evaluate the diplomatic standing of countries. But there is a problem with this approach. Frequently the evidence we use to assess social standing is unreliable. The forensic profile of a country often has more to do with subjective assessments than with objective criteria.

Forensics of Capital argues that the way we tend to understand and analyze politics is deeply flawed. Too often we presume that what accounts for the favorable or disreputable standing of a given country has to do with its relationship to laws and norms and customs. I suggest instead that a country acquires its diplomatic profile through its history of interacting with other polities based on the consensus at which privileged countries have arrived. That diplomatic profile is in a sense a forensic profile: a composite history concerned with whether a country enjoys favorable standing—whether it has transgressed shared protocols. That forensic profile is also a credit profile insofar as other countries use this criterion in deciding if a country is worthy of investment.

It hasn't always been this way. *Forensics of Capital* discusses how the science of forensics emerged during the seventeenth century as the material counterpart to Enlightenment notions of truth. Ever since, it has been the scientific apparatus that we use to calibrate social standing. The forms of social standing we establish then become the basis for granting access to resources. This is true for people and polities alike.

Forensics of Capital breaks from the tendency to focus primarily on the values and ideas that a nation or people espouses. In addition to stated principles, I am interested in the pragmatic acts that establish and reinforce economic and political ties between peoples and polities. In the process, I demonstrate the particular circumstances through which the people and polity of Senegal secured favorable standing in a diplomatic arena that has, for several hundred years, relied on a rudimentary forensic calculus as the basis for adjudicating social standing.

William Pietz coined the phrase "forensics of capital" while contemplating shifts in legal protocols for deciding who owes what to whom that surfaced in the nineteenth century.[13] These developments were occasioned by the emergence of capitalized assets like railroads that fostered the growth of industry but also contributed to widespread injuries and fatalities, provoking new questions about how to assess and adjudicate the monetary value of a human life. These developments also raised questions about what it means for one person, or one country, to be indebted to another and how we ought to understand the social consequences of such a scenario.

Capital is a store of value to which a person or firm has exclusive access. This means that access to capital is premised on a person's or firm's social standing. After all, a person's assets can be seized by the state in the aftermath of a criminal conviction. A person who owes taxes to the state can have a lien placed on her wages. A nation that falls out of favor with international governing agencies might face embargoes and lose access to credit through international financial institutions. For this reason it is crucial to understand the framework for sovereignty in which any given capital network is enmeshed.

ONE

Forensics of Capital

In 1487 Bemoim wrote to John II of Portugal for assistance in defeating his rivals. As part of his plea, the Wolof king dispatched a messenger with a gift of gold plus one hundred slaves for the Portuguese king. John II was sympathetic to Bemoim's cause but, he noted, canon law prohibited him from supplying non-Christian rulers with arms. John II explained that he could accommodate Bemoim's request only if the Muslim king converted to Catholicism.

In 1455 Pope Nicholas V had issued a papal bull granting the Portuguese a monopoly over trade and navigation on Africa's Atlantic coast (a region the Portuguese termed Guinea).[1] Yet for several decades neither conversion nor conquest had enjoyed much success. Despite constantly assuring the clergy in Rome of its interest in spreading Catholicism, the Kingdom of Portugal had thus far done little to establish a strong presence in the region. Instead, commercial ties had mostly been shaped by the whimsy of select traders and diplomats.

Then, between 1475 and 1479, private merchants and soldiers from the kingdom of Castille violated Portugal's Atlantic coast monopoly, gaining access to the prized fort of São Jorge da Mina. They broached land that stretched from present-day Ghana to Nigeria.[2] In response, John II reaffirmed Portugal's access to Guinea and embarked on a much more ambitious project for conversion. Determined to secure unbridled access to the world known and as yet unknown (*cuncta mundi climata omniumque natio-num in illis degentium qualitates*), King John asserted his dominion over the entire Atlantic coast of Africa in his capacity as "lord."[3]

As early as the 1450s, Alvise da Ca da Mosto (more commonly known as Cadamosto), a navigator from Venice, had visited Senegambia on a charter sponsored by Portugal. Ca da Mosto remarked on the intimacy of trade relations between polities in this part of Africa and the city-states of Iberia in ethnographic musings on Wolof customs and strategies of governance.[4] In 1488 Bemoim became the first African sovereign John II had ever hosted[5] when his party of forty, including his son and other close relatives as well as a number of enslaved persons, descended on the royal court.

Instead of remaining seated, as was his prerogative, King John rose to greet Bemoim upon his arrival. In appreciation for this immense display of hospitality, Bemoim genuflected upon reaching the Portuguese king, but John II helped him to his feet.[6] John II made arrangements for Bemoim and his entourage to be dressed in clothing befitting their rank.[7] Silver accoutrements adorned the dining table. The Portuguese king was concerned to greet Bemoim with the diplomatic protocols befitting a sovereign ruler.

It was not long before Bemoim was baptized. John II knighted Bemoim and outfitted him with a coat of arms bearing a gold cross on a red background with the *quinas* (escutcheons) of the Portuguese flag along the border.[8] Theologians and jurists counseled Bemoim privately about the expectations of his new faith. In honor of his spiritual mentor, Bemoim chose John as his Christian name. A short time later he sent a letter in Latin to the pope in which he praised the Portuguese king and conveyed his devotion to the dictates of the Catholic Church.

In accordance with the privileges Bemoim had earned as a Christian prince under the dominion of the Portuguese crown, John II sent him home with twenty caravels brimming with military provisions. The fleet included three hundred soldiers under the command of Pero Vaz da Cunha, who was tasked with building a fort in the Senegal River valley to promote Portuguese commercial interests,[9] in addition to supporting friars and priests who expected to pursue missionary activity in the region.[10] But when Portuguese men en route to this new commercial enclave were devastated by illness, Pero accused Bemoim of treason, murdered him aboard one of the Portuguese vessels, and sailed back to Lisbon.

According to Portuguese law, a person accused of treason should stand trial before the king.[11] Thus it's possible that Pero murdered Bemoim after some sort of dispute, then created a legal justification for killing him. Perhaps Pero believed Bemoim was indeed guilty of treason yet worried that he would be granted a reprieve, since this Wolof king was one of very "few high-ranking converts from Islam" to enjoy such extensive interaction with the Portuguese sovereign.[12] John II was apparently "very displeased" with the murder of Bemoim, yet Pero was never charged with an offense.

By the time the crime had occurred, Bemoim was a Christian. At that juncture, religious affiliation was perhaps the most reliable proxy for social standing. But did Pero somehow enjoy more legitimacy as someone from the Portuguese mainland (in other words, did Bemoim have less authenticity as a Christian because he was a convert?)? By that period, had race, region, or ethnicity already started to creep into the prevailing calculus of social difference in ways we tend to associate with the centuries to come?

Perhaps Pero had deliberately seized on the "ambiguity" of fifteenth-century maritime laws, where a ship's captain was considered a feudal lord over his crew, making mutiny a form of treason, punishable by death—hence the salience of killing Bemoim on a ship rather than on land.[13] However we understand it, the assassination of Bemoim encourages us to think about the way social standing has historically been adjudicated. Bemoim's tragic murder underscores a question that has perplexed legal theorists for centuries: How do we know when a merchant or political official has been authorized to establish commercial agreements and diplomatic initiatives?[14] This event also compels us to ask how rulers from what is today Senegal have historically been characterized and to inquire about the criteria used to arrive at these decisions.

In this regard it is telling that John II never held a formal inquest into the death of Bemoim, even though this Wolof sovereign now enjoyed standing as a Christian prince. By having Bemoim baptized and granting him a coat of arms, King John endowed him with sanctified authority. Bemoim's power as sovereign thus now derived from the Crown's status as God's earthly embodiment. This procedure underscores the historic role of sanctified authority in conferring legitimacy and in adjudicating social standing. Through his anointing as a Christian prince, Bemoim became accountable to the church, on one hand, and the Portuguese Crown on the other.

In what follows I explore the criteria used to determine where a polity, or a person, stands in a juridical regime. I call the calculus used to adjudicate social standing the *forensics of capital*. In deploying this concept, I discuss the diverse factors that have historically shaped Senegal's standing in a world of nations. I demonstrate that political belonging is shaped by strategies for securing political recognition—by protocols for assessing the integrity of a person or polity.

In the process, I reveal that governance has as much to do with pragmatic protocols as with formal treaties. I also show that diplomatic standing does not emerge in some self-evident way from the character or behavior of any given polity. Instead, it is shaped by the consensus that privileged polities and individuals arrive at concerning where a polity and its people stand in a hierarchical system. In spelling out these dynamics, I explain how Senegal has historically managed to secure standing as one of Africa's most stable democracies, and I examine the evidence this judgment is based on.

To make sense of Senegal's political history, it is crucial to revisit the historical formation of the polity. The practice of sovereignty that has structured international trade and governance during the past few centuries derives from long-held beliefs about social standing and divine agency in the context of Latin Christendom. In the aftermath of the Reconquista, these assumptions structured determined efforts to rid the Iberian peninsula of Islamic rule. This notion of sovereignty was also a crucial strategy for winning souls and territories for an increasingly ambitious Christian empire. Theological arguments meshed with pragmatic strategies for securing territory, for authorizing trade agreements, and for forging diplomatic ties. As the polities of Latin Christendom outmaneuvered their rivals in Africa and elsewhere, notions of sovereignty inspired by divine mandate migrated out of Christendom into purportedly secular structures of governance and credit-debt.

Theories of governance tend to presume a polity composed of rational, enlightened individuals. Within this framework, the terms of commerce and diplomacy are forged by the voluntary, self-interested decisions of self-conscious social actors. But what if we begin our analysis of politics from the specific rituals that people use to authorize trade and to solidify binding diplomatic agreements? In what follows, I suggest that important elements of the framework for sovereignty on which we now rely were born from ad hoc rituals for establishing social compacts on Africa's Atlantic coast from the fifteenth century to the nineteenth.

By the time he was invited to Portugal by John II, Bemoim was very familiar with European interests and commercial activity in Senegambia. Six years earlier, Christopher Columbus was engaged in trade along Africa's Atlantic coast—the Guinea coast as well as what came to be known as the Gold Coast. Columbus had even visited the notorious Portuguese fort São Jorge da Mina, becoming familiar with Atlantic Ocean wind systems and cultivating expertise with the navigation instruments he would use on subsequent voyages in the Atlantic. In 1484 Columbus had petitioned John II for resources to make a return visit to the Atlantic coast of Africa. His request was denied. Two years later Columbus showed up in Spain, pressing King

Ferdinand and Queen Isabella for the financial support that would ultimately fund his celebrated 1492 voyage to the Americas.

Bemoim's visit in 1488 has to be read in the context of a burgeoning system of international trade and diplomacy premised on a nascent forensic calculus that sought to adjudicate the social standing of the world's peoples and polities. The inhabitants of Africa's Atlantic coast were, from the Catholic perspective, members of the *extra ecclesiam*—people who did not claim Christianity yet could be construed as subjects of the Catholic Church should they submit to its stated protocols.

From the dawn of Portuguese interest in Africa, ecclesiastical authorities declared a sovereign imperative to adjudicate the spiritual destiny of peoples who resided there. This investment was steeped in a sense of shared humanity. If Iberian merchants and explorers did not deploy the "language of spiritual conquest" as frequently in dealing with Africans as they did when facing off against the indigenous peoples of the Americas, it is because they saw the inhabitants of lands that Muslim residents and rulers hailed from as part of a shared political geography.[15] Initial interactions between Iberian merchants and diplomats reveal that they often considered Africans part of the Old World—having a shared history—rather than the New World.[16] And given the principle of the *extra ecclesiam*, the Catholic Church was invested in asserting the right to adjudicate social standing in the kingdom of God for all potential converts.[17]

This does not mean that relations between rival polities were not coercive at times. The Portuguese applied military force proportionate to their increasing influence and their eagerness to exploit their growing commercial and military advantage. During this period, Christians would routinely kidnap nonbelievers, holding them for *rescate* (ransom), forcibly converting them to Christianity if payments did not correspond to their specified terms. In the eyes of the church, this was a viable practice for converting infidels, who ultimately benefitted from the grace of God whether they realized it or not.[18] *Rescate* was premised on the idea that life in an African polity entailed mortal danger. Thus becoming a hostage granted inhabitants access to a privileged lifestyle. The practice of *rescate* thus foregrounds the prominent role the church played in adjudicating social standing.

In testifying to the eminence of Infante Henrique (more commonly known as Prince Henry the Navigator),[19] the Portuguese chronicler Gomes Eanes de Zurara spoke in glowing terms of the "notable deeds" his lord had managed to "achieve in the Conquest."[20] Yet in the formative years of Portuguese exploration, efforts to establish binding claims to territory, to procure captives for sale, and to secure a strategic military advantage were incremental and ad hoc.

The Reconquista helped to establish juridical distinctions among the inhabitants of the African continent—some conceived as "sovereign," while others were dubbed "sovereignless,"[21] amid the "new taxonomy of difference"[22] that emerged during the sixteenth century. During this time the idea of sovereignty became a way to differentiate between peoples whose lands should or should not be readily exploited—people who could or could not be seized and turned into possessions. Still, it is crucial to note that some of the very same African peoples who had been dubbed "sovereignless," or incapable of forging binding trade agreements, routinely exchanged goods and brokered diplomatic relations with traders from Latin Christendom and the emerging countries of the North Atlantic. Thus the Christian concept of sovereignty, which would ultimately shape notions of government by social contract, entailed a number of assumptions about the alleged profile and supposed standing of the parties to a transaction that were not consistent with how people tended to adjudicate the legal standing of persons and polities in practical terms.

From the fifteenth century onward, traders from different polities operating in the diverse context of Africa's Atlantic coast developed a repertoire of shared strategies for authorizing agreements and establishing rights to territory. As British trader Richard Jobson noted in 1621: "We payd a kind of poor custome, which in the mouth of the river, where the Portingall hath used, is not only greater, but peremptorily *demaunded*, whereas above it is lesse and rather taken as a curtesie presented, which moral kindnesse requires all strangers, comming in the way of amity."[23]

Thus, even where African rulers and merchants did not necessarily secure legitimacy as sovereign on equal terms with European rulers, they established methods for sanctioning agreements their European interlocutors were obliged to accept.[24] As Walter Rodney noted in his study of the Upper Guinea coast, "The word 'contract' can be applied to certain unwritten agreements between the Africans and the Europeans because many of these agreements were based on oaths which were binding under the customary law."[25]

These expectations might cohere as a tax levied on North Atlantic traders, or in procedures that produced sanctified authority akin to what a priest—or in later years a secular judge—was authorized to bestow: "Experienced traders learned to insist that arrangements made with Africans were sworn on some 'medicine.'"[26]

And yet these compacts were ultimately scorned by Enlightenment philosophers, who argued that, precisely because these forms of exchange and interaction maintained an "irreducible materiality," they failed to convey the abstract principles associated with Western forms of jurisprudence. They were, in the language of the time, "fetish oaths" but not legal contracts as such. Still, the "fetish" is useful in charting the formation of an international economic order precisely because the concept did not exist before the sixteenth-century Atlantic trade zone in which it first appeared as the pidgin term *fetisso*. In this context Africans were called "fetisseros" or "fetisheers," their activities translated into verb forms like "to make fetiche" or "to take the fetiche."[27]

The term fetish comes from late medieval Portuguese term *feitiço*, "witchcraft." But it assumed a novel referent in the sixteenth-century Atlantic world. Defined by the chance encounter with natural objects of the material world, the concept of the fetish was used to mark a pragmatic reality: objects that drew competing forms of value together. From the perspective of North Atlantic traders, these objects had been "capriciously chosen and childishly personified." And yet this discourse helps us appreciate the novel challenge that plagued efforts to grapple with the status of the political compacts— and the nature and origin of the value of the material objects—that defined new forms of social belonging and commercial exchange in the intercultural trade zone of the Atlantic coast.[28]

The objects Europeans disdainfully deemed "fetishes" were frequently adorned with colored beads or glass. These technologies of divine intercession, forged from the detritus of a cosmopolitan commercial zone, alarmed Europeans, who placed no faith in priests who could harness the powers of divine agents in the world around them. By the seventeenth century, fetishism had come to define entire social orders allegedly steeped in "a chaotic principle of contingency." If fetishism could be said to have a defining social principle it was "caprice," the eminent taxonomist Carl Linnaeus argued, apparently not realizing that the notion of a capricious social logic is itself a logical absurdity.[29]

This purportedly whimsical way of being posed a problem for European traders concerned to acquire material objects whose value they hoped to stabilize. As early as the 1450s, Ca da Mosto claimed that while people of Africa's Atlantic coast "prized" gold, "they traded it cheaply, taking in exchange of little value in our eyes."[30] The crucial passage being "in our eyes," for in complaining that Africans were unable to appreciate an ostensibly valuable commodity, Ca da Mosto confessed to having a separate and distinct conception of material value. Still, he and other observers remained oblivious to the fact that their own view was by no means objective. Traders and navigators from Latin Christendom and the North Atlantic identified fetishism as a problem because it suggested a world in which objects were not organized according to a discernible logic of commercial exchange. In their view fetishes, deployed in primitive forms of religious ritual, served primarily to cultivate sensuous engagement with the world.

This perspective surfaces in attempts to document beliefs of African peoples as a way to discern whether they are capable of forging binding trade relations and diplomatic initiatives. As fifteenth-century merchants set out from Iberia to explore Africa and, eventually, the Americas, they jotted down the customs, rituals, and preferred methods of exchange that defined the peoples they encountered. Thus Atlantic enclaves of the fifteenth and sixteenth centuries were instrumental in helping to forge strategies of documentation that shaped governance as well as commercial opportunities and scholarship about the world. These forms of documentation might begin as reconnaissance for trade opportunities or military operations, but they could later be deployed as intelligence data for colonial projects or scientific knowledge for scholars concerned with identifying and organizing the peoples of the world.

Recall that 1492, when Columbus set sail for the Americas, was the same year the people of Latin Christendom reclaimed the Iberian peninsula from African and southwest Asian Muslims who for more than seven hundred years had presided over a region extending from the southernmost tip of Europe all the way to parts of what is now France. Thus, in terms of both European continental politics and the emergent territories of the New World, the question of social difference defined trade compacts and political alliances as the supposed essence of a people or polity became central to the way North Atlantic nations ultimately assessed diplomatic standing. Strategies of profiling became essential to interactions between polities. Forensic criteria that involved language and customs of dress and eating, as well as religious affiliation and place of residence, came increasingly to include physiological and physiognomic properties as the question of character, or profile, became crucial to the task of diplomatic coordination. As polities became nations made up of people who supposedly shared a common "character," strategies of commerce fed arguments about causality. The distinction between African and North Atlantic traders as people with distinct customs and ritual practices gave way to the idea that they abided by rather different social logics. And as North Atlantic states established protocols for brokering warfare and commerce through consensus, those who exhibited commercial might and military supremacy gained disproportionate influence in diplomatic circles.

This dual interest in formal diplomatic standing and in vernacular structures of exchange offers a different way to think about the inaugural moments of formal structures for international trade and diplomacy—these dynamics are not merely shaped by abstract principles but by pragmatic concerns. It's worth remembering that the 1648 Peace of Westphalia was accompanied by a series of international treaties for the "protection of private creditors" that North Atlantic nations forged to ensure that new mechanisms of diplomacy would not interrupt commercial opportunities.[31] These compacts were brokered almost ceaselessly from the Peace of Westphalia until the end of the Napoleonic Wars, at which point the nascent corporate form created a disincentive to insist on the nation as the privileged sphere through which to adjudicate commercial interests. During this same historical window, the secular science of forensics was born as a method for adjudicating the social standing of citizens across North Atlantic polities possessed of unprecedented opportunities in commerce and government. Likewise during this time, the discourse of fetishism underwent a series of transformations consistent with the way Enlightenment intellectuals came to understand the African capacity to forge binding economic and political agreements. Because political participation was now premised on legitimate social standing—having satisfied outstanding obligations in the spheres of criminal or civil law—the question of social standing was salient as never before in efforts to grapple with the forensics of capital.

Despite engaging in trade relations with Portuguese merchants since the fifteenth century, Wolof kings never granted them permission to build a fort on Senegal's Atlantic coast. Instead, merchants relied on sparse coastal settlements where they enjoyed intermittent contact with peoples of the Senegal River valley. They sometimes developed partnerships with African women that later waves of European traders would emulate—bonds of matrimony the French described as *mariage à la mode*. These marriages drew elements from indigenous customs as well as Iberian traditions.[32] In fact, the Portuguese dubbed their African companions *signares*, from the Portuguese *senhora*, "wife."

More than any other group, signares played a crucial role in fostering economic opportunities—and, by extension, political possibilities—in early modern Senegambia. Marriages to these female commercial savants were prevalent throughout Senegambia. In what is now Guinea, they were known as *nhara*. In what is today the Gambia, they were called *senora*. Yet the greatest number of these partnerships took place in land that is now known as Senegal, since from the late seventeenth through the nineteenth century there was more commercial activity at Saint-Louis and Gorée than at all the other ports combined.[33]

French trade in Africa had been given new life in the seventeenth century by the improbable success of Jean-Baptiste Colbert. Born in 1619 into a humble merchant family, Colbert would ultimately achieve fame as the man who revolutionized French governance as the close confidant and mentor of the French king Louis XIV. Colbert helped promote a shift in strategies of governance, from the reasoned deliberation of aristocratic intellectuals to a recognition of the benefits deriving from merchant capital.[34] In essence, the age of Colbert witnessed the triumph of accounting as a crucial medium of governance.

It was Colbert who decided in 1658 to reorganize a Norman trading company that had already been operating in Senegal. Working with directors and financiers from Paris, he helped forge a new model for commercial speculation on the Atlantic coast. In large measure due to his efforts, the Compagnie du Cap Vert et du Sénégal helped France dominate commerce in the region for more than a hundred years.[35]

The Compagnie built a fort at the mouth of the Senegal River, on the small island of Saint-Louis. Two hundred miles long and nearly four miles wide, the island enclave had military and commercial advantages. As part of a dense river network, Saint-Louis offered ready access to the African interior. And the treacherous bar that loomed at the mouth of the Senegal River meant that only experienced navigators would even bother to test it. As an island location, Saint-Louis also created some space to maneuver outside the sphere of the Wolof kingdoms that vied for power on the mainland.

The fort at Saint-Louis created new opportunities for settlement. Instead of the ramshackle coastal dwellings that defined Portuguese exploits, the French established durable communities in the shadow of their fort. There they enjoyed constant interaction with indigenous peoples of Africa, free people of color, and people implicated in diverse forms of slavery and servitude. Persuaded by the virtues of this model for trade and settlement, the French added Gorée Island to their empire in 1677 (even if it ultimately served more as a way station for trade than as a formidable base of operations).

In less than a century, the population of Saint-Louis had grown to three thousand. It doubled again by 1785. By that time the population at Gorée numbered two thousand. European settlers included the employees of French trading posts as well as soldiers and military officers charged with securing the region for private investors. Some of the soldiers were marginal people who had been forcibly conscripted or deported to African territories as punishment for crimes in the metropole. Other exiles were disabled or somehow deemed deviant.[36]

Most of these expatriates were men, and French companies prohibited employees from bringing their families to the colony. Consequently, political officials advocated for the right of company employees to marry African women. Governor Julien du Bellay, who presided over Senegal's original capital city, Saint-Louis, from 1722 to 1725, argued that permission to marry would lead traders to establish a more permanent base in the region, eliminating the constant need for fresh recruits. A decade later, Governor Sebastian Devaulx adopted the same stance from a different perspective. Noting that relationships between European men and African women were pervasive, he argued that authorizing marriage would make it easier for the company to manage these "clandestine" unions. These proposals were flatly rejected. Still, merchants forged bonds of intimacy with signares in defiance of these policies.

Europeans waxed poetic about signares. "Their mode of dress, characteristically very elegant," one observer noted, "suits them very well." Antoine Edme Pruneau de Pommegorge discussed the exquisite "beauty" and "intelligence" of signares in his 1789 publication *Description de la nigritie*,[37] praising their capacity to adopt European languages and social norms as evidence of their cultural sophistication. British minister John Lindsay[38] was likewise enthralled:

> As to their women, and in particular the ladies (for so I must call many of those in Senegal) they are in a surprising degree handsome, have very fine features, are wonderfully tractable, remarkably polite both in conversation and manners; and in the point of keeping themselves neat and clean (of which we have generally strange ideas, formed to us by the beastly laziness of slaves), they far surpass the Europeans in every respect.

Lindsay was so smitten that he felt compelled to deride European women:

> [Signares] bathe twice a day . . . and in this particular have a hearty contempt for all white people, who they imagine must be disagreeable, our women especially. Nor can even their men, from this very notion, be brought to look upon the prettiest of our women, but with the coldest indifference, some of whom there are here, officer's ladies, who dress very showy, and who even in England would be thought handsome. You may, perhaps, smile at all this; but I assure you 'tis a truth.

Lindsay was, in other words, convinced that the beauty of signares was un-rivaled on either side of the Atlantic:

> Negroes to me are no novelty; but the accounts I received of them, and in particular the appearance of the females on this occasion, were to me a novelty most pleasing. They were not only pretty, but in the dress in which they appeared, were even desirable. Nor can I give you any drapery more nearly resembling theirs, than the loose, light, easy robe, and sandal, in which we see the female Grecian statues attired; most of which were exceeding white cotton, spun, wove into narrow slips of six or seven inches, and sewn together by themselves. Their hair, for it differs little from wool, very neat and curiously plaited; and their persons otherways adorned, by earrings, necklaces, and bracelets, of the purest gold.

> And indeed I cannot help thinking, that it was to the benefit of the African company in general, and the happiness of those they sent abroad in particular; that, with such promising inhabitants, the French suffered no white women to be sent thither.

Signares were among the most influential social actors on Africa's Atlantic coast during the eighteenth century. The unions they participated in translated into access to wealth and influence unprecedented for persons not tied to nobility. And Lindsay's elaborate description above, singing the praises of the signares' chastity, is partly meant to emphasize that there was no "easy fraternization"[39] between signares and traders. Their reputation for discretion was part of what elevated their social standing, enhancing a desire for them that gave these women access to European wealth and social influence unique to this region and moment. In that sense this politics of respectability had a dual quality—it reinforced the particular contours of gendered authority and access to commerce even as women leveraged a historically unprecedented genre of sexuality to their advantage and on behalf of their kin. Married women accepted social norms and had the same expectations of their husbands.

The aspiring husband was responsible for furnishing a home. After marriage, women were expected to be faithful, to tend the domestic space, to care for their husbands (who at times fell ill from tropical disease or were otherwise fatigued by the exigencies of trade and travel). Signares also blessed their husbands with intimate knowledge of local customs and economic opportunities. It was a husband's duty to provide a slave, as a guardian or mentor, for each of his children. Many of these children were baptized, even though free people of color drew on indigenous religious traditions as well as Abrahamic faiths to establish the rituals and religious sensibilities through which they organized their lives.[40] Because Islam had a presence in the region as early as the eleventh century, it was virtually impossible to disentangle its customs from indigenous practices by this period. And emergent forms of Christianity often mapped onto Wolof customs that had already been shaped by encounters with Islam, creating cosmopolitan religious sensibilities.[41] Senegal would thus evolve a genre of Islam that came to be known as uniquely tolerant.

When it was time for a trader with whom she had partnered to make an overseas voyage, the signare would accompany him to his boat. There she would gather sand from his last footprint and place it in a handkerchief that she would later tie to the foot of her bed. This ritual emphasized her fidelity to their union until he returned, unless she discovered he would not be returning at all, in which case she was released from the covenant and free to remarry.[42]

The characteristics Lindsay attributes to elegance, grace, and charm are partly due to the mixed ancestry that defined free people of color inhabiting Senegal's Atlantic coast. This hybrid heritage helped incubate the social norms that North Atlantic merchants and political officials found familiar and thus pleasing. In essence, signares best embodied the unique social mores that defined the hybrid commercial zone to which North Atlantic merchants had become accustomed. To the extent that partnerships with signares were crucial to forging a colonial presence in the territory, the signare was not merely a medium of desire but a privileged social actor with access to resources and social influence.

Signare Cathy Miller was highly regarded "as a woman of wealth and high social standing" in Saint-Louis during the late eighteenth and early nineteenth centuries. Miller was born in 1760 to the British trader Jean Miller and an African woman whose name is lost to history.

At age twenty, Cathy married Charles Jean-Baptiste d'Erneville of New Orleans. Charles had left his Gulf Coast home to receive training as a French military officer and even did a brief stint in a debtor's prison before arriving in Senegal in 1780 at age twenty-seven. He was tasked with helping France reassert control of the Saint-Louis territory Britain had been forced to relinquish as part of the diplomatic resolution to the American Revolution.

The union of signare Cathy Miller and Charles Jean-Baptiste d'Erneville yielded four children who all became influential merchants and property owners. Nicholas started a trade house before becoming the mayor of Saint-Louis in 1851. And the social ties that Nicholas cultivated testified to the influence that signares wielded. Nicholas's wife, Adelaide Crespin, was the child of signare Kati Wilcok and Benjamin Crespin, a trader from the French city of Nantes. That two of Benjamin's brothers married daughters of Saint-Louis mayor Charles Thevenot testifies to the concentration of power that defined eighteenth-century Senegal's commercial centers. Charles d'Erneville later moved to Gorée, where he partnered with signare Hélène Pateloux. At that juncture, Cathy Miller married the trader Jean-Baptiste Dubrux. Dubrux gave his name to a son who married a woman named Desirée. She was the daughter of signare Marie Paul Bénis and the prominent merchant Jean-Jacques Alain, who came to Senegal from Martinique.[43] In this context, intimate partnerships became one of the primary venues through which capital was organized.

Traders prized virgins and resisted marrying an unmarried woman who had been sexually active. Yet if he did not marry a virgin, a trader would likely pursue a woman who had been married before,[44] since she could demonstrate skills in child rearing, likely possessed privileged social standing, and had perhaps already acquired wealth through commercial enterprise. If a signare remarried, she was expected to raise her new and old children together, though each child would keep the father's last name. The children of a signare usually inherited her wealth. Since virgins commanded the highest bridewealth, there was pressure for women to abide by strict sexual protocols. And both men and women had expectations for fidelity. Since coastal districts tended to be made up of small communities where most people knew each other, these customs entailed strict measures of accountability for European traders, making it difficult for them to engage in casual liaisons with African women.[45]

The significance of these partnerships for the production and distribution of capital prompts us to ask precisely how both parties knew when this agreement had been formally established. Given that *mariages à la mode* drew from diverse traditions, how did parties know when these compacts were binding?

In the absence of formal recognition as a marriage in the eyes of the law—and taking the place of the indigenous wedding ceremonies that Wolof and Lebu peoples were familiar with—an ad hoc ritual known as the "parade of the sheet" endowed unions with legitimacy. "The morning following the consummation of marriage," noted one observer,

> the relatives of the bride come at daybreak and carry off the white cloth on which the couple have spent the night. Do they find the proof they search for? They affix the cloth at the end of a long pole, waving like a flag; they parade

this all day long in the village singing and praising the new bride and her chastity; but when the relatives have not in fact found such proof the morning after, they take care to substitute for it as quickly as possible.[46]

The exigencies of trade and intimacy on the Atlantic coast had provoked changes in the nature of marriage. Typically the Wolof and Lebu peoples of the Senegal River valley would consummate the marriage some time during the first month. Yet as marriages between North Atlantic traders and African women took off, consummation tended to occur during the couple's first night together. The first night after the wedding thus became the occasion to authorize the legal bond between a signare and her male suitor. The "parade of the sheet" was not merely a quaint custom but a ritual procedure for authorizing access to capital. And as a legal procedure, it was riddled with insights that had long vexed legal scholars and political officials throughout the Atlantic world.

Consider Paolo Zacchia's seventeenth-century text *Quaestiones medico-legales*.[47] Zacchia was the personal physician of the popes Innocent X and Alexander VII, as well as legal adviser to the Rota Romana (the highest court of the Roman Catholic Church). In *Quaestiones medico-legales*, Zacchi tried to establish the evidence required to determine if a marriage contract is binding. The legal rationale that North Atlantic polities have inherited centers on whether such a union can be effectively voided (what we think of as annulment) or whether it requires a more elaborate settlement tinged with higher moral, and frequently religious, stakes before it can be dissolved (divorce). As we know, the question of consummation is the governing criterion—rather than the terms of the agreement, the exchange of fluids is what completes the union. It is the same rationale that governs inheritance rights. The argument is that children, born from the "blood" of their parents, "naturally" inherit property rights, while different legal parameters are required to govern compacts among "strangers."

Articulating the logic of consummation, the parade of the sheet relies on the exchange of fluids to authorize a union.[48] More specifically, the "parade of the sheet" provokes critical attention to the relation between "forensic legal objects" (like the sheet) and "capitalized economic objects" (like the resources such unions involved).[49] The "parade of the sheet" was at once a legal innovation that worked to solidify a salient social institution and a ritual for authorizing access to capital. It was also a textbook example of what North Atlantic traders and Enlightenment philosophers routinely dismissed as a "fetish ritual." Meanwhile, if Atlantic trade compacts and theories of governance were dominated by the pragmatic reality and

Enlightenment nightmare of fetishism from the sixteenth century onward, this same historical window encompassed a series of transformations that had lasting consequences for the way social standing would be adjudicated in the Senegal River valley.

In this context, economic and political organization was increasingly driven by patterns of wealth and resource extraction that centered on the Atlantic coast.[50] As burgeoning sugar plantations in the Americas provoked greater demand for African laborers, ships from Europe, Asia, and the American colonies descended on Senegambia to seize, and barter for, bonded human cargo. As Britain and France emerged as the most powerful polities competing for slaves from the region, Senegambia was divided and redivided into "exclusive commercial spheres of influence, which were periodically redrawn in accordance with the fortunes of war."[51]

In this context also, signares were arguably more influential than any other social actors in terms of the way that wealth was distributed throughout Senegal's coastal enclaves. One signare might command as many as thirty or forty slaves. Indeed, some women had been purchased as slaves to become signares in the first place. In these instances Europeans paid for an enslaved woman's freedom in a form of exchange that mirrored the dowry for a purportedly free woman.[52]

Signares would routinely commission male slaves to ship cargo. In fact these men—who, like their owners, were often of mixed heritage—were sometimes referred to as *grumets*, from cognate terms in romance languages meaning "cabin boy" or "ship's boy." From the fifteenth century onward, grumets were hired aboard European ships as pilots and seamen. They had often been reared among coastal populations with nautical expertise that they subsequently leveraged in building and rigging boats. They also worked as private security contractors for river-borne vessels. Since rivers were central to trade, grumets were highly prized in the labyrinthine commercial networks of the Atlantic coast. They spoke a dialect known as Crioulo, described as "Black French" or "Black English," dressed in European-style clothing, and observed Christian customs. For these reasons the children that European traders had with African women were termed *filhos da terra*, "children of the soil," persons with access to Portuguese as well as African networks who spoke languages that derived from both sides of the Atlantic.[53] Grumets routinely exploited their diverse heritage to position themselves as brokers in Atlantic trade circuits.[54]

Lançados were likewise influential in the riverine networks of Senegambian trade. Although they were sometimes of mixed Portuguese and African ancestry, the term might simply refer to a North Atlantic trader who had spent enough time in Africa to be considered de facto native. Unlike grumets, lançados usually were not slaves but free people of color. And while grumets were frequently figured as Christians, lançados participated so extensively in the rituals and customs—the trade compacts and social mores—of African peoples that they were seen as *tangomãos*, "renegades": apostates, people who had shed their Christianity to become de facto Muslim and indubitably African.

Of course, *habitants* are arguably the most influential constituency born from the partnerships signares formed with European explorers, merchants, and diplomatic officials. The term habitant was used when referring to free people of color who usually worked as merchants. They often held considerable wealth and wielded tremendous political influence. Wealth in coastal enclaves like Saint-Louis and Gorée was historically concentrated among twenty to thirty families. By the mid-eighteenth century this dynamic cohered into a concrete identity. These developments underscored how family could function as a form of capital: that is, as a resource—an asset whose value derives from the mobility it affords within the context of an economic hierarchy. British officials, having seized the island of Saint-Louis from France during the Seven Years' War, were confronted with the formidable population of free people of color who controlled its political infrastructure and commercial networks. By the time France reclaimed Saint-Louis in 1758, this constituency referred to itself as habitants, claiming the island as a space of autonomy that French colonial officials were obliged to respect.

In July 1801 the French government sent Louis Henri Pierre Lasserre to the small island of Saint-Louis, just off the coast of Senegal. He was asked to replace Commander François Blanchot de Verly as the formal head of this French outpost. Habitants met his appointment with skepticism. Instead of submitting to Lasserre's authority, they subjected him to a hearty interrogation. Habitants asked Lasserre what it was about his personality that made him think he was fit to rule over them. They quizzed the French administrator about his years of military service and his views on the colonies. Lasserre's habitant interlocutors were sorely disappointed with his responses. They told him they, frankly, were not impressed—that France could have done better by appointing one of the military officers already stationed in Saint-Louis to run the colony.[55]

Three months into his tenure, Lasserre feared that the habitants were plotting an insurrection. He levied a head tax on their slaves hoping to undermine habitant profits and thus prevent them from raising a formidable army against him, as he noted in candid discussions with his superiors. "I think it is very prudent," said Lasserre, "to diminish this too large population; especially of those people who loudly proclaim that they are masters of the isle, that it belongs to them and not to the French."[56] Satisfied that his message had been received, Lasserre established a private firm to control trade on the region's prime commercial artery, the Senegal River. In the ensuing year, Lasserre grew even more confident. He proudly asserted that habitants wanting to ply their trade on the Senegal River would be taxed one-third the value of their cargo.

The habitants balked. Gabriel Pellegrin was imprisoned on July 23, 1802, when he refused to declare slaves he had purchased from a market in Gajaaga and have them inspected by the surgeon general. A delegation of habitants, led by brothers Charles and François Pellegrin, promptly visited Lasserre to demand that Gabriel be released. Lasserre dismissed them.

The following night, two hundred insurgents broke into the fort where Gabriel was held captive. Their number included French colonial troops stationed in Saint-Louis, most of them enslaved people and free people of color who had been deported to Senegal for participating in the Haitian revolution or for joining armed insurrections against the French in places like Guadeloupe.[57] The revolutionaries freed Gabriel Pellegrin. Then they seized Lasserre and marched him, stark naked, to Pellegrin's house. In no time the habitants dispatched the French officer to Gorée Island.

The habitants drafted a letter to the French government, delivered by hand, justifying the insurrection. They argued that Lasserre's investment in generating profit at their expense conflicted with the stated aims of France's 1789 revolution. In their missive, they railed against the "arbitrary acts" that defined Lasserre's style of governance. They found his "despotism" unacceptable, since in their view the French Revolution had demonstrated that republican governance aims to "accord justice and protection to all" and "to repress acts of terror and violence." To fulfill this democratic ideal, the habitants explained, they had deported Lasserre and confiscated most of his property while they waited for France to send them a new governor.[58]

The next month Governor Blanchot—who had preceded Lasserre—was reinstated. François Pellegrin and Jean Blondin, who had delivered the letter, were tried for the insurgency but acquitted. Observers speculated about whether justice had been served. Yet the colonial government seemed primarily concerned with the economic and political stakes of the uprising. Six years later the French government was still urging governors to appreciate "the necessity of good relations with the habitants" by relating "the unhappy case of Lasserre."[59] At a moment when France was still reeling from defeat in colonial Saint-Domingue, now Haiti, the empire was obliged to accept the autonomy that inhabitants of one of its colonies had carved out for themselves.

But these dynamics fit into a longer trajectory concerning the relation between patterns of social differentiation and access to capital. For Wolof kingdoms had likewise developed forms of militarism and credit-debt that drew them into more intimate contact with North Atlantic merchants and politicians operating in the diverse trade zone of what is today Senegal. These emergent forms of commerce and diplomacy were consequently shaped by debates about the physical characteristic and intellectual capabilities of the people who inhabited this part of the world. These discourses fed explicit concerns about the criteria that ought to govern participation in international trade and diplomacy. They also shaped pragmatic decisions about how to understand and adjudicate outstanding obligations.

On June 6, 1701, Lat Sukaabe Faal, ruler of the Geej kingdom, arrested a French trader named André Brüe, along with the rest of the men who had accompanied him to the port of Rufisque. Brüe was director of La Compagnie des Indes Occidentales, one of France's most lucrative overseas ventures. Lat Sukaabe seized 6,000 livres worth of trade goods but refused to release Brüe until the French government paid an additional ransom.

Lat Sukaabe had kidnapped Brüe and his comrades in retaliation for French efforts to monopolize regional trade by seizing English ships in the vicinity. After collecting his ransom, Lat Sukaabe launched an eight-month boycott of the Compagnie that continued after Brüe was replaced with a new company director, Louis le Maître. While Lat Sukaabe ultimately failed in his quest to prevent the French from establishing an exclusive trade zone, he succeeded in persuading them to pay higher taxes for access to water, food, and lumber in Senegambia's Cap Vert peninsula.

Lat Sukaabe had integrated two distinct polities—Kajoor, in the northern Senegal River valley, and Bawol, to the south—into a single empire. The geographic orientation of this Atlantic empire was clear from the name of the dynasty: Geej, Wolof for "sea" or "ocean." Accordingly, Lat Sukaabe sought to capitalize on Kajoor-Bawol's strategic position in a region that nurtured French commercial interests. As the most powerful political entity in a region that bordered French settlements in Saint-Louis and Gorée, the Wolof sovereign realized he could use Kajoor-Bawol's prime location to interrupt access to resources that French ports relied on.[60] And in using boycotts to gain leverage with European merchants, Lat Sukaabe pioneered a technique that his successors would later adopt.[61] When we consider that

Iberian traders of the fifteenth and sixteenth centuries had adopted ransom as a routine practice for adjudicating social standing, it becomes clear that Lat Sukaabe's determined effort to settle accounts meshed with a theory of accountability that had a distinct trajectory in the commercial geography of the Atlantic world.

From the territories that make up what is now Italy and the Netherlands to dynasties associated with present-day France, the late sixteenth and early seventeenth centuries witnessed a shift in tactics of rule from reason to merchant expertise as the ideological apparatus of governance, as noted above. Lat Sukaabe thus promoted a mode of statecraft structured by assumptions he shared with sovereign rulers elsewhere. The decision to seize Brüe parallels the logic of debtors' prisons, which registered as one of the more pervasive ways to resolve an outstanding obligation during that period. If indeed "inventory was capital before capitalism,"[62] Lat Sukaabe deserves credit for his financial acumen. Yet it is not clear that Lat Sukaabe's contemporaries appreciated what he sought to achieve. Instead of seeing the ransom of André Brüe as a legitimate way to resolve an unpaid debt, they viewed Lat Sukaabe's action as an altogether irrational and excessive way to secure compensation.

In 1702 the Dutch trader Willem Bosman published *A New and Accurate Description of the Coast of Guinea, Divided into the Gold, the Slave, and the Ivory Coasts,*[63] which was arguably the most authoritative discussion of commerce and diplomacy in the seventeenth- and eighteenth-century trade zones of Africa's Atlantic coast. Bosman was derisive when discussing the economic and political strategies of area regents. "At several places on the coast," Bosman tells his readers: "Debts are recovered in a very unjust and villainous manner, especially in those places where we have little or no Power, or in some of the Kingdoms. By "villainous," Bosman meant that "A Rascally Creditor" in those places, instead of "asking his Money of his Debtor, and summoning him before the Judges in the case of refusal, seizes the first thing he can meet with, though six times the value of his Debt, without any regard to who is Proprietor."

Under the dismissive tag of "very extravagant justice," Bosman rejected a political system where creditors seized a member of the debtor's family as collateral while the debtor appealed to regional authorities, often kin, who were ultimately expected to determine the amount owed and how it ought to be transferred. Bosman could see in these indigenous forms of jurisprudence only a haphazard system of debt exchange that lacked a universal set of procedures. In Bosman's view, modern commercial and political compacts should be governed by the "law of nations."[64] But Bosman overlooked the fact that ad hoc rituals were pivotal to the way merchants and politicians adjudicated diplomatic standing.

The debut of formal protocols for assessing diplomatic standing is often traced to the 1648 Peace of Westphalia. This event marked the official demise of the Thirty Years' War in the Holy Roman Empire, as well as eighty years of militarized conflict between Spain and the Dutch Republic. The multilateral negotiations that defined the armistice required Spain to recognize the Dutch Republic as a sovereign nation. As a diplomatic event that entailed a series of treaties, and that insisted on the consensus of privileged actors as a protocol for multilateral agreement, this moment is frequently construed as a watershed in the history of sovereignty.[65] And yet, for good reason, some scholars are skeptical that Westphalian sovereignty has ever been reliable as a means for safeguarding diplomatic standing, since—even in the most generous reading—the protocols that shaped the Peace of Westphalia were designed by a few powerful actors, effectively bypassing the interests of most of the world's polities. Further, the stipulated terms of engagement are a poor proxy for the diplomatic and commercial endeavors that North Atlantic polities subsequently pursued. Recent scholarship has demonstrated that the terms of the treaty scarcely obstructed the ongoing political pursuits and commercial aspirations of parties to the contract.[66] Plus, North Atlantic polities were not the only ones pioneering new strategies of statecraft premised on novel approaches to credit-debt.

King Lat Sukaabe taxed his imperial subjects in exchange for protection from slave traders and rival empires. In testimonies laced with swagger, Sage historians of the region's oral traditions insist that Lat Sukaabe would—in testimonies laced with swagger—declare: "You gave me control of your destiny, which I accepted voluntarily. I have lived up to my duty because for ten years your families, your harvests, and your animals have been protected from the pillages which were common before. You owe me a reward, or rather a compensation, because I am the protector of your property."[67]

Dynastic traditions testify to the celebrated ruler's lofty self-esteem. And Lat Sukaabe's knack for military conquest and political ingenuity are only heightened by the story of his rise from "humble origins" to supreme authority.

Lat Sukaabe was born with a physical impairment and used prosthetics to walk from the time he was a toddler. His name, in fact, derives from a Wolof verb, *sukootu*, that "describes the limping walk of someone supporting [himself] on crutches." His brothers, concerned that such a conspicuous physical disability would bring shame to the royal household, persuaded their father, the king, to place Lat Sukaabe with his maternal uncle. Raised in the home of a shepherd, Lat Sukaabe "was healed."[68]

The competition for power between royal matrilineages stemmed from the important role of the maternal family as the "owner" of property, particularly slaves and cattle. The most crucial element of seventeenth-century dynastic traditions in the Wolof empire is the priority assigned to matrilineal descent. This tradition created fierce competition among the male children of a single royal household—conflict between the sons and nephews of a given king figure as a common theme in local oral traditions. Crucial to the emergent criteria for leadership, then, was a process of anointing. Lat Sukaabe's story bears this out, though it's precisely because of the secular and yet mythological quality of his unlikely ascent that he is received as a figure who straddles two historical epochs: the *ceddo* (indigenous, aristocratic) regimes of old and the Islamic dynasties to come.

In the time of Lat Sukaabe, it was prophesied that the son who ate the "slave meat"—the head and feet of a lamb—would be the next king. In this way we perhaps see an effort to retroactively mark the decline of one dynastic tradition in favor of another: in place of a pristine pedigree, the future king cuts his teeth on slave meat. And it's true that, in the age of empire, Lat Sukaabe's power derived from his capacity to command the slaves who would serve as his bureaucrats, staffing every major office. In this framework, slaves occupied the most cherished, and most highly valued, forms of labor: as tax collectors, military officers, and chiefs of agriculture.

In other words, Lat Sukaabe's reign is seen as the triumph of a ceddo regime. Ceddo were warriors who plundered neighboring societies and imbibed large quantities of alcohol, in contrast to the pious customs that characterized governance under Muslim rulers. Uprisings by Islamic intellectuals would define the political landscape of Kajoor during the last few decades of the seventeenth century, and several crucial features of eighteenth-century statecraft stem from trying to contain the "religious wars" that continued to flare up. Yet this question of ceddo (Wolof, *ceddo yi*) versus Muslim (Wolof, *sëriñ si*), has less to do with religious beliefs than with strategies for establishing and regimenting social standing. Wolof aristocrats were notorious for their consumption of alcohol: they hunted and hosted elaborate feasts characterized by music and dance—aristocratic excesses that Muslims of Senegambia found distasteful. Wolof monarchs inherited the throne through their mothers, whereas most Wolof people inherited property through the father's line.

Thus Lat Sukaabe's tenure marked the end of what some scholars call the "old" Wolof regime: it stretches from the moment Kajoor and Bawol were reunified in 1695 until the 1860s, when Islamic reform movements and French strategies of conquest dramatically transformed local structures of sovereignty. This period is also known as "time of slavery," since aristocratic despotism fueled participation in industries associated with the transatlantic slave trade, connecting Senegal's coastal empires to the wider world, with lasting implications for local renditions of sovereignty. By the twenty-first century, more than 40 percent of Senegal's population would identify as Wolof. But the influence of this ethnic group is even more profound, since Wolof is the nation's lingua franca, the tongue that Senegalese people first learn to speak and that they use even more often than French, the official language of education and politics. This dynamic is an artifact of seventeenth- and eighteenth-century empire, as the regions drawn into the orbit of Wolof aristocracies adopted their customs and norms.

Military force was the key to Lat Sukaabe's authority: he effectively managed to subdue political competition in a region where decades of civil war, famine, and chaos had produced divided loyalties. And yet it is his transition from slavery to tariffs and taxes as the primary source of state revenue that registers as his most significant accomplishment. Lat Sukaabe collected tariffs on all goods that passed through the Senegal River valley. Slaves were taxed at the highest rate. French commercial agents readily paid what he charged them in order to access cherished markets, but they also extended credit to African rulers according to rates that were not always consistent or clearly described. And credit could, of course, be embodied in human cargo.

In this sense it is useful to compare these dynamics with the emergence of formal systems for extending credit to merchants in the city-states of Antwerp and Amsterdam in what is today the Netherlands, as well as protocols for making credit available to broad swaths of the male, property-owning citizenry in England with the emergence of the Bank of England in 1694. Because it was not restricted to people with large amounts of capital, the English model of public lending shifted the burden of funding military conflicts and social institutions from the government and the wealthy elite to a public tax base. Accordingly, a model of governance emerged in which the priorities of the Crown and the preferences of a small network of nobility became subsidiary to the concerns of citizens who, because their economic power now fueled government, held the state accountable to their concerns in unprecedented ways. The result was a financial revolution defined by the concept of a national debt, which led England to establish a securities market as well as a currency that circulated throughout Europe and the New World. England thus established what some scholars have termed a "fiscal-military state": a powerful organ of central governance, with an ambitious economic agenda that its powerful navy helped to secure.[69] Thus the new circuits of credit that polities like England thrived on involved new structures of liability. At home, this involved new laws for fining and imprisoning debtors.[70]

We tend to associate the eighteenth century with the triumph of reason and the calculus of difference by which North Atlantic merchants and politicians asserted a distinction between their own capacity for rational judgment and that of their interlocutors in Africa and elsewhere. But it's worthwhile to consider corresponding developments in modes of forensic inquiry. The same context that is credited with incubating the European Enlightenment gave rise to new technologies and procedures associated with heightened structures of surveillance and criminal inquiry, and with protocols for redress—on both sides of the Atlantic.

As Walter Rodney notes in his insightful study of slavery on Africa's Atlantic coast,

> By the end of the sixteenth century the individuals who could be deprived of their freedom by process of law were those condemned to death, those who administered poison or who placed a fatal *fetish* on others. . . . To these it must be added that debts often led to slavery. . . . The slaves obtained in these several ways could be considered in one sense criminals, since they were duly convicted by the law of the land. At the same time, it is clear that customary law in Upper Guinea was functioning in a radically different way during the slave trade era than it did before and afterwards.
>
> Many of the charges which resulted in enslavement were complete fabrications.[71]

It is well documented that criminals were often sold into bondage during the transatlantic slave trade. Here Rodney notes that, as the slave trade escalated, the idea of who counts as a criminal became more expansive. In other words, increasing demand from the transatlantic slave trade shaped indigenous structures of jurisprudence--and not merely in terms of criminal conviction. These developments even shaped the way that African systems of jurisprudence adjudicated what we now think of as an "accidental death":

Crimes were essentially of two sorts: those which were discoverable by physical proof (such as murder, theft, or adultery), and those which were discoverable only because sickness or death had come about. Many deaths were attributable to evil influences, emanating from a *feticeiro*. . . . Africans were prone to come to this latter conclusion when death resulted from accident.

Clearly, offences in the latter category had to be detected in a manner that was quite different from ordinary crimes. It was the interrogation of the dead person by the priest which yielded information as to whether a given person had died because of a "fatal fetish" being placed upon him; and it was the priest who ferreted out the guilty party.[72]

By the nineteenth century this notion of "accidental death" would give rise to the novel legal category of "tort law"—also known as "the law of wrongs"—as legal statutes throughout the Atlantic world (though most notably in England) became ever more concerned with "wrongful death." Yet this sixteenth-century moment, before such jurisprudence became concretized as a separate body of law, is instructive. It is especially crucial to note what characterizes forensic inquiry in this early modern period: the priest was tasked with assessing the nature of the offense. The priest also determined who should be charged and how that person should be punished. The form of inquest Rodney describes, we would classify as a kind of autopsy. As such, the stakes involve the question of causality. For instance, was a personal injury, death, or loss of cargo caused by what sixteenth-century North Atlantic maritime insurance called "an act of God," meaning it was no one's fault, or was someone liable for the offense? The language of "fetish" here marks the potential presence of a medicine or ritual technology (perhaps a poison) deliberately concocted by one person to bring about another's demise. In Europe, toxicology would ultimately provide an indispensable set of scientific criteria by which people could assess causality in instances of sudden, inexplicable death.

As early as 44 BC the Greek physician Antistius had performed a preliminary version of what we now understand as an autopsy when Julius Caesar was fatally stabbed by members of an ancient conspiracy. Yet that medical investigation consisted in a mere examination of stab wounds. The earliest records for a science of forensic inquiry, with implications for legal standing and access to capital, date to sixteenth-century Portuguese sources on the transatlantic slave trade, like those Rodney translated. Similar developments took place in other North Atlantic polities during the same period: in 1533 Charles V of France passed his famous Carolingian Code, which sanctioned the use of "evidence from autopsies" in cases ranging from "infanticide" and "homicide" to "apparent poisoning." This legislative act also provided funds for medical experts to assist in legal investigations. In 1560 a similar society of experts was organized in Italy, and at about the same time the University of Leiden institutionalized the science of medical autopsy. Still, these forms of inquiry proceeded ad hoc until the nineteenth century, when concerns for a science defined by precision and reliability led to greater consensus on methods of forensic inquiry that were institutionalized and shared among North Atlantic nations and their colonial outposts.

Social theorists and historians have thoughtfully critiqued the distinct notion of human agency (possessive individualism) and epistemology (the alleged triumph of reason) that came to define eighteenth-century theories of economy, most prominently in the intellectual stylings of people like Adam Smith and groups like the Physiocrats, who maintained that markets were most efficient when state intervention was minimal, devoting little time in their analyses to the emergent forms of liability that defined access to credit in the period under study. Yet forensic inquiry took root in Smith's native Scotland concurrent with the Edinburgh wing of the Enlightenment, during the same period that witnessed the 1776 publication of Smith's *Inquiry into the Nature and Causes of the Wealth of Nations*. Most notably through a legendary 1780 case in which a doctor discerned that the murderer was left-handed and detectives correctly matched footprints in a muddy bog to a killer who later confessed, "Scotland established itself as a leader in forensic investigation" during the last two decades of the eighteenth century.[73]

It is crucial that we consider theories of causality concerned with economic growth in concert with the mechanisms of social differentiation and protocols for liability that create privileged tiers of economic and political interaction despite the emergence of shared standards for governance and credit-debt explicitly framed as universal, scientific, and objective. Since at least the seventeenth century, governance in North Atlantic polities has in large measure been predicated on techniques for discerning the character of a person, or nation, based on forensic evidence and with translating consensus on these assessments into supposedly value-neutral genres of social standing (for individuals) and diplomatic standing (for nations). For these reasons the birth of forensic science and its implications for jurisprudence as well as for value transfer—here termed the "forensics of capital"—is a more useful guide for making sense of governance than the Enlightenment discourse on reason or the liberal theories of governance based on them that frequently impute a metaphysical essence to persons and polities (as good or evil, legitimate or criminal) without adequately addressing the protocols used to arrive at such decisions or the means for establishing consensus on such matters.

Instead, we might call explicit attention to the moral infrastructure within which commerce and diplomacy take place. Taking the forensics of capital as a theoretical framework calls explicit attention to the fact that theories of causality, as scientific principles, are not "universal." Rather, their legitimacy derives from the way they have been institutionalized and authorized.[74] We might further consider the evidence that structures of governance and credit-debt rely on to adjudicate social and diplomatic standing.

In a related argument, anthropologist and social theorist Stephan Palmié calls our attention to the emphasis that Western jurisprudence has historically placed on "properly individuated human subjects or, to use the more appropriate forensic term, 'persons,' as authors of their actions." It is ultimately to this "highly specific regime of evidentiality"[75] that we attribute facticity, truth, and certainty. This emergent concept of personhood, as a prototype for the citizen, implies "a temporally coherent, skin-bound, self-possessed, and self-identical human subject as the author of his or her actions—or, in a forensic sense, the individual person capable not only of exercising choice in terms of goal-directed behavior, but also of shouldering responsibility for the consequences, intended or not, of his or her own actions."[76] This involves a structure of "accountability" that has implications for social action, historical agency, and economic intercourse.[77]

As early as the seventeenth century, John Locke had argued that "human identity cannot be grounded other than on *personal* terms, that is, forensically."[78] "It isn't enough that we imagine ourselves the same individual from one day to the next, sleeping or waking, young or old, whole or missing a limb. It is our capacity for reflexive self-identification coupled with, or rather upheld by, our sense of responsibility for our past actions that generates the sense of biographically coherent individual identity."[79] Thus the crucial question for Locke is not whether a person *feels* like himself or herself from day to day, but whether that same person can be held *accountable* for individual actions in the world. What we come to understand as a "biographically coherent" personal identity is grounded, for Locke, in the fact of liability.[80] In other words, neither the capacity for social action nor the question of personal recognition is steeped in a general claim about the human capacity for self-governance. Rather, they depend on whether a particular person is seen as the "author" of individual action, an idea that aligns with the theory of property Locke outlines in the *Second Treatise of Civil Government*. Locke begins by insisting that possession of the self (or "proprietorship in one's person") is what makes it possible for people to own property in the first place. For Locke, the modern self confronts nature with his or her (though of course for Locke, *his*) "embodied capacity" to generate wealth. On this basis, Locke argues that "the self that appropriates his or her actions in the creation of wealth" must likewise be held accountable for any "liabilities that arise."[81] In the 1669 constitution that Locke crafted for the British slave colony of the Carolinas, in which he was a stakeholder, the implied subject of the law is likewise "juridically responsible for any deeds freely done or obligations freely contracted."[82] In this sense Locke captures the crucial tether between accountability and accounting that defined governance in the seventeenth-century Atlantic world.

In 1685 the French king Louis XIV passed Le Code Noir, which, besides ordering all people who adhered to the Jewish faith out of French colonies, declared that all persons enslaved in these contexts must be baptized and reared in Roman Catholicism. Yet it also inscribed the distinct legal status of enslaved persons in the eyes of the French government. As article 30 stipulates,

> Ne pourront les esclaves être pourvus d'office ni de commission ayant quelque fonction publique, ni être constitués agents par autres que leurs maîtres pour gérer et administrer aucun négoce, ni être arbitres, experts ou témoins, tant en matière civile que criminelle: et en cas qu'ils soient ouïs en témoignage, leur déposition ne servira que de mémoire pour aider les juges à s'éclairer d'ailleurs, sans qu'on en puisse tire aucune présomption, ni conjoncture, ni adminicule de preuve.

> (Slaves cannot hold offices or mandates that involve the discharge of any public functions. They cannot be made agents, for the running or manning of a business, by anyone other than their masters. Nor can they sit as arbitrators, experts, or witnesses in civil or criminal cases. In cases where their testimony is heard, it can only be used to refresh the memory of judges—it cannot provide the basis for any assumptions, conjectures, or proof.)

Needless to say, these laws were enshrined because colonial entities were well aware that in some versions of Atlantic slavery—like those that defined the Senegal River valley as home to lands and resources the French and British eagerly aspired to secure—slaves had access to capital and wielded political authority that could undercut imperial aspirations. Hence the redundancy of article 31:

Ne pourront aussi les esclaves être parties ni être [*sic*] en jugement en matière civile, tant en demandant qu'en défendant, ni être parties civiles en matière criminelle, sauf à leurs maîtres d'agir et défendre en matière civile et de poursuivre en matière criminelle la réparation des outrages et excès qui auront été contre leurs esclaves.

(Nor can a slave be a party to, or be judged in, a civil matter either as plaintiff or defendant, nor can he institute a criminal action in his own right in redress of a wrong against himself. Only his master acting as his next friend in a civil matter can seek reparations, in a criminal matter, for outrages and excesses committed against the slave.)

Meanwhile these legal protocols, liberal in their efforts to strip enslaved persons of legal standing in the eyes of the law, took few measures to ensure that due process would be observed, even in the way slaves were tried:

Pourront les esclaves être poursuivis criminellement, sans qu'il soit besoin de rendre leurs maîtres partie, (sinon) en cas de complicité.

(Criminal proceedings can be instituted against slaves without involving their masters, except in cases of complicity.)[83]

While it is common to differentiate between indigenous modes of enslavement in Africa and slavery as conducted in Atlantic plantations, with the caveat that the latter entailed treating slaves strictly as chattel (property), scholars less frequently tease out the legal rationale through which persons initially apprehended as human beings were effectively converted into possessions.[84] Nor do they explain how this shift corresponded to broader transformations in governance during the age of the Enlightenment. These developments articulate with the mercantile logic that increasingly defined strategies of governance.

In 1663 the French minister Jean-Baptiste Colbert penned *Mémoires sur les affaires de finances de France pour servir à l'histoire*, a handwritten history of royal finance of which only one copy remains. Colbert never finished the *Mémoires*; still, this text registers shifts in prevailing conceptions of governance, many of which he helped to pioneer, as Colbert biographer Jacob Soll notes: "First, it was a work of political economy, not political history. It was intended to state mercantilist ideology and inform Louis of the financial precedent of past kings. Its detailed reporting of royal accounts suggests that it was for Louis' eyes only. Most remarkably, it contains a long passage almost verbatim from Pacioli."[85]

Fra Luca Bartolemeo de Pacioli, the Italian mathematician, Franciscan monk, and sometimes collaborator of Leonardo da Vinci is the man credited with inventing double-entry bookkeeping, a method that revolutionized financial accounting between the moment it was invented sometime around 1484 and the time it was institutionalized throughout the North Atlantic as the signature strategy for keeping inventory during the century to follow. More than a mere method of keeping exchange in order, double-entry bookkeeping was a tactic for demonstrating the virtue of the merchant who prepared the books. A diligent account was equated with an earnest, noble merchant[86] during a time when commerce was conceived as a secular version of divine grace. Here numbers spoke a divine truth rendered into numerals by God's most diligent earthly scribes.

It was Colbert who trained Louis XIV in accounting based on a system modeled after Pacioli's contributions, a topic the two men routinely discussed. And while it is the Sun King—Monsieur *L'état c'est moi*—whose signature graces royal documents of that age, Louis XIV considered Colbert his guide. The king delegated most of what this emergent science of governance entailed to his trusted minister.[87] Unlike in the city-states of regions that are today known as Italy and the Netherlands, in France double-entry bookkeeping was not yet an official state practice. Still, texts like *États de la dépense et recette du trésor* (The state of expenditures and receipts of the treasury), published between 1662 and 1681, testify to the role of accounting as a crucial element of the royal repertoire in the age of Colbert. Other French ministers would ultimately help to oversee Louis XIV's finances, but even they benefitted from the system Colbert had established.

Louis XIV, renowned for his devotion to Catholicism and disdain for the cosmopolitan and even radical sensibilities that defined merchants and politicians in city-states like those of the Dutch polities, developed numerous reforms in the sphere of accounting that borrowed directly from his declared enemies. During an age when France was engaged in war with England— and at times with the Dutch city-states—Colbert sent his son to what is now Holland (1671), as well as to England and Italy, as part of his training in accounting. Besides noting the technical efficacy with which Dutch polities managed naval forces and levied taxes, the young Jean-Baptiste Colbert (who bore his father's name) remarked on the "order" that defined the approach to inventory emanating from what is now the Netherlands. Colbert eventually commissioned a history of Dutch trade and praised texts that declared the virtues of British and Dutch accounting. As part of his 1673

Ordinance pour le Commerce, Colbert stipulated that all businesses keep double-entry books the government could routinely inspect.[88] As such, accounting became a crucial mechanism for accountability, a formal element of state surveillance and security:

> The European crises of the mid-seventeenth century induced a lack of faith in traditional, literary humanist political culture, and the rise of well-organized, well-armed, and well-financed merchant empires led to the establishment of new political methods. The results were different in each country, but the tools were similar; European states shared not only complex economic, military, political, social and spiritual crises but also comparable responses to them. Feudal government could incorporate neither the evolving merchant culture, with its reform of state finance, nor the exigencies of a growing population.[89]

"The rise of political economy" as a practical science and philosophy of governance, in other words, embodied "an attempt to meet these challenges."[90]

This emergent science of secular governance created strategies for accountability that transformed latent notions of policing and recalibrated social standing, as in the formal creation of bank accounts and police records.[91] But these transformations also produced new ideas about causality, with ramifications for the way people would ultimately understand economic growth.

If the seventeenth century set many of these dynamics in motion with renewed vigor, the nineteenth century provides an appropriate bookend through the proliferation of discrete nations conceived as "legitimate" spheres of commercial and diplomatic adjudication because they were understood to be scientific, objective, and thus not simply rational and appropriate but universal. Any number of nineteenth-century events might be understood as the culmination of this stance. We might note that these events correspond to the birth of wage labor as well as the related rise of the corporation during the first few decades of the nineteenth century. We might see the birth of a new commercial reality in the demise of the treaties designed to protect private creditors stretching back to the time of Westphalia yet ending within a decade of the legal abolition of the slave trade. Or we could focus on the events associated with the demise of these statutes: the end of the Napoleonic Wars between 1814 and 1817, which created a new appreciation for defending each country's right to self-determination (deemed necessary to forge a nation in the image of one's people, even though few if any of these political entities matched the forensic profile their architects imagined them to possess).

That the diverse repertoire of inquiry I am calling forensics has been conceived as the ur-science through which to adjudicate social belonging in the age of secular governance should not, however, lead us to conclude that it is as rational and deliberate as adherents to systems of "scientific jurisprudence"[92] from the nineteenth century onward would tend to believe. For historical concerns with social standing lead, as I have demonstrated, through a tangled web of ad hoc compacts and rituals for authorizing access to capital that draw on the customs of peoples whose forms of governance and notions of value were routinely disqualified from privileged spheres of diplomacy and commerce. Thus it is crucial to understand the calculus used to assess and establish social standing in places like Africa's Atlantic coast. In the mode of governance that came to define this context, we see forms of credit-debt and morality that bear heavily on the question of social standing, where social standing is the means through which access to capital is adjudicated.

While Lat Sukaabe was preoccupied with securing dominion on the Atlantic coast, and even as signares established families and commercial relations with merchants and politicians from the North Atlantic, Islamic intellectuals inhabiting the same region cultivated dissent against the Wolof aristocracy. This had implications for colonial rule in a moment when the French were keen to fortify their territorial presence.

Louis Moreau de Chambonneau of the Compagnie du Sénégal carefully documented the remarkable influence of Nasir ad-Din. Claiming that he and his closest supporters were "messengers of God," Nasir ad-Din insisted that a ruler's primary duty was to protect and provide for his subjects, not to terrorize or exploit them as the Wolof imperium had done. Nasir ad-Din's proposed reforms embodied a forensics of capital emanating from his immediate context: he did not condemn the practice of slavery as a whole, but he sought to have Muslims spared such a fate. He used the rationale that most Muslims belonged to the same ethnic groups and shared the same faith as the warrior aristocrats that Senegambia's ceddo kings had mobilized on their behalf. But Nasir ad-Din did not preach conversion to Islam. His movement was primarily concerned with protesting the forms of injury the people of Kajoor-Bawol were subjected to—with contesting exorbitant taxation and coercive labor practices. The movement surged beyond Mauritania, where it began as "an expression of tension between warriors and scholar-merchants and as an effort" to "destroy the growing commercial hegemony of the European Atlantic trade in the region, which was displacing the trans-Saharan trade." As these religious conflicts spread into the Senegal River valley, they became specifically concerned with advocating for a Muslim monarch (*buur juulit*, in Wolof). Although the movement quickly amassed an impressive following, it fizzled by 1676. The ensuing political turmoil had helped to create a new "aristocratic order" that European slave traders exploited by "purchasing the refugees of war and famine."[93]

Consequently, Muslim learning and political authority became concentrated in the villages of Kokki, Luuga, and Ñomre in northern Kajoor. Lat Sukaabe recognized the political influence of marabouts by offering them royal titles in exchange for loyalty. During conflicts with neighboring polities, marabouts would now be expected to organize military contingents. In the absence of conflict, they served as political representatives for the regions they inhabited. The relationships Lat Sukaabe cultivated with marabouts stemmed from a pragmatic interest in reorganizing and reconstituting sovereign authority in the region. And his approach to statecraft had lasting implications. By giving marabouts royal titles and requiring them to execute state functions like defense, administration, and taxation, he effectively brought them into the sphere of imperial nobility, helping to alienate them from the communities of Muslim scholars who remained skeptical of the aristocracy and deeply invested in critical commentary about state abuses. In the decades to come, opposition to the state would be embodied in Muslim intellectuals who delivered a critique of the aristocracy.

But the Wolof aristocracy was only one of several factions competing for power in the Senegal River valley between the seventeenth and nineteenth centuries. French colonial aspirations would likewise prove crucial new articulations of sovereignty. They would also shape emerging discourses about who fit prevailing criteria for leadership of, and political participation in, the political entity that was on its way to becoming the nation of Senegal.

TWO

Capacity for Governance

On September 10, 1879, French colonial officials persuaded Lat Dior,[1] "king" of Kajoor, to sign a treaty authorizing railway construction in his territory, along with a promise to supply local labor. The treaty of 1879 was the culmination of a sustained diplomatic effort, of clever political strategy by politicians and military commanders on both sides of the Atlantic who seized this moment, and this medium, to cultivate interlocking interests. Though Lat Dior was a powerful monarch, his enterprise relied on funds provided by the habitant Gaspard Devès. In this sense the battle between the French empire and Wolof sovereigns was just one part of a broader landscape in which diverse actors controlled distinct spheres of power and different kinds of resources. The French effort to construct a railroad through Senegal relied on nineteenth-century techniques for determining an African regent's capacity for governance, which has a discernible metric by this juncture. Throughout the Atlantic world, the capacity for governance had increasingly to do with whether an individual or polity could attend to the risks involved with political activity and established clear protocols for assessing liability. But what a risk entailed, and who was fit to manage it, derived from an emergent forensic calculus.

Though French financiers had discussed installing a railroad in west Africa since the birth of locomotive transport in 1830s England, there had long been concern about the commercial viability and the logistic parameters of such an enterprise. By 1857, French colonial officials began hatching plans for a railroad designed to capitalize on Dakar's strategic location as a military installation and trading post. Together with the telegraph, the railroad was imagined as the most efficient way to tether several crucial vectors of trade—the ports of Dakar, Saint-Louis, and Gorée, as well as the territory of Kajoor, which connected them.[2]

France's first effort at a railway in sub-Saharan Africa, the Dakar-Sudan rail line (hereafter DSL), was designed and built by a French firm called the Société de Batignolles. The contract the firm signed with the French government on October 30, 1880, stipulated that the line needed to be completed before April 30, 1883, if Parliament approved all the terms by January 31, 1881. The company was expected to generate one-fourth of the capital for the project (approximately 68,000 francs per kilometer times 260 kms = 17,680,000) by issuing shares, while the rest of the funds would be raised by issuing bonds once the line had been built. In return, the state was to guarantee the company a return of 3,400 francs above operating costs for each section of track that was approved and put into service. This basically amounted to a 5–6 percent annual return on the original investment as long as construction costs matched initial projections. The French government was willing to buttress private investment "because of the supposed risk of the venture." And yet the story of the French colonial railroad is a tale not merely about risk management, but about the way risk is imagined, harnessed, produced, and valued.[3] And the most crucial part of the railroad project involved determining who possessed the capacity for governance in the region where France had decided to install it.

Building a railroad in Senegal required France to carefully weigh the military and diplomatic stakes. Between 1854 and 1859, Governor-General Louis Faidherbe led a series of assaults on regional polities. Breaking with a long-standing diplomatic tradition, he refused to pay tribute to African sovereigns. Adapting battle tactics he had cultivated during his previous assignment in Algeria, Faidherbe established a string of trading posts from Saint-Louis to Médine. Shifting from a primary emphasis on the benefits derived from commerce, the colonial government was now interested to acquire more territory.[4] Since the French had established a presence in Senegal's port cities, the most crucial part of the project involved securing access to Kajoor. By the nineteenth century, Kajoor and Bawol would be the region's most important kingdoms in terms of size and influence.

Kajoor was not yet governed by a written treaty. So Faidherbe decided the French were justified in seizing it. Yet he was aware of the vibrant opposition movement that Muslim intellectuals had established in the region. Communicating with movement leaders, Faidherbe sought support in his plot to dismantle the Wolof aristocracy by suggesting that brutal taxation and forcible repression would cease under French rule.

One consequence of the transatlantic slave trade was the birth of imperial entities that grew powerful in the Senegal River valley by using brokered arms to command territory. The savanna landscape that stretches throughout what is today Senegal made it difficult for large concentrations of people to dwell in a single location. Consequently, Wolof empires were not defined by a single palace inhabited by the royal family and its dependents. Instead, sovereigns often lived in a smaller residence with private security, slaves, and close associates. The king of Kajoor, for instance, had a residence in the port city of Rufisque where he could visit with merchants and politicians from the North Atlantic and elsewhere, in addition to estates scattered throughout the empire.

Aristocrats with close ties to the king included the *garmi*, a man who descended from royalty on both his mother's and his father's sides of the family, and the *lingeer*, a woman from a royal matrilineage whose children would likewise be members of the nobility. Other titles for nobility included *doomi-bur*, "children of the king," a distinction reserved for male children the king might have fathered with women who did not possess a title (including enslaved women). The throne was passed through the mother's side of the family. But in the event that the crown passed to the son of a king, a new royal matriline and line of descent was established.

Wolof aristocracies secured their influence by commanding territory, then conferring noble titles on men who were devoted to the king. Land created the opportunity for nobles to settle their families and acquire slaves, but also to assess tribute and to secure labor from area residents. Kings had to carefully weigh the stakes of creating new nobility and granting land, which meant empowering people who might one day oppose the sovereign. And no king could remove a noble without risking adverse political consequences. Yet if this practice was prone to risk, Wolof sovereigns also controlled the most powerful mechanism of liability, since military might generally outweighed any promise of land or title, or any other juridical claim.

Wolof empires grew powerful during the transatlantic slave trade as trafficking in human cargo granted them access to cotton from Asia as well as alcohol and other manufactured products from around the world.[5] Wolof aristocrats also acquired horses, used in slave raids to generate even more revenue and to expand their dominion. During an especially intense period of warfare and famine during the 1750s, Senegambia produced large numbers of slave exports even though the region produced only 10 percent of all slaves shipped across the Atlantic during the eighteenth century—and even fewer at later periods.[6] Thus the significance of this region's history with the slave trade has, in one important sense, less to do with sheer numbers than with the relation between slavery and transformations in militarism and credit-debt on Africa's Atlantic coast. Wolof polities charged Europeans for access to Atlantic trading posts, forts, and markets. At one point Senegambia produced 75 percent of the grain France acquired from Africa through trade, a product that local merchants routinely taxed at coastal cities like Saint-Louis and Gorée. Meanwhile, by the end of the eighteenth century Wolof polities were completely dependent on France for the arms they used to battle each other and to raid small-scale societies for slaves.

Wolof empires were made up of people from diverse walks of life. There were agriculturalists who produced crops and weavers who toiled to make cloth. Some people prepared food, while others were domestic servants. Having people devoted to these various tasks freed the elite for leisure, but it also enabled them to focus on warfare and commerce, which generated revenue and translated into political privilege. Meanwhile, the imperial state commissioned people from different caste groups for countless tasks. Apart from slave bureaucrats who commanded the military, some enslaved persons managed elite households and farms, while others provided private security and strategic counsel. Their status as slaves explains their unique access to privilege: denied social mobility, they curried favor with their owners for income and opportunity. Thus, even as slaves were technically bound by law to "serve" their "owners," a dynamic political landscape emerged from the power they were able to command.

The closeness rulers enjoyed with trusted slaves and confidants yielded political demarcations that did not map evenly onto ideas of individual autonomy. The term *geer* was used when referring to people who owned or worked on the land, whether slaves and modest farmers or the sovereign leader of the polity. Since the term *geer* cut across economic distinctions, nobles distinguished themselves from slaves and peasants through lineage. In contrast to people with intimate ties to the land, *ñeeño* evolved as a term for inherited caste occupations: *géwél* (praise singer or bard), *tëgg* (blacksmith), or *uude* (leather worker). The privileged standing that *geer* enjoyed derived from the opportunity to shape their own economic fortunes through the harvest and from cultivating ties with their patrons and allies among the aristocracy; *ñeeño*, meanwhile, earned income from projects that people commissioned (often people with greater wealth and social standing). Over time, the distinction between *geer* and *ñeeño* acquired the appearance of a natural division, and the differential orders were maintained by strict social taboos concerning intermarriage.[7]

The strict association that emerged between Wolof peoples of lower standing and the aristocracy marked a contrast with people who enjoyed other ethnic affiliations. If slavery was central to statecraft in Wolof empires, Sereer peoples were defined by their aversion to it. They tended to inhabit the dense forest region that they conceived as a kind of refuge. Wolof aristocrats frequently characterized Sereer as "peoples without god, laws, or king," in a forensic calculus that made these uncivilized peoples easier to enslave. In pursuing missionary work among Sereer, the Saint-Louis métis Abbé David Boilat rejected widespread allegations that they were "thieves and murderers,"[8] noting that this ostensible ethnic characteristic was in fact a tactical position that derived from the Sereer's relation to the political economy of slavery in the region:

> Fearing they would be captured and sold into slavery, [the Sereer] resolved to close off their territory to all strangers. This is why they assassinate anyone who dares to enter their villages. . . . Their greatest crime was to fight for their liberty and independence, for the defense of their fields and forests, for the free possession of their herds, but above all for the inviolable liberty of their wives and children, who were hunted like wild beasts in order to reduce them to servitude and slavery. Alone in the midst . . . [they] regard slavery as a crime.[9]

Lebu peoples were likewise marginal to the power centers that defined the Senegal River valley of the eighteenth and nineteenth centuries. Known for their prowess in fishing, Lebu populations had steadily made their way from the interior to the Atlantic coast. Lebu oral traditions speak of marriage and intermixture with peoples close to the coast, who "taught them techniques for harvesting the riches of the sea." This suggests that Lebu societies derived from intermingling between Wolof speakers from the interior and Sereer fishing communities along the Atlantic coast. Meanwhile, Wolof settlements emerged in the least fertile regions of the Senegal River valley. In this context, a highly stratified social order emerged, including aristocrats, free persons, highly skilled caste workers, and enslaved persons. The imperial quality of Wolof polities made it easy to mobilize labor for digging wells and to conscript "military specialists" who guarded against attack from "mobile desert warriors who periodically erupted into the region, especially during prolonged periods of ecological crisis."[10]

The most strident critics of the Wolof aristocracy tended to be Muslims who lived in areas abutting the empire. These intellectuals construed imperial sovereigns as corrupt tyrants, and the customs and rituals of ceddo warriors came to signify decadence. Although Wolof elites initially managed to fend off the opposition, the forms of militarism and political engagement that surfaced in this moment would have lasting implications.

In November 1859 there was an uprising in the Ndiambur district against the sovereign leaders of the Geej dynasty. Muslim insurgents circulated rumors that they were being armed and supported by French colonial authorities. Royal slaves employed by the Wolof imperial military responded by burning dozens of villages to the ground, destroying stores of recently harvested millet and groundnuts.[11] Despite not achieving many of their goals, insurgents struck a blow at the Wolof aristocracy. The uprising revealed the cleavages within local polities between wealthy aristocrats, Muslim intellectuals like those who had led the rebellion, and French colonial officials who tried to play different sides off against each other as part of their strategy of conquest. This conflict helped to reconfigure the relation between Islam and the Wolof aristocracy. As their military efforts proved unsuccessful, Muslim leaders began to invest hope in a critique of French colonialism as well as the ceddo regime. Ceddo would ultimately embrace Islam for pragmatic reasons having to do with shifts in the broader political landscape. But because their aristocratic lifestyle veered away from the piety[12] that took root in smaller Muslim settlements, this version of Islam was widely viewed by critics as a veneer rather than an earnest engagement with the faith.[13]

This is not to suggest that there was no contact between *ceddo yi* (people with ties to the court) and *sëriñ si* (people with ties to vernacular forms of Islam): the former were associated with government and warfare and the latter with education and agriculture, and people in the two constituencies would sometimes exchange gifts and favors. Ceddo might offer Muslim priests land, cattle, slaves, and other items of value for religious protection in the form of blessings or talismans that might be tied to the body for protection in battle. Still, as Islam proliferated among people of the Senegal River valley during the nineteenth century, aristocratic power and the forms of enslavement through which it was constituted unraveled. The most significant event for opposition forces was, of course, the emergence of a new Muslim order in Bawol in the 1890s, headed by Cheikh Amadu Bamba. Under his leadership, Murids built on a long-standing tradition of intellectual and social critique to challenge the Wolof aristocracy. Even after that imperial structure fell apart, Murids would confound colonial administrators by erecting an infrastructure of peasant cash cropping that joined newly emancipated slaves together with migrants and disciples. As such the history of Sufi Islam articulated with the legal abolition of slavery to produce a new economic and religious landscape in the aftermath of emancipation. But these developments were still some way off.

Just as the Ndiambur rebellion of 1859 was taking off, the French government granted Faidherbe the funds he had requested to start developing Kajoor. At the same time, the French minister of colonies was adamant that Senegal not be plagued by the relentless bloodshed that had characterized colonial Algeria. French policy stipulated that indigenous peoples were to retain control of their land. French commercial interests centered on undermining the juridical standing of Wolof kings and replacing them with leaders more amenable to French interests.

French forces were alarmed by the quick defeat of their comrades in the uprising of 1859 and based their next steps on trying to discern which constituency would ultimately prove most powerful. French intelligence networks revealed intense competition for sovereign authority.[14] Colonial officials realized they could not fully anticipate or control political power plays in the region once they observed the improbable ascent of Lat Dior, who came to power at the behest of Demba War Sall, a "royal slave." Demba War Sall was a high-ranking political official commanding a retinue of armed slaves on behalf of the Geej king until the Maajoojo empire seized control of the region. In 1861 he seized on Lat Dior's unique pedigree in order to position him as heir to the Geej dynasty in a scheme to reclaim territorial dominance.[15]

Though Lat Dior could not trace descent to a former king as the rules of succession stipulated, he was part of the Geej matriclan. He also had close family ties to royal bureaucrats who had converted to Islam during a time when indigenous authority was under increasing pressure to accept the religion for commercial and diplomatic reasons.[16] Aided by Demba War Sall's military expertise, Lat Dior inflicted a series of military defeats on his rivals. But Majoojo Faal had received sanction as the legitimate ruler of Kajoor from French colonial officials. As such, he continued to claim sovereign control of the disputed territory. With two kings claiming legitimacy, Kajoor fell into a prolonged state of political crisis until French military officials finally succeeding in expelling Lat Dior and his allies in 1864.[17]

But in 1870 Lat Dior seized power in Kajoor. Under Demba War Sall's guidance, he dominated the region from 1870 until 1886. Lat Dior's rise to power in 1870 involved extensive negotiation with French colonial officials.[18] He also allied with wealthy and influential habitant merchants in Saint-Louis. In fact, Lat Dior's tenure as sovereign was distinguished by his economic acumen. He arranged to have prisoners from military conflicts serve as forced labor on groundnut plantations; consequently, his reign witnessed tremendous growth in crop production. Despite being credited with economic prosperity, Lat Dior struggled to win full approval from area Muslims and remained vulnerable throughout his tenure as king.[19]

Conflicts had been especially troublesome in 1875, when Muslim soldiers from Kajoor and nearby Jolof launched an uprising. French officials helped Lat Dior fend off the opposition. Thus his policy going forward would to a significant degree involve managing his "political debt to French."[20] This created a dynamic in which Lat Dior was pressured by three competing constituencies. Besides the French, relations had become increasingly tense with his mentor, Demba War Sall. At the same time, members of the Muslim opposition bristled at the violence he had visited on their fallen comrades.

If Louis Brière de l'Isle had embraced the 1879 treaty that authorized the railroad as a way to secure Kajoor for the French, Lat Dior was concerned to ensure that French lands did not become a haven for slaves. Enslaved and free persons sought refuge in Jander and Ganjool because French colonial officials helped them evade the pervasive forms of warfare and kidnapping that proliferated in the decades following the legal abolition of the slave trade. As part of the treaty, the French also promised to keep the railroad territories free from any military presence.[21]

Yet it's not clear that Lat Dior fully understood the documents he was encouraged to sign: amid the circuitous language, there was no direct reference to railway construction, and the term locomotive appears only one time. It's likely that French authorities hoped to confuse him with their convoluted language, perhaps even to fudge their promises, as they had done with the revolutionary leaders of Guadeloupe and Saint-Domingue during the struggles for territorial autonomy that raged during the last decade of the eighteenth century and into the nineteenth.[22] Lat Dior had primarily been interested in securing French support to defeat political rivals. Yet by 1881 he was uncomfortable with the terms of the agreement. And either because he believed he had been duped—or perhaps because he had never planned to uphold it anyway—he rescinded the 1879 treaty.[23]

About this time, Lat Dior caught wind of the French authorities' plan to launch steamships down local rivers, which had long created convenient avenues for usurping imperial sovereignty.[24] Concerned that this development would give France an unanticipated military advantage, Lat Dior threatened to wage war against any further effort at railroad construction in Kajoor. The French secured the clandestine support of Lat Dior's allies (who joined with him in fighting the colonial military while secretly plotting his demise).

When Lat Dior tried to interrupt these plans, he was drawn into battle at Dexxele and killed through a conspiracy assisted by Demba War Sall.[25] In his capacity as a top-ranking adviser to the Wolof monarchy, Demba War Sall had long believed that Lat Dior made too many overtures to the Muslim opposition, and he would ultimately play a significant role in helping the French suppress Islamic insurgency in the region. This alliance was in many ways detrimental to both parties: in partnering with agents of conquest, Demba War Sall earned the ire of regional sovereigns. By attaching itself to Demba War Sall and by extension the Geej dynasty, the French government inherited long-standing enemies of the Wolof aristocracy.[26] Still, with military resistance drastically diminished, agents of the DSL could now address daily operations.

The colonial military seized control of Kajoor on December 20, 1882, then embarked on a program of rapid railway construction, completing the Dakar–Saint-Louis segment of the line by 1885. But the haphazard process of construction that defined this venture proved that sovereignty was primarily not about durable governance but about intersecting commercial interests and cross-cutting political aspirations.

After all, the French state had no clear idea of what construction would cost. And the engineering firm that built the rail line was not obligated to share its books with the French government. Plus, by the time construction began, the state had already pledged to guarantee a 5–6 percent rate of interest, even though government bonds were selling for between 3 and 4 percent at the time. This meant the Société could turn a profit of 7.6 million francs on its projected investment of 17.7 million (5 percent rate of interest divided by 3.5 percent on government bonds multiplied by 17,680,000 francs initial investment = 25,260,000 gross revenue and 25,260,000 gross revenue minus the 17,680,000 initial investment = 7,580,000 francs net profit). And though the contract required that "maximum operating expenses" be clearly delineated, it did not stipulate when the firm must disclose this information. Reviewing the contract, the finance minister remained concerned that "all risks" were being "charged to the state" and concluded that under these conditions it would be cheaper for the government to construct the railway itself. But he faced opposition from other political officials who felt the government was still under too much financial strain to go it alone.[27]

The scheduled government payment of 12,680,000 francs (48,769.23 francs per kilometer) would be disbursed as each segment of the line was accepted.[28] The Société thus had an incentive to have each section of the emergent rail line approved as quickly as possible. Construction protocols stipulated that each segment of the rail line be secure enough to manage the flow of crews and construction materials needed to lay the track. Beyond these minimal requirements, the engineers took shortcuts whenever possible. They relied on fragile embankments to secure rails. They used ramshackle lodges for station service whenever they could get away with it. Knowing that routine service would require a more elaborate infrastructure, the firm used the advance it had received from the state to cover expenses until rail segments were finished. They planned to funnel future expenses through the state treasury once the government began to provide public transportation. This way, the Société could avoid using any of the profit it had earned during construction to maintain the line.

In April 1884 an inspector drew the governor-general's attention to several risky features of the railroad embankment. First, engineers used inadequate soil to secure rail lines. They also used unapproved excavation methods for laying track. Finally, workers routinely relied on inferior materials, including spikes that buckled under the weight of railroad cars. But the process used to verify completed sections of the rail line and to authorize payment of government subsidies left much to be desired. Local ad hoc commissions could sanction rail lines before the governor of Senegal had a chance to make an assessment. And despite the crucial role these commissions were expected to play, they were filled with people who had very little knowledge of the specifications. This invariably led them to approve sections of the rail line that were incomplete and inadequate. The Dakar-Sudan rail line (DSL), of course, wanted rail sections reviewed as favorably and as quickly as possible: the sooner decisions were made, the sooner the payments would arrive, which benefited the Société more than the French government or the inhabitants of the colony.[29]

The DSL was heralded as a benign way to enhance commercial opportunities and to promote commerce in Africa.[30] Yet the public relations campaign used to acquire funds and to generate public support relied on a battery of half-truths. It is true, as proponents argued, that the proposed path of the railway would traverse flat terrain. But it was not true that rail stations would be built in densely populated areas, providing transportation to eager consumers, as tended to be the case in Europe. Nor was it true that Africans welcomed the railroad, as proponents insisted. It certainly was not true, as the Société claimed, that cheap labor was readily available: the transatlantic slave trade and the local skirmishes it fostered had depleted the most likely source of labor in the region: young men.[31] Meanwhile, the forms of coercive labor that persisted after the legal abolition of the slave trade drew in a disproportionate number of young women, whose labor included reproduction.[32] And the railway scheme was as oblivious to ecological conditions as to population dynamics, even if it would be informed by, and help to reshape, both domains of social life.

Averse to addressing this problematic enterprise, French colonial forces installed Samba Laobé Fall as the new head of Kajoor. Samba Laobé Fall had joined forces with the French military and with Demba War Sall in the conspiracy against Lat Dior. He began his tenure in good standing with the colonial government, in part because he helped the French erect a formidable infrastructure for communications that was also an apparatus of surveillance. He allowed the French to fill Kajoor's railway stations with telegraph lines. And when jaded former employees ambushed a paymaster's railway car, Samba Laobé Fall had them arrested. The new sovereign of Kajoor also helped to promote commercial development of the region.[33] When peasants balked at the prices France offered for their groundnuts, Samba Laobé Fall pressured them to accept the terms. Despite his efforts to remain in good standing with colonial officials, he was often caught between his constituents and his French collaborators. Colonial officials had persuaded Samba Laobé Fall to let them secure one hundred to three hundred meters around each rail station for commercial activities. Yet they complained when he made parcels of lands in adjoining territories available to local merchants. Meanwhile, merchants protested that they were being pressured to pay taxes both to the king and to the colonial officials (even if they exploited these competing conceptions of sovereign authority as much as they were frustrated by them).

Samba Laobé Fall had established close ties to area merchants. Given this, he was more attentive to their interests. Colonial officials grew tired of being excluded from these arrangements and plotted to diminish his authority by splitting Kajoor into several provinces. Samba Laobé Fall quickly lost favor with the French, proving that diplomatic standing was embedded in a morality of credit debt (where the capacity to enact taxation involves defining the moral infrastructure exchange). These developments also demonstrated that political legitimacy primarily derived not from the will of the people but from the exigencies of French colonial rule and from the forms of political contestation that defined regional politics.[34]

Since the French had so skillfully dismantled political authority in the region, there was little in the way of a direct challenge to French hegemony by the time the rail line was nearing completion in 1884. Thus, instead of armed resistance, acts of sabotage appear to account for the most notable early challenges to the DSL. In 1884 more than twelve hundred meters of pickets marking the railroad trace disappeared from a segment of the line that ran through Kajoor.[35] On a different occasion, railway tracks were deliberately filled with detritus designed to derail moving trains.[36] At times vexed area residents fired projectiles at moving trains. As a consequence, DSL executives hastily arranged to have European workers removed from these areas while they scrambled to come up with a solution, revealing a direct connection between emergent forms of labor management and strategies of resistance. On hearing of these violent confrontations, colonial officials initially planned to massacre the inhabitants of two villages they deemed responsible. But military operations ultimately focused on maintaining tighter surveillance on trains passing through contested territory.[37]

Colonial authorities charged with investigating these events ultimately discovered that railroad employees had initiated the violence. Their assaults on area residents ranged from barring access to wells and other crucial resources to seizing and detaining innocent bystanders near sabotaged railway tracks. The acting governor of Senegal insisted that railroad employees respect African inhabitants of the region. DSL personnel, meanwhile, argued that their African neighbors were at fault and threatened to meet recurrent protests with greater force.

The resolute stance of railroad personnel heightened disgust for the French presence. Instead of evaluating the coercive nature of their presence, DSL officials complained that their African interlocutors lacked the capacity for peaceful civic interaction. Railroad officials routinely offended the surrounding population and hastily introduced foreign workers whose ignorance and blatant disregard of social norms only heightened disdain for the railroad project. They sought to resolve conflict through increased reliance on new technologies of detainment, security, and surveillance.

Despite the railway's investment in using forensic technologies to adjudicate social standing, there was nothing for gathering reliable intelligence. In December 1884, rail workers reported an armed attack by a crew of eight armed Sereers, which turned out to two unarmed Lebus trying to collect payment for food they had prepared and served to the laborers. In an 1886 dispute, a stationmaster at Kelle mistook a trader from Saint-Louis for the agitator in a dispute that he was actually trying to help mediate,[38] demonstrating how unwieldy the politics of suspicion would prove to be in this context.

On September 10, 1886, when a train inadvertently killed some cattle, area villagers protested at the nearest rail station. Furious, the officer commanding the fort of Louga tried to fine the villagers, threatening to hang the culprits if they refused to pay. The chief of N'Diambour obliged by hanging the alleged perpetrators yet still collected fines from among them. On a different occasion, during Governor-General Jules Genouille's brief absence from the colony, a group of traders accosted the railway station of Tivaouane to recover a pair of escaped slaves who had taken shelter there. The French commandant at Thiès ignored the issue, but the local merchants who sought to recover their bonded human cargo were accused of trespassing on French territory. Samba Laobé Fall, was angry about French authorities' obstructing local commerce. French officials responded by threatening him with arrest if he tried to intervene. Concerned that colonial officials were taking too many liberties on territory that he governed, Samba Laobé Fall threatened to expel traders from Tivaouane unless they paid him the taxes he had demanded. Genouille sent an officer to N'Dande with orders to have the king's request clarified, but tension between these competing sovereigns intensified when Samba Laobé Fall refused to meet with the French emissary. Tempers grew short, and the officer ordered a mounted charge into the Wolof king's camp. Samba Laobé Fall's men were taken by surprise, and their leader fled, only to be killed soon afterward.

Samba Laobé Fall's death triggered a power vacuum, and colonial officials worried that violent competition would erupt among area leaders who hoped to succeed him. The emphasis in French colonial policy shifted from finance and construction to security and surveillance, in hopes of protecting investments like those embodied in the railroad. Still, colonial officials had to be careful how they managed Kajoor, since installing an extensive system of taxation, as they someday hoped to do, was likely to trigger a response they were not sure they could contain. Colonial authorities finally decided to split Kajoor into six districts, each to be governed by a *chef de province*. Each one presumably had his own interests and ambitions to pursue, making it unlikely that they would unite against the French. Colonial officials were concerned that Demba War Sall would leverage his extensive influenced against them. So they put him in charge of Kajoor's federated system[39] as a way to make him accountable to French authorities. Meanwhile the flaws in the built infrastructure of the railroad that ran through Kajoor became more pronounced with time. Although the route was complete by October 1885, its many flaws required constant attention and excessive repairs. The DSL generated tremendous deficits that the French treasury was contractually obligated to underwrite. The railroad ultimately became, in the words of one French colonial official, the "umbilical cord" of the colonial administration: an element of infrastructure designed to guarantee the health and vitality of the territory. By 1912 a French inspector of public works insisted that "neither material nor moral progress is possible in our African colonies without the railroads."

Colonial officials were fixated on moral progress because nineteenth-century Africa was thought to linger in premodern excesses like human sacrifice and fetish worship of various kinds. British merchant and adventurer Henry M. Stanley used the preface of his 1885 book *The Congo and the Founding of Its Free State: A Story of Work and Exploration* to make the case that railroads proved the most reliable way to mesh capital assets with the infrastructure Africa desperately needed. Published in a year that coincided with the Berlin Conference, where European powers like Britain, France, and Germany established clear domains of interest in the African continent, Stanley's proposal included calculations of "the rate of exploitation per mile per population density along the coast," though his project was not merely a commercial mission but a civilizing one. For, in Stanley's mind, until railroads cut a clear path into the African hinterland, "the road" would remain "unsafe for the more amiable people of the interior" owing to "the rapacious petty chiefs" who allegedly "dwell[ed] along the route."[40] Thus Stanley's commentary was not merely a fanciful projection, but a discourse on the forensics of capital that calls into question the profile of African polities and peoples. His critique has to do with whether African people and polities deserve diplomatic recognition in the framework for international governance that emerged during his time.

THREE

Problem of Accountability

In 1892 the French military invaded Dahomey, bringing down a civilization that had been described with gothic intensity in a newspaper a few years earlier:

> Rien de plus sinistre, en effet, que ce coin de la terre africaine où l'on pratique encore en grand les sacrifices humains. On coupe les têtes, on arrose de sang la tombe des rois morts, on enterre tout vivants dans la fosse royale les serviteurs du souverain décédé.

> (Nothing is more sinister, indeed, than this corner of Africa where people still practice human sacrifice. Heads are severed, blood sprays the graves of dead kings, and the servants of the deceased sovereign are buried alive in the royal tomb.)[1]

Europeans had long been engaged in trade relations with Dahomey: the reigning king had in fact provided a royal throne for display at the Great Exhibition of 1851 held in London's Crystal Palace.[2] Despite their familiarity with this African polity, North Atlantic traders and diplomats had long also maintained concerns about the social logic that ostensibly governed it.

In his 1871 account of eight months spent in Dahomey, the British traveler Alfred J. Skertchly chronicles the royal attire of King Gelelé, which included a "fétiche umbrella, black with white skulls[,] the stick crowned with a real cranium,"[3] though he is more distressed still to see what has become of the "skull of Bakoko, king of Ishaga," slain by Dahomean king "Gelelé's own hand." It had been boiled and polished smooth. The lower jaw had been removed to ornament Gelelé's royal stool,[4] Skertchly explains, citing a ritual practice popular from Benin to Dahomey where military leaders waged "spiritual terror"[5] by harnessing the life force that resided in the skull and bones of a vanquished enemy. Of course, British and French travelers found fetishism in a range of ritual practices, as Skertchly demonstrates in his account of a Dahomean recipe for fertility that he calls "a woman's fetiche": "And if she is childless, she smears [the image of Khevoysh, the thunder god] with palm oil and ground maize mixed with the blood of a fowl."[6]

Note the reference to palm oil. Since the 1840s, the term "civilization" had been used as the antithesis of fetishism in European military and political discourse—in travel writing and in journalistic accounts of Africa. But "civilization" was also used to reference economic and political transformations that included "European-style modern commerce and cash crop production, especially in palm oil, and the active suppression of the slave trade" after it was officially abolished by the British Slavery Abolition Act of 1833 and the Slave Trade Acts of 1842 and 1843.[7] Yet the most sensational aspect of the transition from slavery to contract labor, characterized by the deceptively simple term "legitimate commerce,"[8] had to do with the anxiety that African sovereigns were, in the absence of Europeans, likely to enslave or sacrifice their subjects. Even more dramatically, these ideas were often joined, as in Skertchly's remarks about the rationale for large-scale sacrifice: "The Dahom[e]ans believe that a person exists in the other world in a rank similar to that occupied by the deceased before death. Consequently, it is necessary to supply the deceased monarch with slaves. . . . This in a great measure is the cause of the continuance of the human sacrifices."[9]

Dahomey dominated commercial activity in a region that had interested French merchants. Diplomats and emissaries had been pressuring the king of Dahomey in earnest since at least 1851 to sign treaties promoting more extensive trade relations. French officials had also been urging the king to end the practice of human sacrifice, in which servants and other social marginals (the demographics most likely to be sold and shipped overseas during the transatlantic slave trade) were ritually sacrificed. Meanwhile, the fact that thousands of soldiers were sacrificed in French military interventions hardly factored into European discussions about the stakes of conquest. Newspaper accounts placed as little emphasis on French mortality rates as on French commercial interest in the region, praising this North Atlantic nation for having destroyed a polity whose sovereign allegedly subjected the populace to horrific treatment with no valid justification. And yet the crucial issue is not the objective conditions of daily life in Dahomey but the moral logic of warfare. Thus the characterization of Dahomey by European travelers and amateur ethnographers as a lair of fetish tyranny, far from being a crude piece of sensationalism, is something to consider very carefully.

From its origins in the sixteenth century through the first half of the nineteenth, European traders and colonial officials mostly regarded the capricious social logic they dubbed "fetishism" as a nuisance. Yet by the end of the nineteenth century—after decades of using this term as a synonym for "barbarism," in explicit contrast to "civilization"—fetishism came to mark societies structured through wealth in people, meaning credit in blood. In this moment the term "fetishism" no longer merely referred to the deistic worship of material objects. It now indicated social systems that induced horror because they allegedly relied on the threat of human sacrifice as a technology of state violence. These polities were horrific because the social logics that governed them amounted to "a jumble of superstitious nonsense," to cite one of the period's leading religious scholars.[10] As colonial officials construed fetish rule as arbitrary and despotic, they concluded that this form of government could not be reformed—the only solution was to conquer and dismantle it.[11]

Amid these developments there was a stated commitment to "scientific jurisprudence." Both the move to eradicate debtors' prisons throughout Europe and the effort to consolidate colonial empires involved strategies of policing and militarism designed to transform the "present-oriented spender into a future-oriented saver."[12] These projects sought to replace governance steeped in whim with rational methods for accumulating capital.

The nineteenth-century liberal discourse concerning African sovereigns who clung to primitive notions of embodied value ignored the fact that the emergence of debt adjudication strategies that did not rely on the monetary value of a human life was a novel development in Europe.[13] After all, it was essentially during the same period—the aftermath of the formal abolition of slavery in Britain in 1833, amid the birth of formal wage labor—that the idea of adjudicating monetary value through the human body fell out of vogue in North Atlantic nations[14] (though the traffic in human cargo, in which many Americans and Europeans continued to participate in African coastal settlements and in Cuba and Brazil, makes it difficult to periodize these developments in any absolute way). As I noted above, a number of statutes were passed in 1830s Britain testifying to the newfangled idea that the human body should be construed as a secular, "modern" entity—no longer too sacred for scientific inquiry, yet too precious to be considered merely an object of monetary value. In like fashion, the 1848 Fatal Accidents Act stipulated that, in accidents involving injury or death to a human being, compensation would no longer be directed to the state (a law that had historically relied on treating the offending object as an "accursed" entity and the absolutist king as God's earthly embodiment) but to the person injured or to the family of the deceased. And the amount to be adjudicated would no longer be based on the value of the offending object but on the projected lost wages of the injured or deceased party. The official birth of policing during this time—which created national precincts to regulate commerce and institutionalize domestic security and which eventually restricted the use of a standing military to regulate citizens' affairs—corresponded to this new attitude. Human life was precious. And modern. The corresponding economic logic: people should enter into contracts that are mutually beneficial so long as they do not affix monetary value to human life, now deemed priceless.[15]

Liberal reformers, in Europe and the territories that North Atlantic nations controlled, remained concerned that "the legal relationship between creditor and debtor—had yet to rise beyond its supposed barbaric underpinnings." Determined efforts to promote "legitimate commerce" surfaced as a critique of "the explicit right of the creditor to seize and sequester the body of the debtor." In essence, this liberal attitude suggested that "the laws governing credit and debt were clearly not conducive to fostering a fully 'civilized' society" amid an enduring dialectic "between barbarism and civilization."[16]

This was not to rule out the role of debt altogether. Far from it. Instead, the task was to identify the *cause* of indebtedness. Upstanding citizens were expected to contract debts that carried reasonable terms. Citizens in favorable social standing could be counted on to deliver payments according to a schedule, based on the established value of an object, through methods deemed objective, reliable, precise, and thus judicious. And as "barbaric" debtors were eradicated from the heart of North Atlantic nations (via debtors' prisons) and supposedly driven from the face of the earth (through colonial conquest), "legitimate commerce"[17] surfaced as the preferred rubric for sanctioned forms of economic exchange.

Few examples capture this emergent attitude as well as the 1892 conquest of Dahomey, which ultimately involved soldiers from the African continent in large numbers on both sides of the conflict. Colonel Alfred-Amédée Dodds, who hailed from a prominent habitant family, commanded more than four thousand troops in a military invasion that was explicitly conceived as an effort to eradicate one of the few remaining barriers to the spread of "civilization" in Africa.

Dodds, born in Saint-Louis in 1842, served in the French army. Having directed French forces during the "Boxer Rebellion," or Yihetuan

Movement, that surfaced in China between 1898 and 1901, Dodds led a French campaign that has since been known as the Second Franco-Dahomean War. During this time the powerful African empire become a client state for France before its ultimate demise. Note that Dodds was not a colonial conscript. A métis (sometimes referred to as an octoroon in British reports because he had one-eighth African ancestry), Dodds qualified as a French citizen under laws regulating the Four Communes.

Besides officially ending slavery in all territories, the Revolution of 1848 offered France's Caribbean colonies, henceforth known as *départements*, the power to send a representative to the French National Assembly. This decision simultaneously led to a general election in which all *originaires* or habitants who had been residents in the Four Communes for at least five years could vote. In 1872 Saint-Louis and Gorée were officially granted most of the rights of French citizens. Rufisque joined the consortium in 1880, and Dakar followed in 1887, as residents of select districts in Senegal became the only Africans under French colonial rule to enjoy this opportunity. By 1900, electoral participation was so widespread that some colonial administrators were ready to reverse their decision, fretting that this increased sense of political autonomy might lead other colonies to demand the same treatment. However, by that time local politicians were already developing measures to solidify this unique status. Blaise Diagne returned from the metropole where he had attended university to become the first black African elected to the French parliament in 1914.[18] Diagne realized that France was desperate for more soldiers to fight in World War I, so he strategically recruited thousands of troops, securing the rights of his Senegalese constituents by providing permanent guarantees of French rights in exchange for military service.[19]

From the moment French merchants first began constructing trading posts on Senegal's Atlantic coast during the 1650s until the first few decades of the nineteenth century, French political officials preferred to use force intermittently. They usually relied on compacts with African merchants and political officials to access resources. Yet the French approach to resource acquisition had changed by the time Louis Faidherbe became governor-general of Senegal in 1859. Faidherbe wanted to revive commercial interest in Senegal through a concerted effort to acquire territory rather than relying on disparate trading posts that were at times difficult to secure. To execute his plan, Faidherbe drew from what he had just learned from waging a series of military campaigns in Algeria. In the process, he modified protocols for recruiting troops and for linking conscription to citizenship.

Faidherbe was keen to secure troops from the indigenous population. He stressed to recruits from places like Saint-Louis and the Cap Vert peninsula that they were "French" and thus obligated to defend the commercial interests of their true homeland against those of area sovereigns. These conscripts fortified French forces, as did groups of soldiers arriving from territories like Algeria. Owing to Faidherbe's aggressive program, military service was, for the first time, linked to citizenship.

The tradition of using slaves with extensive experience to protect merchant vessels and cargo was nearly two centuries old by the time Faidherbe arrived. But because slavery had been legally abolished in France in 1848, these efforts now required merchants to commission troops or to solicit volunteers (even if coercion remained a mainstay of recruitment).

As Faidherbe helped France secure territorial control of the region, he simultaneously worked to convince habitants that supporting his military efforts would fortify political belonging. Amid these developments, the eighteenth century had witnessed a growing skepticism about using the military to suppress popular uprisings. As I have noted, it was during this period that many North Atlantic nations moved toward a tiered model of law enforcement, with police reserved for the domestic populace, and a standing army to battle external threats.

The first police forces of note were made up of plantation society militias. They banded together to secure and recover enslaved persons who were relentless in trying to flee and forge their own settlements. In the South Atlantic (whether the US South or Caribbean isles), these ad hoc police forces petitioned local legislatures for the right to carry arms (restricted at that time to formal military personnel). They donned similar attire (so they could recognize other planters devoted to a similar cause).[20] But the model of policing that would ultimately take root throughout the Atlantic world—made up of a central authority with precincts reproduced throughout the country—comes from Britain, as I noted above. And it is no coincidence that it was born in 1833, just as slavery was abolished (making all subjects of the monarch purportedly British, in contrast to alleged outsiders). Nor is it a coincidence that national policing, as such, began in France in 1848—the same year that slavery was finally abolished throughout the French empire.

In this nineteenth-century moment the standing army, now distinct from a domestic police force—was charged with defending the presumed territorial integrity of the state. Thus, to conscript colonial subjects for a national enterprise meant instilling within them the sense that they all were "sons of the soil"—all citizens, even those of mixed ancestry who had spent all of their lives in Africa. Meanwhile, France used these newly weaponized subjects to secure liability for commercial contracts. Soldiers could also be used to punish adversaries who sought to evade or obstruct commercial and political ambitions. Amid these dynamics, Faidherbe played up the unique enfranchisement of residents in the Four Communes—he encouraged them to differentiate themselves from the indigenous peoples and empires surrounding them.[21]

Thus, political representation became a proxy for investment in the French *mission civilisatrice* as Faidherbe and others insisted that African empires were dominated by an arbitrary, despotic logic that structured customary beliefs and social institutions. It is crucial to recall that, from 1859 to 1886, French efforts to secure territorial control of Senegal had been undermined by warfare between rival polities, as well as between Muslim marabouts and Wolof aristocrats. As such it was only "during the *peace* that followed" that "France began constructing a colonial state."[22]

Throughout the latter part of the nineteenth century, France, Britain, the United States, and other North Atlantic polities would institute reforms that we now associated with the emergence of the nation-state—with the birth of commercial and political legitimacy. A mode of economic and political consolidation emerged during the last decade of the nineteenth century that is frequently described as a genre of conquest. It likewise involved displacing African debt regimes with methods for adjudicating value perceived as more rational, modern, and scientific.

Recall the argument that ethnographers like Skertchly made: that "fetiche people" could benefit from economic and political transformations sweeping across the world only if indigenous methods for assessing the relation between sacrifice and debt were eradicated. The implication is that primitive notions of debt adjudication would be replaced by voluntary agreements and rational explanations for the loss of life. This assertion would bear witness to novel techniques for managing death through justifications for the loss of human life that could presumably be adjudicated by rational means. Incidents that fell within this category included acts of self-defense and fatal accidents (now explained by recourse to scientific causality rather than metaphysical agency). Rational events that justified the loss of life also included military service exemplified by African-born officers and conscripts fighting in North Atlantic armies (though warfare waged by African polities was excluded from this framework). Recall that Max Weber equated the emergence of the standing army with the birth of the state: as part of its "monopoly on violence" with consequences for diverse legal subjectivities and genres of social belonging.

Every society has its own methods of forensic inquiry, of assessing the meaning and material worth of a lost life, especially when that loss appears accidental, inadvertent, or morally dubious.[23] Yet from the nineteenth century onward European commercial agents in the Atlantic arena began to argue that purportedly "African" methods for inducing death (for instance, those that derive from sorcery or human sacrifice) should be extinguished. This was generally achieved through military conquest specifically aimed at displacing forms of debt exchange deemed primitive. These naturally included slavery, but also *panyarring*, which entailed having a creditor seize a member of the debtor's family as payment for an outstanding obligation. British and French military civilizing missions sought to eradicate this practice. Yet they did not simply ignore but encouraged pawning—the practice of offering a member of one family to another as "security for an unpaid debt"—as a benign "substitute for slavery." In practical terms, the latter practice also helped foster the spread of capitalist monetary debt as a prevailing social logic.[24] Thus, modern notions of liability were forged within a distinct moral infrastructure, where voluntary alienation became a prerequisite for legitimate commercial exchange, and where sponsorship by a sovereign state endowed forms of militarism and policing with political legitimacy.

Still, force was only one mechanism of accountability. It's worth asking why the French adopted a rather different approach in the colony of Senegal. Rather than guaranteeing fidelity to a specific economic and political arrangement through conquest, the French were obliged to negotiate an economic relationship with newly emancipated slaves and with a demographic that had previously been deemed a threat to national security: the Murids, led by Sheikh Amadu Bamba.

By the turn of the century, slavery as a central feature of Senegalese social life continued to undermine French claims that they had instituted a "modern" economic and political infrastructure. French colonial officials insisted they had eradicated slavery in their oldest, best-organized, and most prosperous colony in Africa—the one that was most secure, with the oldest history of policing. But they were assailed by newspaper reports that Wolof aristocrats, including some of their allies—were trafficking in human cargo, especially young girls. Slavery had been abolished throughout the French empire in 1848, but it had continued under the guise of "adoption" (*tutelle*). Adoption could be a coercive form of labor. The concept could also be used to camouflage emergent forms of prostitution. In either case, the practice was reminiscent of legalized slavery.[25]

French strategies of conquest during the last decade of the nineteenth century centered largely on suppressing the slave trade to consolidate economic practices—these included an effort to institutionalize very specific notions of wage labor and the character traits most suitable to undertaking it. French officials encouraged slaves to leave their masters. But formal abolition undermined efforts to establish durable ties with the Wolof aristocrats who retained nominal control of the Senegal River valley and relied heavily on coercive labor. The French generally refused to sanction any person's legal claim to dominion over another, but this tactic was easier to adopt in principle than to carry out.[26]

Colonial officials were anxious about the social, economic, and political consequences of emancipation. They feared what happened in Caribbean territories, where former slaves became workers cognizant of their market value and thus eager to negotiate for fair wages. But they encouraged emancipated slaves to explore new possibilities for labor because they knew that slavery was the basis for imperial power in Senegal. They hoped that without slaves the Wolof aristocracy would crumble. And it did. But colonial officials struggled to account for and manage this newly emancipated population. Although they had established commercial and military supremacy in the region, French efforts to shape social and political aspirations, to control patterns of settlement and migration, met with mixed results.[27]

From the 1890s onward, people settled lands that could be used to cultivate groundnuts, which suddenly brought increased prices in international markets. These agrarian societies incorporated migrants displaced by warfare and economic crisis. As these communities grew, new gender and generational hierarchies emerged. The peasant household became the preferred unit of social organization as men sought women with whom to reproduce and build homes. These men expected their partners to manage domestic organization so they could generate revenue for the household in a market system increasingly stratified by gender.

This did not mean that agrarian workers, former slaves, and migrants were indistinguishable from each other. Modes of caste and comportment that had been institutionalized during the transatlantic slave trade retained traction in the aftermath of emancipation.[28] French intelligence on the state of slavery in Kajoor and Bawol parsed the different categories of slavery salient in the Senegal River valley, complete with French renditions of Wolof terms. The three main categories of slaves were *les captifs de la couronne,* "slaves of the crown," or *Diam-Bour* (from the Wolof, *jaami-bur*); *les captifs de case,* "household slaves," or *Diam-Sayor* (Wolof, *jaami-sayóor*); and *les captifs de terre,* "slaves of the land," or *Diam-Dioudou* (Wolof, *jaami-juddu*).

Crown slaves—more or less equivalent to the category of royal slaves, high-ranking slaves in the Wolof aristocracies of old—were bureaucrats. They served as royal administrators or, at times, executives. *Jaami-bur* owned slaves, lands, and herds of animals. They were usually wealthy. They had, of course, enjoyed historical proximity to Wolof elites as acquaintances and confidants, as private security, and as military officers. In other words, they were part and parcel of the aristocracy, enjoying many of its benefits. What distinguished them as slaves was merely their juridical standing (belonging to someone else) and their social status (as people under the dominion of others). But this status did not make them marginal. The onset of French colonial rule changed the nature of slavery and servitude in the region. Many slaves who had enjoyed privileged positions in Wolof empires—people who had once commanded their own slaves—were now reduced to tilling soil or tending animals. Crown slaves were obliged to provide their masters with gifts and aid on request. As colonial conquest reconfigured trade relations, crown slaves were increasingly besieged by their patrons for the bridewealth sons needed to marry, for wedding gifts, and for other monetary contributions.

Jaami-juddu were employed at their masters' behest. They did not labor for themselves, nor could they own property. All food, clothing, and shelter was provided by their masters. They were burdened with arduous tasks and routinely subjected to harsh punishment for the slightest infraction.

Jaami-sayóor (household slaves) might perform any number of tasks crucial to managing the household, from rearing elite children to household chores. The status within a household and degree of familiarity with a family that this kind of slave might achieve naturally varied. In addition, the *jaami-sayóor*'s status, and his or her placement within the broader family structure, changed during the course of a lifetime. *Jaami-sayóor* could marry, but only if the master granted permission. The bride's master might force the presumptive groom to pay bridewealth, even if her parents had the same expectation. Masters sometimes granted *jaami-sayóor* the right to a separate residence, but this might mean that her future children would likewise be part of the master's household. So, even while enjoying more privileges than a *jaami-juddu*, no *jaami-sayóor* could effectively construct an autonomous household.[29]

By the nineteenth century, *baadoolo* (a Wolof term meaning powerless) became pervasive to describe an increasingly prevalent genre of labor and distinct social position: people who sowed crops as a way to generate income. This term has a negative connotation, owing to its origin as a slur coined by Wolof aristocrats for petty farmers who worked the land instead of generating revenue from militarism, slave trading, or taxation. Agrarian workers preferred the Wolof term *beykat*, "farmer," to describe their lifestyle. But the term *baadoolo* as the original frame for what was taking place is telling, since that term derives from farms against which elites levied heavy tributes. *Baadoolo* also owed a profound political allegiance to nobles, in contrast to the *beykat*, who exercised their autonomy not simply through their commercial strategies but through the uprisings they sometimes initiated against unjust taxation and political coercion. With the birth of the Murid movement in the later nineteenth century, these agricultural settlements came to embody an alternative sphere of authority from the colonial state. The *beykat*, as a social actor empowered to construct an autonomous vision of family, emerged between the French conquest of the region during the last decade of the nineteenth century and the onset of World War I. Previously, peasants were subject to the dictates of more influential social actors, whether royal slaves, habitants, or Muslims who had been granted imperial titles of nobility.

Colonial officials seized on these new economic developments to create a political infrastructure that could draw on and ultimately benefit from new structures of credit-debt. European import and export firms engaged in commerce with Arab and African merchants. They forged trade networks with local merchants and peasant households. The peasant household became especially salient as an individual unit of economic organization once traders began to offer extensive access to credit as a way to eliminate traders who tried to position themselves as brokers for *beykat* who wanted to access markets elsewhere. Yet the forms of credit *beykat* were obliged to use carried exorbitant interest rates, making colonial officials worry that escalating peasant debt would undermine the trade in groundnuts that they profited from.

A *boroom-ker-ga* (or senior male) led each peasant household, where he lived with his wife, or wives, children, and other relatives who recognized his dominion. His primary task was to establish a regime of labor that accounted for the age, gender, and status of the household members. In calculating family members' contributions to the collective enterprise, the *boroom-ker-ga* also brokered their access to food, land, and to the family inheritance. The most active workers in any *beykat* household tended to be women or those in various forms of informal indenture (perhaps even slaves, if any were present) and young, unmarried men dubbed *surga*.[30]

The preferred labor scheme of groundnut production had been adapted from historical patterns of millet production: men cleared fields, prepared the ground for seeds, and harvested mature plants. Together, men and women sowed seed and weeded. And after the harvest, women and young children shelled the nuts. In this geography of domesticity, men did jobs at some remove from the residence, while women executed tasks that kept them close to the household. Women shelled nuts and coordinated child labor as well as child care. They fetched water from wells. They pounded millet. Women were chiefly responsible for cleaning and maintaining the residence in addition to planning and preparing meals. Where the *boroom-ker-ga* had more than one wife, each woman harvested her own plot and could sometimes keep profits from the crops she grew. The *boroom-ker-ga* coordinated the activities of family members who were generally denied direct access to household profits.

In a place where female labor was crucial to so many enterprises at once, young male laborers, or *surga*, assumed central importance as the workers whose time was easiest to predict and manage. Consequently, groundnut productivity was increasingly based on tabulating the number of *surga* in a given household, extracting as much value as could be gained from their labor until they married and founded their own households. But since *surga* worked within the family household until they were ready to marry, they were also dependent on the *boroom-ker-ga* for bridewealth. Thus, apart from the exigencies of family hierarchy, there was economic pressure to be productive and to remain in good standing with the *boroom-ker-ga*. Even when *beykat* households employed slaves, *surga* tended to work the same hours (though—like wives—they would sometimes be granted their own plots of land to farm for extra income).

Unmarried daughters in a *beykat* household were not granted land, however. For extra income they worked on plots their mothers owned, under the expectation that they would leave the household if they received a marriage proposal. While *surga* saved to pay bridewealth, their female counterparts anticipated generating capital for their families through bridewealth.

The two most significant economic developments in the territory of Senegal during the nineteenth century concerned infrastructure for transportation and commerce (steamships, ocean ports, railroads, telegraph lines) and structures for credit-debt, through which European standards of value were institutionalized. Colonial standards of measure translated goods harvested in Africa into prices on the international market, rendering concrete practices and products into an abstract, purportedly universal, equivalent. In contrast to the time of slavery, prices would no longer arise from the subjective impressions of area traders, or from reconnaissance that yielded practical information about translocal markets. As peasants eagerly cultivated groundnuts, French merchants settled on prices that reflected demand from European cities.

Wolof peasants were the first farmers in all of West Africa to prepare cash crops for annual export. Groundnut production took off during a moment when the prices of most other exports fell, making them a crucial commodity for peasant households trying to brace against fluctuations in the international marketplace. Before the onset of major groundnut cultivation, local agriculturalists sold grain to French traders and to merchants from across the Sahara. But with burgeoning demand and escalating prices, cultivation of groundnuts quickly eclipsed grain production. By the second decade of groundnut production, exports from Kajoor and Bawol increased from 20,000 metric tons per annum to 100,000 metric tons, while millet yielded only 1,000 metric tons. Groundnuts generated a yield as much as 50 percent higher per hectare because prices for equivalent amounts of groundnuts and millet were the same even though groundnuts were the central ingredient in a broader range of goods. Also, the price of millet fluctuated more widely, being much lower while farmers were getting rid of their surplus and much higher in the weeks and months preceding a harvest.[31]

Beykat used earnings from groundnuts to buy livestock, especially among small-scale societies like the Sereer, or to save money for the bridewealth of sons who hoped to marry, especially among the Wolof. In either instance, the groundnut economy was the basis for economic and thus social autonomy. But these dynamics were intensely gendered. The groundnut was the means by which young men gained social mobility at a time when marriage was the most significant marker of adulthood—the ritual practice most closely tethered to the conditions for achieving economic autonomy and changes in social status. Because *beykat* were now earning more income, they could buy a broader range of goods. By 1903 they accounted for at least one-third of Senegalese imports.

The *beykat* household as the dominant mode of economic organization reflected the failure of plantation agriculture in Senegal. *Beykat* were much more productive than the agricultural ventures wealthy aristocrats endeavored to forge. At this time, the economic aspirations of various elites were shaped by Caribbean plantation economies. Apart from Cuba and Brazil, slavery had been abolished in most of the world. Yet on the west coast of Africa, coercive labor regimes tailored by the transatlantic slave trade had been carefully integrated into local social institutions and were thus available as a means of capital accumulation.

Agriculturalists experimented with botanical gardens and set up research centers to select privileged strains of seed and to determine which products yielded the greatest value as pharmaceuticals. But despite a renewed investment in sorting methods and agricultural techniques, the plantation model quickly fell apart, in no small measure because of the trouble estate owners had in enticing and retaining labor. Plantation agriculture further vexed the French because this system favored *originaires*, transferring economic power and land to a group whose privilege was already difficult to regulate. Wealthy Senegalese merchants conceived of their lands not simply as sites for plantation production, but as property they could rent out and tax, and on which they could hire or rent out laborers for diverse enterprises. Having wealthy elites acquire lands in new districts meant that their commercial might and political influence would no longer be mostly restricted to the Four Communes. Instead, métis like Hyacinthe Devès threatened to undermine the territorial sovereignty of the colonial administration and to create competition for labor and capital.

The failure of plantation agriculture encouraged French colonial officials to grant Wolof farmers and landowners greater autonomy. In 1903, Governor-General Ernest Roume decided to recognize customary law, which meant that area merchants could develop their own systems of land management and acquisition. Although this ruling protected *beykat* claims to land, it did not prevent them from being taxed heavily by *sëriñ* (Muslims bearing noble titles) or *laman* (Wolof) landowners.

And because there were sometimes multiple claims to the same territory, the French strategically intervened to moderate disputes. If they agreed to abide by customary law, the French also helped to reshape it by adjudicating conflicts through fines and by determining how and when taxes could be levied on a crop.

As a means of capital accumulation that generated a higher crop yield at a much lower cost, *beykat* households flourished. Their efficiency derived from a structure that was intensely hierarchical, even if it ultimately came to seem natural, mapping onto a trajectory that Europe shared, in which a discrete family unit became enshrined as the norm.

Groundnut production fell off a bit around 1905, vexed by area droughts and by French transformations in colonial governance that intensified surveillance and taxation. Production continued to expand in the decades following emancipation, even during times that were troublesome for most crops. The success of groundnuts stemmed from their significance in peasant households, both from their routine profitability and from the fact that groundnuts could be easily rotated with other food crops in cycles that maximized the fertility of the soil. These dynamics help explain what drove widespread migration to territories beyond the dominion of French colonial officials and slaveowning Wolof aristocrats. They also help explain why French colonial authorities so feared Muridism both as an ideology and as a new form of economic organization, and why they found it insurrectionary even in the absence of any specific plot to overthrow the colonial regime.[32]

By the nineteenth century, a new economic and religious agenda cohered under the leadership of Cheikh Amadu Bamba. Bamba would prove to be the figure most vexing for French colonial rule. His rise to prominence is especially intriguing in that he shared a relationship with Lat Dior, the deposed leader and subsequent icon of indigenous resistance. When Lat Dior was keen to fend off French colonial forces in the 1860s, Amadu Bamba's father had served at the dynastic court as both a teacher and a judge. In fact, Bamba's father was so highly esteemed that he served for a time as Lat Dior's spiritual guide.

The structure of Muridism differed dramatically from that of the Tijani order, prominent among Senegalese elite who had been educated by the French. The Tijani coalesced in coastal cities and in territories adjacent to the rail line. They tended to be outspoken critics of colonial rule. By contrast, Amadu Bamba sought to cultivate a base among rural agriculturalists.

Amadu Bamba actively recruited the descendants of men who had been high-ranking political officials in regional empires, making colonial officials fear that he had political aspirations of his own. Yet Bamba never tried to mobilize his constituency toward explicitly political ends. Instead, his influence derived from the teachings he circulated and the ornate Islamic poetry he wrote. His critique of colonialism assumed the form of a distinct lifestyle: he encouraged his followers to follow a strict schedule of meditation, discipline, and labor that their spiritual leader, or marabout, would provide. Meanwhile, he promoted an approach to labor steeped in a religious ethic that he and his followers established.

Based on faulty intelligence from suspicious rivals and detractors, the French colonial government twice exiled Amadu Bamba: to Gabon from 1895 to 1902, then to Mauritania from 1903 to 1907. These tactics of intimidation bolstered Bamba's notoriety, leading scores of his followers to populate the city of Touba, which soon became sacred ground for members of the Murid brotherhood. By 1910 French colonial officials had decided that, unlike members of the Tijani brotherhood, who had at times directly challenged colonial rule, the Murids had no interest in staging a resistance movement. Further, Bamba had effectively helped to reconfigure the Senegalese economy: the legions of young men who flocked to rural areas in search of Bamba's teaching paralleled the emergence of rural agricultural households as a pervasive way to earn a livelihood. Seeing in the structure of Murid religious authority a formidable bureaucracy, French colonial officials delegated groundnut production to the marabouts of this religious order and generated revenues for the colonial state through tariffs levied on the industry. In the process, colonial officials helped to forge a new profile for the Murid—follower of Bamba, peasant agriculturalist, emissary of foreign finance capital—that continues to animate economic hierarchies well into the twenty-first century.[33]

At the same time, economic strategies and religious sentiments were only two genres of accountability that would define governance in Senegal during the nineteenth and twentieth centuries. For despite achieving independence during the twentieth century, the Senegalese state would ultimately fashion a distinct political trajectory that was neither reducible to nor completely distinct from the colonial infrastructure it had inherited. The element of that infrastructure that forms the basis for the next chapter is Senegalese militarism. Far from obstructing the path to democracy, as tends to be the criticism of African nations with active militaries, Senegal's armed forces are routinely credited with helping it secure diplomatic standing as a moral exemplar—a leader of economic and political reform in Africa.

FOUR

Diplomatic Profile

The taxi lets me off at the corner, near the US embassy in Dakar. I weave between the bunkers in search of Lieutenant Colonel Matthew V. Sousa, chief of the Office of Security Cooperation for the US Army. I knew that Sousa was largely responsible for shepherding the agenda of AFRICOM, US Africa Command. His office is nestled deep in a web of ramshackle buildings. From the exterior it is not clear which ones are inhabited, or by whom.

A few minutes shy of my appointment time, I slip off my backpack and empty my pockets. An overzealous civil servant hurries me along. Yet there are a few people ahead of me in line. So, even after I comply with the specified protocols, my eyes have time to graze the notices affixed to the wall. I read about a Black History Month essay competition. (*I hadn't realized this is even a holiday in Senegal.*) I also see a memo notifying Senegalese people that they are not authorized to join the US military. (*What made them think they could?*) I come across a plaque paying tribute to the employee of the month. (*No wonder he's so eager.*) Just then, a towering, broad-shouldered figure strides into the room from an adjoining staircase to the left. He scans the room for "Dr. Michael Ralph." I raise my hand cautiously. He nods. He moves forward, apologizing for the Senegalese officer who is now eyeing my cell phone suspiciously. Just as he instructs me to turn it off, Sousa slides it out of his hand, giving it back to me. "Ça va," Sousa says casually.

Sousa leads me up several flights of stairs toward an office apart from a common area cluttered with desks and nameless people busy at work behind neat stacks of papers and Post-It notes in every conceivable size, shape, and color. He begins quizzing me even before he makes it to his seat.

Do you speak Wolof?
Yes.

And French?

Oui.

And . . . you teach at NYU?

Yes. In the Department of Social and Cultural Analysis.

But your degree is in—

Anthropology

From—

The University of Chicago.

Sousa strips off his cap and slides into his seat, satisfied. He asks what he can do to help me.

I am interested in the role that Senegal plays as a leader of economic and political reform in Africa. I am also interested in what Sousa makes of diplomatic ties between the United States and Senegal. But my interview happens to fall on the sixteenth day of the January 25 uprising in Cairo's Tahrir Square. I am suddenly eager to know how the lieutenant colonel understands this protest movement in the broader context of African politics.

His terse response catches me off guard.

"It's exciting."

My ears perk up.

I wonder if Sousa thinks it would be "exciting" to see mass demonstrations continue to spread across Africa and southwest Asia. I wonder if he thinks it would be "exciting" to witness an uprising in Dakar, as was the wish of many participants to the World Social Forum, then being held across town. Thus far there hadn't been much insurgency except for student protests against the brand new chancellor of the Université de Cheikh Anta Diop. He was altogether unaccommodating, leading organizers of the 2011 WSF to host most sessions in tents on the campus lawn. But then, this season of Arab revolt that was also a season of African revolt had caught the global left by surprise. It felt like there were more panels about third world debt crisis and climate change than any other topic. And yet the momentum sweeping across Africa and southwest Asia had finally infused the proceedings. The day before, as I was headed to the US embassy for my interview, a friend told me about a protest scheduled to take place at the Egyptian embassy in Dakar later that afternoon.

In the meanwhile, I'm trying to make the most of my time with Sousa, knowing there are pressing matters elsewhere.

In response to a pointed question about AFRICOM, Sousa insists that US Africa Command is principally concerned with providing a service to Africa—with helping Africans cultivate more intimate knowledge of security, since "security is crucial for economic development." According to Corporal Steve Denning,[1] the United States' role is to provide "training" in techniques of security: the idea being that African militaries trained by the United States and Britain and France will be better positioned to foster economic and political stability in their home countries. In this theory of diplomacy, democratic nations with the most powerful militaries are best equipped to provide this form of tutelage.

In line with this argument, US, British, and French military officers and diplomats alike insist that Senegal is tops on the list of Africa's most democratic nations, one of the few countries where, in the words of one US embassy official, "civilians control the military, rather than the other way around." In his view this was what made Senegal unlike most other African countries. In the words of General Richard Tompkins,[2] "Senegal's military operations are more sophisticated than most other countries in Africa because the officers are well-educated," though Corporal Denning put the matter more crudely: "In some of these countries, officers have essentially proven themselves through leadership in the bush." Fishing for a better way to convey the context of civil strife in sub-Saharan Africa, he cleans it up, "in the field." Then Denning continues, "As a result, they may know how to fight, but they don't know military strategy or appreciate what's at stake in the concept of security." As examples, he cites Guinea-Conkary, Mali, and Côte d'Ivoire—all former members of Afrique Occidentale Français (the French colonial empire in West Africa)—as sites where such training has made a significant impact. In the view of the military officers and embassy officials I interview, Senegal, better than any other former French colony, appreciates the relation between security and economic development. As far as Sousa is concerned, "former British colonies like Uganda," have even more profound appreciation for the relation between this distinct notion of security and economic growth.

It is an odd comparison. Of course, George W. Bush routinely commended Uganda for the instrumental role it played in what he had dubbed the "global war on terror." Still, President Yoweri Museveni has been criticized for all kinds of political malfeasance. A widely cited 2011 report by the US Social Science Research Council cited the Ugandan military for numerous atrocities and incidents of improper conduct. And the fact that Museveni came to power through a military coup means this tradition of fostering "civilian control" over the state military apparatus is more complicated and contradictory than US military personnel and embassy officials were suggesting.

Sousa seems distracted during our meeting. And as we part, his face seems resolute. Pensive. "Let's just say, there's a lot going on," his parting words and partial explanation. After the interview, I move quickly from the US embassy to the Egyptian embassy in Dakar, where many protestors have just arrived from the World Social Forum. A few short hours later, Egyptian President Hosni Mubarak finally cedes power to the Supreme Council of the Armed Forces in Egypt, as protests give way to celebration and celebrations bleed into strategy sessions concerned with developing a more comprehensive critique of Senegalese president Abdoulaye Wade.

Visiting the US embassy in Dakar during the height of the "Arab Spring" would later feel like foreshadowing. Exactly one week after my interview with Sousa, a Senegalese veteran, still dressed in his military uniform, set himself on fire in front of the presidential palace. The timing is impossible to overlook, since the formal debut of the "Arab Spring" is often linked to Tunisian shopkeeper Mohammed Bouazizi's self-immolation to protest political corruption and economic stagnation.[3] In 2008 a veteran named Keba Diop likewise set himself on fire in front of the presidential palace, claiming the government had defaulted on promised payments.

Political scientists and specialists of international relations often rely on normative guidelines for democratic governance when assessing the political stakes in a given nation. Anthropologists, by contrast, focus on the rituals, practices, and characteristics that define social life. But both approaches rely on the assumption that objective circumstances provide an accurate portrait of governance. How does the perspective of privileged actors shape the way we view social dynamics? To what extent is the diplomatic standing of a given polity shaped by factors beyond that country's control? And what might taking these dynamics more seriously mean for the study of politics?

The favorable standing of people and polities is often understood to derive from whether they adhere to well-established laws and norms. But there is a problem with this approach. Frequently the evidence we use to assess social standing is unreliable. The forensic profile of a country often has more to do with subjective assessments than objective criteria. The concept of forensics is usually deployed in relation to policing, marking the protocols used to adjudicate the social standing of someone who is allegedly responsible for a crime or a civil infraction. But the tendency to privilege specific kinds of evidence and to use that evidence as the basis for moral judgments is likewise used to evaluate the diplomatic standing of a given country.

The privileged standing that Senegal has been assigned by influential nations like the United States shapes the way Senegalese military personnel see their country—at least from the perspective of Colonel Birame Diop, whose military assignments require him to routinely engage with these dynamics.

Colonel Diop joined the Senegalese Armed Forces as a high school (*lycée*) student in the national military academy. He did not succeed in his first attempt at the entrance exam. But after a protracted student strike—and the state's subsequent decision to break the strike by terminating students—Diop earned a spot on the vacant roll that now had plenty of availability. He went on to a distinguished career as a fighter pilot. He received training from Egyptian and Moroccan military officials. Through these accomplishments, Diop rose to the rank of colonel. He now spends a great deal of time working closely with the British, French, and, most notably, US militaries, consulting with officers from these disparate locales during their visits to Dakar as well as traveling abroad to lead and participate in seminars.

Soon after returning to the United States from my visit to the US embassy in Dakar, I caught up with Diop. He was in New York on his way to Washington, DC, for a seminar. We had initially planned to meet near my NYU office in downtown Manhattan, but he called on the day of our appointment to confess that he did not know New York geography as well as he had presumed. He was visiting friends and family in Harlem's burgeoning Senegalese community and wanted to know if we could meet uptown instead. I agreed and joined him at a coffee shop near 125th Street. There I encountered the towering figure of the colonel, dressed in a well-tailored navy business suit. We exchanged pleasantries and sat at a table in the corner.

Intrigued by the way US embassy officials and military officers characterize the Senegalese military, I was keen to ask him about the nation's prominent role in international peacekeeping missions. Without a moment's hesitation, Diop fired back a response so detailed that I wondered if it had been rehearsed:

> There are several stages in what we might call the peace process. Peacekeeping is but one of them. And, in fact, you can't always move right to peacekeeping.
>
> If there is no peace, then we deploy strategies for peace building. Once we have established protocols for peace, we can reinforce them through measures of accountability, through peace making and peace enforcement. Once we have built peace, we can turn our attention to maintaining peace, or what you are calling "peacekeeping."

Sketching this model for achieving and securing peace on a scrap piece of paper, Diop carefully detailed his framework for establishing what

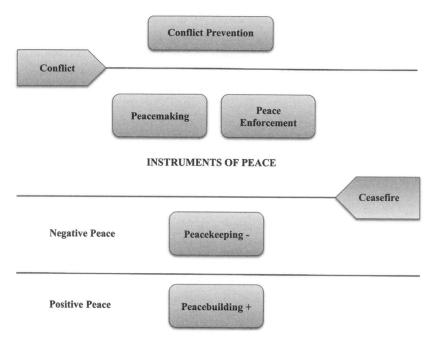

1. Diagram I later constructed from Diop's sketch on a Starbucks napkin.

professional political scientists call the "democratic peace" while speaking in the first person as if reflecting on the countless peacekeeping missions he has participated in. Diop visits the United States each year as part of a fellowship program that offers a few representatives from nations across the African continent the chance to receive instruction from senior US military officials. Diop, who has participated in these initiatives for more than a decade, is now tasked with hosting seminars for neophytes.

Until about a decade ago, managing the US military presence on the continent of Africa was largely in the hands of the US Middle East Central Command (CENTCOM). But with the formation of AFRICOM in 2003, the United States officially established a military presence on the continent. Though Stuttgart, Germany, is the site of AFRICOM's official headquarters, the prominence of US military officials at the embassy in Dakar has led critics to ask if this initiative constitutes a new imperialism.[4] I point out that critics have inquired about successive trips to Africa by US presidents, especially to oil-rich nations like Ghana and Nigeria. Some observers, I remind Diop, are concerned that these developments might be part of an effort to court—to extract—precious resources under cover of diplomatic aid and promotion of fair trade.

To my surprise, Diop does not dismiss these critiques. In fact, he insists that economic and geopolitical interests can never be ruled out entirely. In partial appreciation for the critics I cite, he offers a powerful if enigmatic observation: "I tell my students that nothing ever goes away. It only changes form. Before, the US and USSR had a cold war. Now the US has a cold war with China."

Presumably, as in the cold war of old, the US and the Republic of China are both vying for influence with wealthy and powerful nations of the world as well as trying to curry favor with resource-rich, numerically significant countries of the global South. Perhaps in this new cold war they are pursuing military advantage through proxy armies, engaging protocols for international governance on their own terms, with their own interests in mind. At the very least, I found this analogy intriguing because even in the "objective" realm of print journalism the United States and China are frequently construed as two emergent axes of security and economic development.

Consider the *New York Times* article of August 8, 2012, chronicling US investment in Africa. Centering on then US secretary of state Hillary Rodham Clinton, the feature points out that she is accompanied by representatives from Boeing, Wal-Mart, FedEx, and General Electric—corporations seeking to cultivate a much more substantial presence in Africa. Noting that more than six hundred US firms have offices on the continent, the *New York Times* remarks that "China" actually "anticipated" a commercial boom in Africa "long ago." From a podium in Dakar, Senegal, Clinton emphasizes that the United States has deliberately pursued a more judicious path. "The days of having outsiders come and extract the wealth of Africa for themselves, leaving nothing or very little behind, should be over in the twenty-first century," Clinton declares emphatically in a passage the *New York Times* notes was "widely interpreted as a swipe at China."[5]

Meanwhile, if the United States has lagged behind China in commercial ventures, it maintains a dramatic advantage in security—or "security training," in the deliberate language of US military personnel and embassy officials. Besides AFRICOM, the US Central Intelligence Agency has partnered with the Transitional Federal Government of Somalia to establish detention sites in Mogadishu, Somalia, for interrogating suspected terrorists.[6] The Pentagon has a base at Camp Lemonnier in Djibouti, which sits on the Gulf of Aden, across the Red Sea corridor from Yemen. The Department of Defense has personnel stationed in "US embassies across Africa, including

21 individual offices of Security Cooperation responsible for facilitating military to military activities with 'partner nations.'"[7]

But the relation between militarism and economic development that Diop, Denning, Sousa, Tompkins, and countless others refer to is more intriguing still. If Senegal's distinguished military experts and battalion commanders are trained by the combined efforts of British, French, and most notably US officers, many of the African nations that have been construed as "rogue" or "terrorist watch list" states have been trained in this other axis. Isaias Aferwerki, the president of Eritrea, received extensive military training in China that he would later use to help his nation wage a successful liberation struggle against Ethiopia. Eritrea, a territory Italy acquired in 1882, was sacked by the British during World War II as part of an Allied campaign targeting the fascist regime. Eritrea then became a British mandate—a quasi-sovereign territory, dubbed incapable of fully governing itself in the League of Nations international treaty regime—until 1951, when it became part of a joint federation with Ethiopia. But having forged a distinct social and political identity over some seven decades, the inhabitants of Eritrea were reluctant to concede autonomy. The ensuing decades witnessed a bitter liberation struggle that reached a formal resolution in 1993 when Eritrea was recognized as a sovereign republic by the United Nations.

Yet Eritrea has generally scoffed at protocols established by international governing agencies like the UN and international lending agencies like the International Monetary Fund and World Bank, widely understood to establish the parameters for economic and political legitimacy—for the modes of state comportment that count as good governance. Thus, within two decades of formal independence, Eritrea has been dubbed a "rogue state" for rejecting UN recommendations and pronouncements. It has earned a place on the US Department of Homeland Security's terrorist watch list for allegedly supporting Islamic "terrorists" like al-Shabaab, accused of fostering chronic political instability in Somalia. Meanwhile Eritrea has pursued a vision of economic growth that conflicts with prevailing notions of good governance even though it has proved especially lucrative.

The Eritrean economy is focused on mining and extracting resources as a way to strengthen its economy, with a particular emphasis on gold reserves. Economic experts, especially those working for international governing and lending agencies, routinely condemn this approach to market growth, as do leaders of economic and political reform in Africa. Abdoulaye Wade has insisted in numerous international fora that African nations ought to center their plans for growth on monetary policy and structural adjustment loans. Despite enacting a "rogue" development plan, Eritrea was cited by the highly esteemed Economist Intelligence Unit as arguably the fastest-growing economy in the world. One year later, Eritrea was ninth among all countries in the world in raw economic output as measured by real gross domestic product. In 2014, Eritrea was still regarded by the EIU as one of the world's fastest-growing economies.

In this regard, Eritrea presents a stark contrast with Senegal. Still, it is crucial to grapple with, rather than take for granted, what a particular economic course and genre of militarism mean for a country's diplomatic standing. Part of what accounts for the differential standing that countries like Senegal and Eritrea enjoy has to do with the mode of economic enterprise that dominates each nation's political aspirations. Part of what differentiates them concerns military operations. Whereas the Eritrean military is allegedly in league with terrorists, Senegal's long-standing participation in UN peacekeeping missions contributes to the idea that it is a democratic leader.

Far from merely building on its distinct history of colonial militarism, Senegal's exemplary reputation emerges from the unique mode of statecraft it cultivated in the immediate aftermath of independence and from the pragmatic strategies it has pursued ever since. If Senegal is only one of several former colonies whose soldiers earned privileged standing in an emergent sphere of international diplomacy through colonial conscription, this nation has used military service to build and broker esteem in diplomatic fora in novel ways since achieving independence in 1960. Since the advent of UN peacekeeping missions Senegal has, relative to its size, deployed more troops than any other nation including the United States.

During its first official peacekeeping mission, Senegal was still part of the Mali Federation, together with the former colony of French Sudan. The Mali Federation deployed troops to the Democratic Republic of the Congo in 1960, in the aftermath of a coup d'état that saw Prime Minister Patrice Lumumba kidnapped, then executed by the general of his standing army. A local merchant turned charismatic leader, Lumumba had political aspirations that articulated with the Pan-African sensibilities of Kwame Nkrumah of Ghana and Julius Nyerere of Tanzania. Lumumba used his inaugural address to reject the historic violence of the Belgian colony and to articulate a new economic and political destiny. But the prime minister's fiery speech isolated his own president, who was more ambivalent concerning Belgium-Congo relations. Lumumba raised the ire of the Belgian king, who had attended the ceremony. He also raised the ire of powerful economic and political interests keeping tabs on these developments. There is now consensus among historians that the US Central Intelligence Agency colluded with the Belgian government and the Congolese military in the precocious leader's ouster from power and his assassination a few days later.

The Congo is a fascinating place from which to track the relation between domestic political organization and diplomatic standing, since, as early as 1876, King Leopold II of Belgium had explained away his imperial ambitions as a modest effort "to open to civilization the only part of our globe where it has yet to penetrate, to pierce the darkness which envelops whole populations,"[9] though the Congo Free State would ultimately gain notoriety for the countless laborers who suffered amputations for the smallest infractions. The Mali Federation authorized peacekeeping forces to the Congo on July 14, 1960, after having been freed from colonial rule four months earlier. At that juncture, the Congo had been independent for only two months.

On August 2, 1960, the first troop deployment left Dakar after two weeks' preparation for one of "the very first uses of the 'blue helmets' symbolizing UN forces,"[10] though it is perhaps important to note that France helped outfit the Mali Federation forces—to ensure that they were "equipped to the nines with every necessary piece of equipment."[11] The Mali Federation lasted two more years, after which time Senegal continued to participate in peacekeeping missions. Mali's military would likewise be active during the decades to come but would be plagued by military coups that undermined the prospect of democratic governance. Meanwhile, consensus would build that Senegal constitutes one of the few countries in Africa where—as Sousa had insisted—*civilians control the military rather than the other way around.* Given their shared genealogy, it is striking that Senegal is heralded as a democratic leader whose military helps spread democratic governance, whereas Mali is characterized as a nation whose military has fostered corruption. In other words, to the story of the *tirailleurs* conscripted from across the AOF (Afrique Occidentale Français, or French African territories) there needs to be added the story of the postcolonial reconstitution of the Senegalese military as a peacekeeping entity. This perspective is pervasive in military discourse, which routinely projects assessments of Senegalese character backward into a moment when Senegal was not yet an independent nation-state.

In writing about the Mali Federation's 1960 UN effort in the Congo, US Air Force captain Roy Dietzman writes, "The mission of the deployed battalion was to restore peace in the former Belgian colony of the Congo which had been thrown into chaos with their new-found independence."[12] But note that Dietzman's 2003 study is called "Forty-Two Years of Peacekeeping:

A Review of *Senegalese* Participation in Peacekeeping Missions." Here, whether the 1960 UN mission is construed as part of Senegal's or Mali's history makes all the difference. Dietzman refers to troops from the Mali Federation as a "Senegalese contingent" and frequently refers to the "Senegalese Armed Forces" (SAF) as the subject of his forty-two-year history, effectively excising its inception as part of the Mali Federation.

In Dietzman's view, Senegalese soldiers operate with "exacting effectiveness."[13] He sees their dedication to peacekeeping as a tradition they belong to as "the outward manifestation of a constant will of Senegalese diplomacy to hold a particular position of high regard in the world, and particularly in Africa." It is tempting to read this 1960s trajectory against the background of the surge in independence among African nations that defined the decade. But scholars have argued convincingly that the 1940s set in motion the chain of events that translated into independence for many African nations in the 1960s.[14] Thus we should consider the dynamics that defined postindependence Senegal in concert with the broader context of World War II and the birth of the United Nations as a crucial actor in an emergent framework for international governance. During this period, the mandate for international governing entities and international lending agencies to promote peace and preserve democracy cohered into a shared structure of liability involving new regimes of credit-debt and militarism that are too often taken for granted.

In the aftermath of World War II, US presidents Franklin D. Roosevelt and, later, Harry S. Truman took advantage of the fact that diplomatic and commercial heavyweights like Britain and France were financially drained to leverage the United States' own position. The US government helped to establish international lending and governing agencies, which created elaborate protocols to evaluate nations invested in good standing in a growing diplomatic community. The US government oversaw a shift in sovereign finance where the US dollar became the basis of international currency markets. The Marshall Plan would fund and foster efforts to rebuild Europe. Meanwhile, the United States brokered an end to military conflict, adopting an aggressive agenda for peace. Since the first part of the twentieth century had witnessed "more warfare, of greater destructive intensity, than at any other time in world history,"[15] the United States self-consciously promoted the idea of a "democratic peace."[16] This principle was subsequently enshrined as a governing premise of resolutions the United Nations and other governing agencies would endorse.

"Democratic peace theory" is one of the most influential theories of governance. It is arguably the "most powerful liberal contribution to the debate on the causes of war and peace." It is essentially born of the idea that "democracies rarely fight one another because they share common norms of live-and-let-die" as well political "institutions that constrain" an otherwise pervasive "recourse to war."[17] This theory constitutes a critique of the realist presumption that international politics is the science of securing and sustaining economic and military advantage. Democratic peace theory is also notable for emphasizing the character or profile of a nation as a proxy for political behavior. In that sense, it is likewise a critique of structural and materialist accounts of international politics.

Insofar as democracy is often assumed to be the default template for a just society, we should think carefully about whether prevailing assumptions align with empirical realities. The most alarming feature of democratic peace theory—as recent research has demonstrated time and again—is that there are numerous, often blatant, inconsistencies between the diplomatic standing a country manages to secure and the behavior that nation has historically exhibited. And this in part has to do with the fact that "democracy" is a privileged mode of diplomatic standing.

Supporters of democratic peace theory insist that it "socialize[s] elites to act on the basis of democratic norms whenever possible." Yet in this formulation a "democracy" is bound to observe peaceful norms only with another "democracy," not with a nondemocracy. Casting another country as a nondemocracy has historically been a convenient way for purportedly democratic countries to gain political leverage. Democratic peace theory also tends to overlook the fact that many countries, including the United States, struggled for much of their history to secure diplomatic standing as "democratic." Even in the midst of the conventions for ratification that resulted in the United Nations, the US government worked actively to deter African American leaders from raising concerns about legalized segregation during deliberations about human rights. They were concerned that widespread knowledge of rampant racial discrimination in state industries and public institutions would undermine the United States' effort to cast itself as a diplomatic leader.[18]

The idea that democratic nations are accountable to their vast constituencies is a central feature of democratic peace theory. Often this is not the case. As a recent example, consider the advent of military campaigns in Iraq and Afghanistan during the twenty-first century, where the United States neither relied on congressional approval nor consistently consulted the electorate before embarking on a new militarized course of action.

It is perhaps true, as democratic peace theorists insist, that democratic nations rarely declare war against each other. Yet even during the Cold War era, the United States and the Soviet Union used economic and political leverage to bolster their allies in what was essentially a proxy war.[19] And during the past few decades, the United States has increasingly relied on military engagements by special operations soldiers, on private security contractors, and on targeted killings using unmanned aircraft to alleviate perceived threats to national security. As such, the idea of "peace" that lurks behind democratic peace theory has little traction analytically. And insofar as an interest in fostering "peace" coincided with a new age of economic and diplomatic leverage in the aftermath of World War II, we should ask whether what we are calling "peace" might not bring its own genre of economic and military advantage for nations understood to be "peace builders" and "peacekeepers." In this context we should perhaps think more carefully about what it means that three of the countries that sit on the UN Security Council, three purported beacons of democracy—the United States, Britain, and France—are responsible for training the Senegalese military in matters of security.

Since independence, Senegal has been involved in more than twenty missions in at least eighteen countries involving more than twenty thousand troops. "Their reputation has risen to such a level," says Dietzman,[20] "that their presence proves to be impossible to circumvent on the African scene for any operation wanting to be credible."[21] And Senegal has leveraged this credibility at key moments in its political history to shape regional politics and to strengthen ties with its allies.

The Cold War made the idea of international peacekeeping especially contentious. With both the United States and the USSR being permanent members of the UN Security Council, either nation could exercise its veto power to undermine a concerted effort to intervene in international conflict situations. As the Cold War fizzled, these nations relaxed their veto power, and the United Nations gained unprecedented influence as a governing body that could adjudicate political tensions between and within nations.[22] Over the past twenty years, this position has fed an increase in the number and duration of formal peacekeeping efforts: in these, the Senegalese Armed Forces have distinguished themselves among the world's nations, but most notably among African countries. Senegal would go on to establish a track record for providing UN peacekeeping missions with more troops per capita than any other nation. This rate of participation is staggering when you consider that the SAF, with every branch combined, number only thirteen thousand troops, plus an additional six thousand from the *national gendarmerie*, or federal police. Indeed, the singular commitment Senegal has made in this regard has forged a diplomatic record that is exceptional in more than one sense. Senegal was the only African nation to provide troops for Operations Desert Storm and Desert Shield in 1990–91. And this was no small sacrifice. Although the SAF lost fourteen soldiers in Liberia, sixteen in Lebanon, and two in Rwanda during the 1990s, ninety-three soldiers died in a Gulf War plane crash, which says something about the tremendous stakes this diplomatic tradition potentially entails.

The praise lavished on Senegalese soldiers tends to focus on four characteristics. First, they can be deployed quickly (taking only four days to prepare for service in Desert Shield and Desert Storm). Second, Senegal privileges a "homogeneous contingent," which means the same group is "deployed for the duration of the operation with no rotation of forces." Third, the Senegalese government is willing to accommodate missions that extend for a "long duration" (anywhere from six to fifteen months).[23] Finally, Senegal prefers to send high-ranking officials trained in US, French, and British military academies. Here peacekeeping bears an uncanny resemblance to a very different multilateral strategy for global improvement: structural adjustment. Structural adjustment is likewise concerned with measuring the economic and political aspirations of individual nations against a standard that international governing organizations have established. Structural adjustment also uses experts to instruct recipient nations about the normative mechanisms best suited to produce a successful outcome.[24] Senegal's relation to both peacekeeping *and* structural adjustment has implications for the nation's diplomatic standing. In the context of peacekeeping and structural adjustment, Senegal benefits from sanction conferred by the British, French, and US governments.

On January 17, 2005, Senegalese President Abdoulaye Wade addressed the audience assembled for the Seventeenth Annual World Bank Conference on Development Economics in Dakar, Senegal—only the second time this forum had been held in a "developing country." Directing his attention to the challenge of financing economic growth in Africa, Wade plunged right into the issue of indebtedness:

> So far, African countries have relied on their own domestic efforts and on external aid to finance growth. Unfortunately, external aid has often led to large, unsustainable, indebtedness.
>
> There is now a global consensus on the need for debt cancellation. Prime Minister Tony Blair of the United Kingdom and President Jacques Chirac of

France, among other world leaders, have publicly supported the idea. I have
been given the honor of preparing an African seminar on debt issues.

After citing the endorsement he has received from the sovereign leaders
of France and Great Britain, Wade directs his attention to the circumstances
most favorable for economic growth and cites "good political governance"
as the key factor. In Wade's view, good political governance enables nations to manage their own resources to create the "domestic conditions"
necessary to "attract foreign capital." In this line of argument, good public
governance—like good political governance—is about "democracy, human
rights, and everything else within the power of the state." It also means
working to solidify "good private governance" by "creating a business-
friendly environment." In figuring good political governance as a composite of good public governance and good private governance, Wade gestures
to Senegal's exemplary diplomatic standing to justify his assertion that he
has been granted the authority—the sanction—to establish mechanisms for
debt adjudication that other African nations are expected to heed.

In his address, Wade spoke at length about the "capacity" of Senegal's
natural resources to accommodate health, gesturing toward the privatizing
of electricity and the liberalizing of the groundnut sector. More than 70 percent of Senegalese people live in rural areas, earning income through plant
and animal resources (livestock, cotton, and fishing). But the hierarchies
that structure labor all but guarantee that returns will be concentrated in
the hands of a select few. Much has been made of the shifty marabouts who
employ armies of orphans to beg for money on Dakar streets, generating
profits from which these young people are excluded.[25] But most industries
are structured by a similar form of generationism. More than 60 percent of
the population is under age twenty (nearly 50 percent are under fifteen).
And of the 50 percent of the population that remains chronically unemployed, more than 40 percent are categorized in official statistics as "urban
youth." For more than twenty years, Senegal has been seeking the remedy
for economic stagnation in loans sponsored by the World Bank and the
International Monetary Fund. Senegal secured its first loan from the World
Bank in 1967 and has since been approved for more than 120 loans and
credits that amount to nearly US$2.5 billion. This staggering number con-
stitutes one of the lowest disbursement rates in sub-Saharan Africa. Still,
it has been more than two decades since Senegal has been able to meet its
annual obligation to lending agencies.

The World Bank requires Senegal to eliminate the "administrative, legal, regulatory, and fiscal impediments to private investment," especially where "foreign direct investment" is concerned, which proves that this sort of debt management program is not merely a repertoire of fiscal policies but a mode of statecraft. If the Senegalese tradition in peacekeeping proves there is no neutral territory in international diplomacy, neither is there any where market mechanisms are concerned. The structure of debt that Senegal endorses means it is constantly subjected to programs for good governance established by international financial institutions instead of the institutions that voters, intellectuals, and activists might bring to bear through principled debate and concerted action. Moreover, these debt relief programs rely on a very particular sense of accountability, suspending the most vexed questions for postcolonial polities: Who or what is responsible for the debt? Who is liable for it? And what happens to the citizens of a nation that spends most of its resources trying to make good on debts to foreign creditors? Even debt relief, far from being a benevolent gesture, works to secure a social field in which the present government of the indebted nation is held liable for a debt that is adjudicated through international financial institutions that operate with a very narrow conception of just governance.

In April 2010, the IMF and the World Bank announced that Senegal would be awarded $850 million in debt service relief, with "more likely to follow," with both institutions citing the nation's "political stability" and "broad ranging structural reforms," including privatization and deregulation of the economy. The Paris Club, a financial consortium of affluent nations including the United States, Britain, France, and Russia, among others, offered to provide an additional $400 million on learning the news. Leaving no room for speculation, the IMF and the World Bank cited the "reduced role of the state in the economy" and the "improved business environment" as Senegal's most important reforms. Six months before receiving this distinction, Wade had actually been accused of trying to bribe an IMF representative with €133,000 in cash, which he insisted was simply a farewell gift. Meanwhile, a diplomatic cable dated February 2010, two months before this announcement was made, reveals a US ambassador engaged in private conversation with Wade about the rising tide of corruption throughout the Senegalese government.[26] In this sense, the fraught nature of Senegalese peacekeeping missions combines with its status as a leader in debt management to suggest that "stabilizing" any diplomatic or economic scenario turns out to be rather more vexed than it is taken to be in prevailing discourses on good governance.

The loans that the IMF and World Bank made available to Senegal as a testament to "good governance" suggest that if the forensic profile is a kind of diplomatic profile it is also a credit profile. Senegal's standing as a leader of economic and political reform in Africa underscores that the national character it has been assigned equates to subjective estimates about its moral integrity. Whether the people of Senegal rely on the same evidence to assess the profile of their polity, and whether they draw same conclusions, remains another matter entirely.

After all, Senegal's diplomatic profile has in part to do with pragmatic responses to contentious international events. The September 11, 2001, bombing of New York City's World Trade Center enhanced Senegal's diplomatic standing. Senegal did not merely support the United States' campaign against terror, it pioneered an African coalition dedicated to the same goal. In the process, the people of Senegal were reminded of the uneven stakes that a diplomatic profile entails. They were further reminded that a diplomatic profile is a forensic profile, subject to strategies of surveillance and detention whose consequences are difficult to predict and even more difficult to constrain.

FIVE

Forensic Profile

The Senegalese American hip-hop rhythm and blues singer Akon soared to the top of United States music charts in 2004 with his autobiographical gangsta ballad "Locked Up." The track chronicles Akon's frustration with being profiled, harassed, and ultimately imprisoned by law enforcement officials. Though Akon's narrative centers on his experience in the United States, the sense of captivity outlined in his hit song—with its chorus, "I'm locked up, they won't let me out"—parallels events that took place in his native Senegal the year before.[1]

On July 8, 2003, US president George W. Bush visited Gorée Island. According to those interviewed, US military personnel arrived around 4:00 a.m. that day, accompanied by bomb-sniffing dogs. Soldiers evacuated people and then searched their homes. They moved most of the island's residents onto a sandlot soccer field. Once packed to capacity, the field was barricaded. The small packets of water haphazardly distributed provided little relief for the crowd during the eight hours some people spent in that spot complained—from 6.00 a.m. until 2.00 p.m.—though Bush's entire visit took place between 11:00 a.m. and 1:00 p.m. All cell phone communication was disabled during this time.

The reaction of the local population can be distilled into a Wolof phrase that a friend, Bineta, scrawled in my notebook: Da fa mel ni Jaam moo ñëwaat, which she translated, "It was like slavery had returned."[2] Until that moment, I had seen the term *jaam* used only in connection with different historic categories of enslaved persons (*jaami-bur*, "slaves of the Crown"; *jaami-sayóor*, "household slaves"; *jaami-juddu*, "slaves of the land," etc.). In what sense does this idea of the Senegalese citizen as a slave cue us to the forensic profile that emerged on Gorée Island that day?

During several years of ethnographic fieldwork and more than a decade of research in Senegal, I encountered few people who self-consciously identified with the legacy of slavery except in the most casual sense. So it's especially intriguing that the Bush visit led people to characterize themselves in a way that was both distressing and unfamiliar. In what follows, I want to explore what this latter-day figuration of Senegalese people in the grip of "slavery" means for the social standing they enjoy at home and abroad. More specifically, I am interested in what the coercive treatment of Senegalese people suggests about the way they were assessed and characterized by security forces. We cannot possibly know the forensic calculus US security forces and their Senegalese collaborators used to establish potential risks to the security of the US president on July 8, 2003. But the proposition of this chapter is that the forensics of capital provides a lens through which to assess this event in the context of broader economic and political transformations.

What does it mean that a soccer field was the place where island residents were detained? Bush's visit occurred the year after Senegal's national soccer team achieved widespread acclaim for an upset victory over France in the 2002 World Cup. That milestone grew out of a determined effort through which former French colonies, as well as players from these polities in the metropole, settled on soccer as a way to distinguish themselves, and to assert their potential, in an emerging context of international diplomacy and goodwill.[3] The idea of an enclosed field as a security mechanism with the power to detain and sequester Senegalese citizens—to turn people into *jaami*, or slaves—establishes the theoretical parameters through which this chapter examines the question of social belonging in postindependence Senegal.

In part this means considering the way Senegalese Islam is heralded and promoted as a uniquely peaceful, cosmopolitan variant of the religion. For it is crucial to consider the crude conflation between Islam and terrorism that proliferates in international diplomacy, and that surfaced in Bush's Gorée Island address. In his remarks, we see how secular governance articulates with a post-Reconquista Christian ethos. The triumph of the former polities of Latin Christendom and those of the North Atlantic has intermittently been framed as a "war" against Islam, even if it is couched in the language of a humanitarian crusade against Islamic fundamentalism.[4] In this formulation, a nation like Senegal that is characterized by a version of Islam understood to be earnest and pious is frequently contrasted with other African polities. Observe that widespread consternation about the alliance between militarized insurgents in Mali and in Algeria is rarely framed as a geopolitical conflict but is seen as a war by democratic nations against Islamic insurgency or even as part of the fight against a specific terrorist network known as al-Qaeda. Of course, Islamic groups sometimes understand themselves this way. But note that the stipulated Christian investments of a nation like the United States, even with the references to God and country that heads of state dabble in—and that Bush stressed during his speech—does not lead foreign policy analysts to view US geopolitics through the lens of some specific interest in promoting Christian practice and doctrine. Part of what I want to accomplish in theorizing social belonging in Senegal is to understand how the idea of Senegal as a nation of pious, earnest Muslims helps structure the forensic profile of the polity and, at a different level, its people.

With these concerns in mind, this chapter explores a series of related events that begin with the tragic events of September 11, 2001, which set the stage for Bush's visit to Senegal nearly two years later. My aim is to demonstrate how the forensics of capital might occasion a more careful analysis of the way a diplomatic profile functions as a kind of forensic profile.[5]

Before the tragic events of September 11, 2001, were even ten days past, Senegalese president Abdoulaye Wade had already formed an African coalition to fight terrorism. What the nation lacked in firepower, it made up in enthusiasm. Positioning himself as a representative of the African continent, Wade declared that his coalition condemned the terrorist acts committed against the United States and pledged that, following the lead of the Western coalition fighting terrorism,[6] he would create a committee of African nations dedicated to the same cause. Wade expected this collective to include wealthy African nations like oil-rich Nigeria as well as some of the continent's diplomatic leaders like South Africa. He assured the world he would do his part to ensure that no African nation financed or otherwise enabled terrorist activities.[7] Complicating Bush's stated investment in a "crusade" against Islamic terrorism—an anachronism bristling with Reconquista imagery—Wade remained convinced there were no clandestine terror networks in Senegal, a country that is more than 90 percent Muslim.

By the time Wade's summit was convened in Dakar on October 17, it boasted fifteen African heads of state.[8] The resulting document, the Déclaration de Dakar, was ultimately signed by twenty-seven nations dedicated to keeping Africa free of all terrorist activity, whether motivated by political, philosophical, ideological, racial, ethnic, or religious concerns. The signatories insisted that the guidelines of the United Nations and the African Union (formerly the Organization of African Unity) offered the best blueprints for fighting terrorism and recommended that this "pact against terrorism," proposed and coordinated by Senegal, be ratified through official protocol.[9] Thirteen days later George W. Bush would publicly affirm his appreciation for Senegal's newest foreign policy objective at the Forum for African Economic and Commercial Cooperation. At this same event, Bush announced that the United States would create a $200 million fund to stimulate private investment for countries in sub-Saharan Africa and would offer American corporations certain protections against risk to encourage interest in the continent.[10]

African economic recovery was a prominent issue in the world that year. In January 2001 Abdoulaye Wade had unveiled his Omega Plan, which stressed the need to improve physical and human capital in Africa and to bring continent-wide development plans under the aegis of a single international authority.[11] The project was formally introduced to the public during an international conference six months later. Eventually the Omega Plan was combined with South African president Thabo Mbeki's Millennium Partnership for African Recovery program. The result was NEPAD, the New Partnership for African Development, an initiative the United States endorsed, alongside other donor nations.[12] The United States had so quickly become one of Senegal's most important financiers and political supporters that French president Jacques Chirac held talks with Wade in 2004 to "remind" him which country had historically been his greatest ally.[13] This newer alliance, more meaningful for both countries since 2001, started to assume its present contours during the Cold War. Although Senegal has operated differently from many socialist nations in its historical reluctance to align itself with other socialist or communist countries, it was never intimate with the United States either. This trend started to change in the 1980s when the Reagan administration started to see Senegal as a "friend and potential ally" based on its resolute opposition to Cuban and Soviet influence in African politics.[14]

The war on terror offered the perfect occasion to bolster this alliance:[15] Bush's $200 million investment fund sent a message that the United States was prepared to support Senegal's foreign policy both rhetorically and financially. Since African nations are frequently expected to demonstrate their commitment to democracy as a precondition for receiving foreign direct assistance, Senegal's fight against terrorism signaled that the country was committed to sustaining and enhancing democratic political institutions.

For Bush, nations who did not vow their support for the fight against terror would ultimately sabotage it. He sought to recruit allies in diverse international arenas—and these domains did not have to be explicitly political:

he threatened to boycott US participation in the 2002 World Cup if other nations did not demonstrate a satisfactory commitment to fighting against the encroachment of global terrorist networks. Ultimately, however, Bush must have been pleased that he decided not to do so, because the US national team reached the quarterfinals. This was the subject of a friendly conversation with Wade. As they met in 2002 to discuss each country's newest foreign policy initiatives, the two presidents joked that if both teams continued to excel in their divisions the United States and Senegal would face off in the World Cup championship.[16] At the same time, soccer was becoming increasingly significant locally. Thus, even as Senegal worked to bolster public faith in its commitment to democracy by pioneering an African coalition against terrorism, it was pursuing another course of action that likewise involved enhancing the country's image in the world.

This leads me back to a question posed at the outset: what are the implications that residents of Gorée Island could experience slavery again for the first time on the island's only soccer field? To grapple with this question, I draw from key events surrounding the political campaign of then-president Abdoulaye Wade, as well as Senegal's participation in the World Cup the year following 9/11—the year before Bush's visit.

In 2000 Abdoulaye Wade became Senegal's third president because he managed to secure the support of Senegal's most powerful and disaffected constituency: young people. In a nation where more than 50 percent of the population is under twenty[17] and where "urban youth"[18] constitute more than 40 percent of the total 48 percent unemployed population,[19] the "youth" labor problem is the nation's most significant economic obstacle.

From the moment he declared victory in the 2000 presidential elections, Wade registered an ambition to make young people the engine of national productivity. His inaugural speech, in which he referred to youth as the country's most valuable "resource," builds to a climax that closes with the motto that immediately made him famous: "There is no secret [to success]: you should work, work some more, work a lot—always work" (Il n'y a pas de secret: il faut travailler, encore travailler, beaucoup travailler, toujours travailler). Wade's words were memorialized and resurface in a number of popular *mbalax* songs throughout Senegal. "Il faut travailler, beaucoup travailler, encore travailler, toujours travailler . . ." is always the refrain.

The most popular rendition was made by the group Pape et Cheikh. But as this version ends the chorus changes, the most significant word in the mantra transformed by the duo's effort to index what they surely hoped would be the outcome of all this hard work, "Il faut gagner, encore gagner, beaucoup gagner, toujours gagner" (You should win, win some more, win a lot, always win).

As Senegal marched through qualifying matches for the 2002 World Cup, national enthusiasm increased with every victory. News that the team had been officially selected occasioned an impromptu parade as the populace flooded downtown Dakar in celebration of this momentous achievement. President Wade cut short an official trip to France so he could party with the national team at home: "At this time it's the most important thing that could happen to any country, and I will join the team and the nation in celebrating by reducing the amount of time I was expected to stay in Paris."

The nation's chief executive stressed the significance of this event for the entire populace—and for posterity—"My deepest congratulations go to the courageous Lions who have made history for Senegal"[20]—as he resurfaced a short time later wearing the jersey of striker El-Hadji Diouf to join the "madness" that characterized local celebrations, according to one spectator.

A few days later, Wade held a special ceremony and concert at the presidential palace where each team member was presented a bonus of 10 million francs CFA (then approximately $15,000);[21] this in addition to cash rewards offered by the nation's wealthiest residents and families. From the perspective of El-Hadji Diouf, the team's best but also its most controversial player, people were acting as if Senegal had already won the World Cup.[22]

The drama was heightened once fans realized that Senegal was slotted to battle France in the first round. Supporters stressed the geopolitical dimensions of this occasion: "Senegal-France is an historic match. . . . This is the European country that colonized us. And, God willing, we will beat them." The government, to galvanize support for the team, promoted the slogan that the Lions de Teranga—as the team is affectionately called—hail from *Le Sénégal qui gagne* ("the Senegal that wins"). Where the slogan came from is not altogether clear, but in the days, weeks, and months leading up to the match against France, the motto appeared on flyers, posters, and signs across the country. *Le Sénégal qui gagne*. Once emblazoned across the nation, the phrase stuck.

El-Hadji Diouf seemed to understand profoundly the political consequences of this postcolonial drama. As the team had swept through qualifying competition on the strength of his eight goals, he found himself commanding the Senegalese forces for this important battle. "It's like being the leader of a country," he explained when asked his feelings about the ensuing match against France.[23] So when Senegal pulled off the 0–1 upset victory, fans poured into the streets of Dakar, gravitating, significantly, to Le Place de l'Indépendance and the presidential palace. Red, yellow, and green Senegalese flags, hats, scarves, T-shirts, and African-style *boubous* were the only acceptable attire to commemorate the occasion.

One supporter, Omar Ly, extended the meaningfulness of this event beyond Senegal's national boundaries. In his words, it was "a victory for black people everywhere." As he elaborated, "I'm Senegalese, but I've lived in the U.S. and France. I've experienced racism. I'm so happy to be here for this."[24] Whether in terms of the old or new superpower ally, this win communicated an important message.

Yet the victory camouflaged a complicated relationship between Senegal and its former colonizer. In the months leading up to the match, Khalilou Fadiga, who scored the game-winning goal, had been quoted as saying it would be difficult for him to play against France: "The truth is that I know the streets of Paris better than the streets of Dakar." Fadiga had left Senegal when he was six. He grew up in France. These factors would make it tough for him to line up against the representatives of a place that was so special to him. "But," he was careful to add, "if I play in the World Cup finals, I've got to try my best to beat them."

Fadiga's loyalties ultimately rested with his ancestral land. "I feel Senegalese," he eventually concluded, "When I was home, everybody would speak our language, and we listened to Senegalese radio and music. We ate Senegalese food." The significance of his heritage went even beyond his acculturation: "I share both [French and Senegalese] cultures, but I have a lot of family over in Senegal, and my color is Senegalese."[25] The superstar's affectionate testimony highlights an important paradox. Many of the Senegalese players spend at least as much time in Europe as they do in Africa— often more. To the extent that they spend most of the year playing for club teams—in France, Switzerland, and England, for instance—they are seldom in Senegal.[26] Yet they are its emissaries on important diplomatic missions such as this one.

This seeming contradiction exposes a significant feature of Senegalese social life, especially during the postcolonial period: whether professional athletes, musicians, students, politicians, merchants, or professors, the persons occupying the highest ranks of power and wealth are those who have spent some period absent from the nation.[27] Socioeconomic mobility in this context means moving out to move up.

Still, this team of citizens with multiple national allegiances was constituted, in the World Cup moment, as a coalition of the nation's best talent.

Suddenly *Le Sénégal qui gagne* referred not simply to a nation with the ability to win. It referred to a country that had proved it could win—that it was destined to prevail.

Le Sénégal qui gagne. Supporters delivered the chant when welcoming the national team back home. It was a slogan that immediately evoked the euphoria attached to victory over France.

The president was quick to associate himself with this turn of events. Declaring a national holiday in honor of the team's win, Wade appeared at the national parade in a vehicle with the top open so everyone could see him juggling a soccer ball to commemorate this important event. Wade had been in office only two years at that point. His presidency had coincided with Senegal's eruption onto the world scene as a soccer team of renown. His undying emotional and financial support for the squad made him a national hero of sorts, even as his opposition criticized what they considered vulgar opportunism. "Our president is trying to capture this performance of the Senegalese boys, but I think it is very childish . . . because [this victory] is not the result of" some "football policy," said Amath Dansokho, leader of the Independence and Labor Party.[28] For some people, the president had done little—in terms of sports or politics—to influence the successes for which he credited himself.

That year, Senegal would win again before tying a match and losing another to finally exit World Cup competition. But the team had already made history, affirming a place in the international spotlight for the country and its president.

What are we to make of the team's success and of its ability to put a positive spin on Abdoulaye Wade's tenure at the nation's helm? The national soccer team's improbable World Cup success had eclipsed the government's inability to cope with recurring energy shortages as well as the countless jobs lost to agricultural stagnation amid the escalating numbers of young people crowding urban areas in the previous decades in search of work.

Without offering an elaborate treatment of the gender issues under consideration, Dansokho provokes us to consider them by complaining about how Wade appropriates the success of the national soccer team. Indeed, one of the most prominent features of economic liberalization in Senegal has been the way it valorizes masculinity in aspirational narratives. From overseas traders to athletes, Senegalese success stories frequently privilege male subjects with extensive access to foreign capital. This tendency is tied to the way Senegalese politics has been characterized, during the past several decades, by increased reliance on structural adjustment and on donations from wealthier nations. The state, instead of building a national infrastructure, has largely relied on private investment to engender economic revitalization. In the process, the masculinity of the trader—like that of the athlete—is institutionalized as a kind of prerequisite for access to foreign capital. The nightmare version of this fantasy centers on unemployed young men, who are ridiculed for being idle despite battling decades of chronic unemployment. Meanwhile, the crucial role that women play in rearing the nation, as well as attending to the educational and economic aspirations of the populace, remains woefully underappreciated and undertheorized by scholars. Where the "spectacle charm" of masculine authority is concerned, it's significant that—like President Wade—each of the best players on the national soccer team consults a personal marabout who receives the lion's share of credit for the individual prowess of an athlete. The same kind of relationship obtains with high-ranking Senegalese politicians.[29] As such, the science of masculine efficacy turns on the practice of anointing, even if evidence of efficacy is inevitably introduced ex post facto.

Athletic competition presumes an idealized subject. Just as teams—or firms—try to select the individuals most capable of attaining desired results, a key aspect of Senegal's investment strategy involves convincing potential donors that it has achieved a form worthy of their investment:[30] democracy according to a profile sketched by international governing and lending agencies. Otherwise a country is considered unfit for sponsorship and disqualified from competition altogether.[31] NEPAD, after all, summoned "African leaders to put their houses in order in exchange for foreign direct investment."[32] The male-focused image of success and emphasis on foreign investment that structure Senegal's pursuit of prosperity thus articulate in a discomforting way with the soccer field that became the site of the political spectacle that provoked comparison with this region's most inhumane historical traffic in human commodities.

Several people I interviewed insisted that, during George W. Bush's visit to Gorée, the entire population of the island was taken to a soccer stadium and locked inside. I later learned it was a sandlot soccer field, barricaded to prevent escape. Yet by referring to the field as a solid fortification, interviewees suggested that for them the makeshift barriers had become concrete enclosures.

Although US foreign policy in Senegal has crystallized through the successive visits of different presidents, interviewees contrasted the repressive treatment that accompanied Bush's arrival with the enriching experience of hosting Bill and Hillary Clinton in 1998. "Bill would be in the countryside playing with little children," a thirty-something female vendor insisted. Hillary, meanwhile, participated in a debate on female genital mutilation.[33]

President Barack Obama's visit to Senegal in 2013 would, like the Clinton visit, be regarded fondly—meaningful socially but also intellectually and politically, like the Clinton visit. After meeting with President Sall at the Palais de Président, Obama met with the chief justice and even set aside time to speak with activists and social justice leaders supporting diverse causes before drawing his trip to a close.

Bush's 2003 visit was deemed coercive by contrast: reporters noticed that, even before the US president arrived, security personnel had placed his anticipated hotel under strict surveillance.[34] They leveled age-old baobab trees to enhance visibility and ultimately detained much of the island's population on a soccer field. And few people missed the profound irony that all this took place a few feet from the historic Maison des Esclaves (slave house or slave dungeon), responsible for the tourism that provides this island economy's primary revenue.

In recent years some scholars have challenged Gorée's historical legitimacy as a central port in the transatlantic slave trade, suggesting that the current site of the Maison des Esclaves served primarily as a private residence for one Anne Pépin.[35] Although Pépin sometimes engaged in minor forms of overseas exchange and occasionally held enslaved Africans in the basement of the residence,[36] the Maison was apparently not the pivotal site of Atlantic dispersion it is often imagined to be.[37] Given all this, the slavery discourses that emerged in the aftermath of July 8, 2003, seem at best exaggerated and at worst unjustified.[38]

The Bush visit, though, ultimately hinges on a profound irony: the technique of coercion used to subdue Senegalese people in that moment[39] reproduced the way enslavement historically occurred on Gorée Island more faithfully than any event that has ever occurred at the Maison des Esclaves, for slavery in this locale typically did not proceed through dungeons and warehousing. Instead, enslaved Africans were usually herded together and bound in open-air *captiveries*,[40] waiting to be loaded on ships that would send them across the Atlantic. The residents of Gorée Island conveyed to me that, except for a few invited guests, they were treated similarly on July 8, 2003.

So though Bush's speech was ostensibly directed to the people of Senegal, many were too busy fighting heat exhaustion and too far removed from the podium to hear his address. The speech nevertheless had a discernible structure and an audience. Thus we might consider how this address could be read for what it reveals about Senegal's diplomatic relations with the United States, from within the context of an impromptu detention camp.

With the power and resources given to us, the United States seeks to bring peace where there is conflict, hope where there is suffering, and liberty where there is tyranny. And these commitments bring me and other distinguished leaders of my government across the Atlantic to Africa.

—George W. Bush, Gorée Island, July 8, 2003

Beginning sometime around 11:45 a.m., the US commander-in-chief immediately situated his remarks in the context of transatlantic slavery:

For hundreds of years on this island, peoples of different continents met in fear and cruelty. Today we gather in respect and friendship, mindful of past wrongs and dedicated to the advance of human liberty.

At this place, liberty and life were stolen and sold. Human beings were delivered and sorted, and weighed, and branded with the marks of commercial enterprises, and loaded as cargo on a voyage without return. One of the largest migrations in history was also one of the greatest crimes of history.

Below the decks, the middle passage was a hot, narrow, sunless nightmare; weeks and months of confinement and abuse and confusion on a strange and lonely sea. Some refused to eat, preferring death to any future their captors might prepare for them. Some who were sick were thrown over the side. Some rose up in violent rebellion, delivering the closest thing to justice on a slave ship. Many acts of defiance and bravery are recorded. Countless others, we will never know.

Here Bush endorses resistance as a feasible strategy for Africans who refuse captivity. Perhaps Bush believes that when faced with a "crim[inal]" or tyrannical regime, people ought to pursue their freedom by any means necessary.

And yet Senegal became an important ally of the United States at this historical juncture because of President Wade's expressed disdain for Islamic jihad waged by Muslims who see the United States as an imperial regime. Bush certainly could not be speaking about them. The "war on terror" entailed identifying militants associated with an international axis of evil, not commending people who declare themselves revolutionaries in the face of a political superpower. This phraseology, then, is devoid of a more specific argument concerning the conditions under which insurgency is appropriate. Perhaps this explains why no specific personages or sites of struggle are named, though Bush would be more specific at other moments in his speech.

> Those who lived to see land again were displayed, examined, and sold at auctions across nations in the Western Hemisphere. Because families were often separated, many were denied even the comfort of suffering together. . . .
>
> In America, enslaved Africans learned the story of the exodus from Egypt and set their own hearts on a promised land of freedom. Enslaved Africans discovered a suffering Savior and found he was more like themselves than their masters. Enslaved Africans heard the ringing promises of the Declaration of Independence and asked the self-evident question, "Then why not me?"

Bush establishes a parallel between the people of Senegal and the descendants of "enslaved Africans" who now live in the United States. Such a move is strategic rhetorically, since in 2001 the US government was criticized for leaving a United Nations conference on racism in Durban, South Africa, where many believed it would have been asked to issue an apology for its participation in the transatlantic slave trade and to deliver a formal statement concerning its position on the issue of reparations for African Americans. By establishing a correlation between African Americans and Africans in Senegal, Bush commends the latter while paying homage to the former—yet he avoids detailing a specific commitment to either population.

Bush speaks of the church's role in the slave trade but does not condemn it. Instead of addressing the contradictions that structured Christianity in the context of plantation enslavement in the United States, Bush submits that European Christians were not Christian *enough*. Thus Africans who discerned spiritual lessons in the Bible taught Christians what they really needed to learn about humanity, so all those "generations of oppression" could not "defeat the purposes of God," intentions that perhaps align with Bush's tendency, in the aftermath of the devastating World Trade Center attacks of September 11, 2001, to deploy "religious arguments that encourage[d]" the US military's "aggressive tendencies" in his speeches.[41]

> In the struggle of the centuries, America learned that freedom is not the possession of one race. We know with equal certainty that freedom is not the possession of one nation. This belief in the natural rights of man, this conviction that justice should reach wherever the sun passes leads America into the world. . . .
>
> African peoples are now writing your own story of liberty. Africans have overcome the arrogance of colonial powers, overturned the cruelties of

apartheid, and made it clear that dictatorship is not the future of any nation on this continent. In the process, Africa has produced heroes of liberation—leaders like Mandela, Senghor, Nkrumah, Kenyatta, Selassie and Sadat. And many visionary African leaders, such as my friend, have grasped the power of economic and political freedom to lift whole nations and put forth bold plans for Africa's development.[42]

The narrative of "liberty" that figures prominently in this speech glorifies African "fathers" of independence: a roll call that includes Léopold Sédar Senghor and someone Bush refers to as his "friend," who remains unnamed. Most likely he is referring to Abdoulaye Wade: note that it is the same language President Barack Obama used in his remarks on the Senegalese elections of 2012. Here Bush commends Wade for having "grasped the power of economic and political freedom to lift whole nations and put forth bold plans for Africa's development." Further, Bush affirms his support for NEPAD, an initiative that promotes economic liberalization and that "sees global integration as the key to Africa's development."[43] Wade, as I have noted, was one of the proposal's main architects and is one of its biggest advocates in Africa.

But invoking the proverbial fathers of independence has implications for the forensic profiles of African nations and leaders. Note that the British colonial regime considered Kwame Nkrumah the "epitome of a dangerous demagogue." British officials demonized Nkrumah until it appeared that his United Gold Coast Coalition was likely to realize its ambition of independence for Ghana, at which point it promptly shifted course to embrace him.[44] In a similar reversal, Nelson Mandela was considered a terrorist by South Africa's apartheid government. Yet on the brink of a new age, the regime seized on his standing as a political prisoner, leveraging his freedom as part of a deliberate strategy to transition out of apartheid without having to initiate a massive redistribution of resources.

Because Africans and Americans share a belief in the values of liberty and dignity, we must share in the labor of advancing those values. In a time of growing commerce across the globe, we will ensure that the nations of Africa are full partners in the trade and prosperity of the world. Against the waste and violence of civil war, we will stand together for peace. Against the merciless terrorists who threaten every nation, we will wage an unrelenting campaign of justice. Confronted with desperate hunger, we will answer with human compassion and the tools of human technology. In the face of spreading disease, we will join with you in turning the tide against AIDS in Africa.

We know that these challenges can be overcome, because history moves in the direction of justice. There is a voice of conscience and hope in every man and woman that will not be silenced—what Martin Luther King called a certain kind of fire that no water could put out. That flame could not be extinguished at the Birmingham jail. It could not be stamped out at Robben Island Prison. It was seen in the darkness here at Gorée Island, where no chain could bind the soul. This untamed fire of justice continues to burn in the affairs of man, and it lights the way before us.

May God bless you all.

And with that benediction Bush ends his speech, though his audience is by no means clear. Given that most Senegalese citizens in the immediate vicinity were locked away, it seems the speech was aimed not at them but at an audience located elsewhere who would apprehend an address mediated by print journalism, snapshots, and televisual snippets.

What was he saying to *them*? Bush's initial concern with the African American protest tradition blends easily, in the latter part of his address, with the political inclinations of all "Americans," embodied by the Reverend Martin Luther King Jr. African Americans, as far as Bush was concerned, had joined his "unrelenting campaign for justice." But in speaking of a shared commitment to "dignity . . . [i]n a time of growing commerce across the globe," Bush implicitly references the legacy of Senegalese traders in the United States, by now so prevalent that a section of Harlem's renowned 125th Street market has become known locally as Le Pétit Sénégal. In that regard, we might revisit Bush's statement that "one of the greatest migrations in history is one of the biggest crimes of history" with greater attention for the argument he inadvertently advances about the implications a forensic profile has for social mobility.

While theorizing the activities of Senegalese actors in US commercial spheres, some scholars have been complicit in reproducing the dubious notion that their success grows exclusively from a work ethic that sets them apart from their African American peers operating in shared contexts. In some of the literature, the African American traders who work alongside Senegalese merchants are, understandably, beyond the scholar's analytic focus.[45] Elsewhere, though, writers uncritically recycle the ethnoracial stereotype that in "entering legally, working furtively, leaving harmlessly," the Senegalese trader is a model citizen.[46] The anthropologist Paul Stoller,[47] in his discussion of New York City's Senegalese traders, disputes the assumption that they are all law-abiding citizens but nevertheless imbues them with a devotion to their work ethic, which implies that other people occupying the communities in which they tend to operate fail to achieve comparable levels of prosperity because they do not apply themselves to the same principles. When these merchants arrived in the Big Apple for commercial opportunities in the early 1980s, Stoller tells us, they immediately applied to the Consumer Affairs Board for vending licenses. As a result of the excessive harassment state agents rained on them, the traders quickly racked up thousands of dollars in fines. So these vendors quietly allowed their licenses to expire, then "continued their operations outside the regulatory aegis of New York City." This, from Stoller's perspective, is a success story even though these merchants had willingly entered the unregulated—and illicit—informal economic sector. Stoller and others consider this not as an indication of the harassment traders racialized as black are likely to experience, but as one more example of the way "West African merchants in New York City use their familial traditions to construct long-distance trade networks in North America." Stoller is especially interested in the way African actors use the perceived cultural impoverishment of African Americans as an economic advantage—as a strategy for marketing "Afrocentricity."[48] Little regard is shown here for the way African Americans manage to develop economic opportunities despite battling state-sponsored forms of social exclusion[49] or the moments when Senegalese traders and African Americans embrace shared categories of racial or cultural identification,[50] at times in the context of illicit enterprise.

When Akon released the hit single "Locked Up" in 2004, he was joined by the African American rapper Styles P. Styles, who to date has garnered more critical attention than commercial sales, is well known for gritty tales about drug trafficking and for his argument about hypocrisy in the criminal justice system. Appropriately, Akon enlisted Styles for a song that discussed his own trials with law enforcement. The album, tellingly titled *Trouble*, hit shelves soon after Akon was released from prison for an auto theft conviction. Subsequently, he formed the label "Konvict Musik," and soon appeared in songs from a range of rap artists—from Snoop Dogg to Young Jeezy to Eminem. In 2005 Styles P joined Akon in Dakar for a concert; during their stay the Senegalese artist was declared a "youth ambassador"[51] besides being received at Wade's presidential palace. In this moment, Akon embodied the Senegalese emigrant's success story: son of the famous percussionist Mior Thiam, Akon was raised in the United States, where he eventually became a top-selling recording artist. Yet what separates this story from others of similar ilk is the sense that Akon came of age in unmonitored economic enclaves alongside African Americans who were dedicated to the pursuit of profit even when their pragmatic interests conflicted with legal statutes. For Akon this entailed being the "leader of a national car-theft operation."[52]

To his credit, Stoller is sometimes concerned to highlight the sociological context that Senegal's "astute entrepreneurs" inhabit as they seize the "economic advantage" to be gained from the new forces of "global restructuring." Yet what is meant to be a flattering portrayal of Senegalese vendors unfortunately—in overstating the role of "familial traditions"—reproduces a primitive sense of African genius, which is ultimately a dehumanizing gesture. Stoller's Senegalese traders are charming and quaint. Their success does not derive from skill in quantification, analysis, strategy—tactics we might otherwise associate with successful merchants.

Perhaps most crucially, Stoller's sense that Senegalese immigrants to the United States invariably understand themselves as separate and distinct from African Americans is empirically wrong.[53] Akon, when questioned by police about the stolen luxury cars he regularly resold, strategically used American stereotypes about Africans to his advantage, "[I would speak] with an accent as if my English ain't no good . . . like I didn't know what they're talking about. . . . [The police] bought it. And I stuck with that story forever."[54]

Stoller's assessment ultimately relies too heavily on an absolute irreconcilability of racial categories that, in quite a few instances, sabotages his analysis. In place of this ethnic reification, I suggest greater recognition for the way that the same forensic criteria can be deployed in distinct yet overlapping profiles. While conducting research—in Dakar and in New York City—among Senegalese basketball players who aspired to play professionally in the United States, I regularly encountered players who insisted they had a natural advantage over competitors from other racial categories simply because they were "black, just like African Americans."[55]

These dynamics were palpable during my first trip to Gorée. I was with Mark, a graduate student in psychology from Howard University who was, like me, in Senegal to conduct research for a doctoral dissertation. Mark was interested in seeing Gorée Island because he hoped it would let him connect with a vital part of his ancestral legacy, one that geographical distance and financial obligations had previously prevented him from experiencing. Mark once asked some of our Senegalese friends if they would accompany him to Gorée. He was outraged when they enthusiastically offered to join him for a swim at Gorée's beautiful beaches. Mark was disgusted by the thought of relaxing in the same body of water where some of his ancestors

had drowned centuries before, even if the US dollars he carried still contributed to Gorée's booming "heritage" tourism. Thus Gorée establishes
a complicated set of relationships for vacationers, merchants, and visitors
that is too easily elided in some of the scholarly literature and in Bush's
Gorée Island address. In fact, the commercial dimensions of heritage tourism inadvertently overlap with the commercial ambitions of a postcolonial
nation that no doubt hosted the US president because it hoped there might
be some economic benefit.

In his speech, George W. Bush emphasized the need to make Senegalese people "full partners in the trade and prosperity of the world." The alternative—
not being full partners in trade—is linked, in his view, to all manner of
social problems, including the spread of AIDS and civil war—both infec-
tious diseases that apparently run rampant in Africa. Not to "move in [this]
direction," too, would fuel the efforts of "merciless terrorists." Senegal's
historical mission, in Bush's view, would not allow it to do that, given the
way its present geopolitical projects dovetail with the spirit that sustained
Martin Luther King Jr. in his Birmingham jail and Nelson Mandela in his
Robben Island cell. These leaders endured imprisonment to awaken a sense
of "hope" that dwells in the "human heart" of every "man and woman."

Bush's message was apparently directed at all segments of the population, which explains its gender-inclusive phraseology. Yet the leaders mentioned were all men. How are Senegalese women to understand the part
they play in the "full partnership" that the country's historical arc is leading
it to embrace in the world? Will this "partnership" be realized for them as
well? Or does their exclusion in Bush's speech correspond to the way the
enslavement of Senegalese people is silenced as a necessary part of this new
economic enterprise?

What of the specific images used to anchor Bush's address, in particular
the sense conveyed toward the end of his speech that King and Mandela
communicate to the world a powerful message of "hope"? Who, after all,
was charged with maintaining "hope" for the Senegalese people detained,
during that same moment, in the center of the island where they live? This
question apparently is not mine alone: *espoir*, the French word for hope, was
scrawled on the wall of the Gorée Island site where Senegalese people were
forced into captivity.

The word has a special significance for me, based on my research and
travails in Senegal. As I moved back and forth between Chicago (later, New

York) and Senegal, friends would invariably ask how I could help them advance their careers. They nearly always used the term *espoir* to articulate their aspirations. My friend Lamine,[56] a sculptor, once asked if I might join him in a new commercial venture. If I could front the money for a major purchase of wood from Mali, Lamine suggested, he could produce sculptures in bulk, then split the profits with me. He recognized that this was a long-term investment but was sure we both stood to gain. "I know it's a lot to ask, Michael," he conceded, "But you're my last hope [*dernier espoir*]."

Some months after a research trip to Senegal in 2002, I received a letter from Pierre, a security guard in the home where I had stayed. He asked if I knew of any security or law enforcement jobs in the United States that he might be suited for. As the letter drew to a close, he too made sure to tell me I was his *dernier espoir*.

Significantly, I think, the phrase of note was *dernier espoir*—always in French, even for friends who usually spoke only Wolof and conceded that they were barely literate in the European language. I still struggle to grasp the semantic significance of communicating the concept in French, but I suspect it has do with the sense that opportunities exist in a context connected to the elsewhere. Senegalese people usually learn Wolof from the moment they are born. French, as the language of official business and formal education, dwells in a register of expanded possibility. *Espoir*, as an index of desperation, stood opposite another term used to express the prospect of prosperity: *gagner*.

Lamine and Pierre (who don't know each other) both used to say they needed my assistance because, in Senegal, it was *difficile à gagner quelque chose*. Among others, a former basketball player I once interviewed likewise insisted that "in Senegal, it is *difficile à gagner quelque chose* [hard to find a job] unless you are well connected [*bien placé*]." The phrase *difficile à gagner quelque chose*, though relatively simple, resists translation; the sense being communicated is that it is "hard to gain something" or "hard to find work." But *gagner* was usually deployed by interviewees to speak about prospects for earning money. They hoped this or that opportunity would enable them to "earn" an income. *Gagner*, then, means at once to "find," "win," or "earn" revenue: *Il faut toujours gagner*. In this context, being imprisoned on Gorée Island during a visit from the "leader of the free world" reminded Senegalese people of the extent to which they are "trapped" in a marginal economic and political position, just as it led other Senegalese citizens I interviewed to conclude that, although the treatment they received was indeed "unjust," the Bush visit was something the country "needed" to improve its stature in the world of nations. It's hard to divorce this idea of "winning" from the material implications that different genres of victory have for diplomatic relations and fiscal decisions.

Senegal first began to pursue World Bank loans during the tenure of Robert McNamara, who had served as the US secretary of state during the Vietnam War. As president of the World Bank, McNamara was concerned that the bank play an "explicit role in shaping the direction of urban governance and in framing the ideal relationship between states, markets, and citizens"—a tradition that by then was already several decades old.[57]

From the moment it became involved in World War II, the US government had been strategizing about how to craft and institute "new international financial institutions for the post-war era."[58] This meant in part suppressing communist influence. But McNamara also explicitly saw his task as helping former colonies reconfigure the relationship between burgeoning urban centers and agricultural communities. More crucial still, he was concerned to modernize the inhabitants of emergent nations through policies designed to convert them from threats to democracy into stakeholders in a new vision of governance. McNamara was concerned that, in Dakar and elsewhere, cities were being flooded by people in search of work, with dire implications for national security, as he noted in a 1975 speech at the World Bank's annual meeting: "Historically, violence and civil upheaval are more common in cities than in the countryside. Frustrations that fester among the urban poor are readily exploited by political extremists. If cities do not begin to deal constructively with poverty, poverty may well begin to deal more destructively with cities."[59]

Arguing that "cities [are] an expression of man's attempt to achieve his potential," McNamara insisted that it was "development's task to restore it." In this regard, it's crucial to note that Dakar was a top priority, site of the bank's "first targeted attempt at urban development" when it approved an $8 million loan in September 1972. Instead of establishing state-sponsored public housing, the bank drew on the theories of neoclassical economists like Milton Friedman to emphasize the role that "public choice" and "self-help" ought to play in urban development projects. The idea was to "upgrade" the environments that newly arrived urban residents had fashioned for themselves. In the process the bank effectively fortified burgeoning slums.

The emphasis on choice, coupled with the World Bank's abiding concern that all projects be profitable, proved disastrous. To reduce costs, the bank designed dense residential areas with very little infrastructure and scant space between dwellings.[60] The plans took longer than expected to implement, and even when the housing took more than a decade to erect, it often lacked basic sanitation. Visiting the construction site two years into the project, President Senghor insisted that "all households in the project should have private water taps and toilets," though the residents could by no means afford to pay the utility bills or maintenance costs. Meanwhile, the Senegalese state was "legally bound by agreements it had signed with the World Bank." So "the implementation of the project continued," despite the state's visible discomfort.[61] As these developments unfolded, Senegal sank deeper and deeper into debt.

Far from being regarded as a coercive presence in fiscal matters, maintaining good standing with international lending institutions like the IMF and World Bank continues to be a proxy for good governance. How much did Senegal suffer from a commitment to secure favorable standing from international lending and government agencies? At what cost to Senegal's forensic profile as a leader of economic and political reform in Africa? It would be easy to dismiss the profile that Senegal has assumed on the world stage; the more difficult task is to make sense of its ramifications in terms of both the way Senegalese people are regarded and, more important, how they are treated.

***

We tend to associate a "forensic profile" with the characteristics police assign to suspects based on place of residence, race, family background, occupation, and socioeconomic status. Of course, a passport is a mechanism of forensic profiling as well—it chronicles a person's history of international travel. A passport is also used to adjudicate an individual person's diplomatic standing: it elaborates the individual relationship to a given legal regime and indexes the status of the polity that issued the document. It is in this latter sense of the forensic profile that I want to consider Bush's insight that slavery was both a "crime" and a "migration." If so, what implications does his inadvertent restaging of the transatlantic slave trade have for the economic and political aspirations of Senegalese people?

Prevailing theories of social difference reveal a startling paradox. For some scholars, race, gender, sexuality, national origin, socioeconomic status, and the capacities or deficiencies a person is considered capable of demonstrating have everything to do with social and economic possibilities. From a different perspective, scholars argue that social difference as a medium of social mobility is on the wane; that perhaps economic standing remains a by-product of stratification, but too great emphasis on these dynamics amounts to "identity politics." This perceived stalemate is intriguing from the standpoint of forensic protocols like an individual passport or a driver's license or a credit score. These technologies establish a profile of the individual that is indispensable to accessing capital and to participating in the life of a given polity, giving the lie to any intellectual project that might seek to displace forms of economic and political standing in favor of an emphasis on identity or any effort to jettison the question of social difference altogether.

Insofar as Senegalese people do not generally self-consciously identify as a people victimized by the transatlantic slave trade, it is crucial to ask why the 2003 internment provoked this sort of association. And what are we to make of Bush's conceit that slavery is both a crime and a migration, as well as his seeming obliviousness to the coercive treatment his visit occasioned? Apart from triggering new forms of historicity among Senegalese people, does this event have discernible ramifications for the forensics of capital?

In a time of economic desperation, moments like July 8, 2003, emerge as an opportunity for Senegal to attract a capital commitment that could potentially reverse its economic course. The victims of the "enslavement" that characterized Bush's Gorée Island visit might be skeptical of the message he promoted, but a message need not be well received to transform a social context. For at least the second time, delivering a speech at Gorée Island helped a US president cultivate a foreign policy agenda in Africa while strategically evading the consequences of the United States' historic participation in the transatlantic slave trade. Consider this lengthy excerpt from *U.S. News and World Report* about Clinton's visit to Africa in 1998:

> In stopovers in Africa last week, President Clinton was careful not to issue a formal apology for America's slave past, but rather to express regret and contrition. One . . . factor—rarely discussed by the White House—is concern over the legal implications of an apology. If Clinton, as head of the U.S. government, issues such a statement, it could increase legal, as well as moral, pressure for reparations to the descendants of slaves. . . . That's why the White House is particularly grateful for the Rev. Jesse Jackson's defense of Clinton's handling of the issue. White House officials say privately that Jackson, who accompanied Clinton to Africa, has been especially effective in giving Clinton credibility on the apology question within the press corps and, they believe, with many African-Americans.[62]

Regarding the forensics of capital, we might conclude that "slavery" emerged as a way to categorize the injustices perpetrated on Gorée Island because a discourse on slavery is always a commentary across competing regimes of value: the interior emotional complexity of the human condition versus the economic value that can potentially be extracted from laboring bodies.[63] Since African nations must demonstrate fitness for democracy as a prerequisite for foreign aid, events like Bush's July 8th visit can have concrete economic consequences and "legal implications." Countries like Senegal cannot simply declare that they are committed to democracy; their devotion to this political ideal must be demonstrated, just as a legally binding promise cannot simply be affirmed but requires the additional element of "material consideration."[64]

William Pietz offers an example that makes this point forcefully. In referring to the cinematic version of John Grisham's novel *The Client*, Pietz describes a scene where a young boy expected to testify about the mob murder he witnessed "hires a sympathetic lawyer by handing her a crumpled dollar bill": "The real transfer of even this nominal sum can cause a contractual relationship, in this case the lawyer-client relation, to come into existence. . . . Although she accepts the dollar, the lawyer does not regard it as a partial payment for her services. It is just [a retainer,] the technical requirement for establishing the contractual relationship."[65]

On the face of it, the scenario Pietz discusses here has little to do with Senegal or the events that took place on July 8, 2003. No formal legal document was prepared to confirm Senegal's commitment to democracy or even to ensure that the United States would represent the country in any legal arena.[67] Still, in being packaged and presented using the same techniques deployed by those who enslaved Africans centuries before, the population of Gorée appears as a bundle of value that, while not exchangeable in any concrete form, signifies Senegalese consent to the terms of this informal contractual arrangement. This is the reason that, although "the requirement to give up control over some material object that in value might be a mere trifle might sound like a pointless formality or an empty ritual left over from a more primitive age, consideration . . . as a positive doctrine and concrete legal reality . . . has [in fact] survived to the present day both as a legal object in judicial decisions and," even more relevant to this case, "as a practical reality in social transactions."[67] In this "transaction," Bush traded on the capital afforded by the virtual enslavement of Senegalese citizens for his own purposes: to cleanse the United States of any culpability concerning its historical involvement in the transatlantic slave trade, ironically, by restaging the exchange of bonded Africans.[68]

The concept of consideration emerged in Anglo-American law during the sixteenth century, at precisely the moment England sought to displace Spain's military dominance in Europe and its territorial acquisition in the

Americas. In fact, the concept emerged as a partial response to a rather specific problem—how to differentiate a gift from a commodity, how to convert a "subjective promise" into an "objective obligation." The implication here is that Senegal did not merely "promise" to support the United States' campaign against Islamic terrorism from a distance. Instead, the Senegalese state allowed its people to be detained during a visit by the US head of state, which inadvertently produced material evidence of Senegalese support in the form of a material consideration.

Consideration might seem an inappropriate concept to invoke, since there was no formal exchange at Gorée as there is with a legal retainer. Yet at least in Anglo-American law, where the notion of "material consideration" operates, it is not crucial that the second party formally take possession of the object tendered. "Consideration is a social fact brought into being by the voluntary alienation of a valuable material object":[69] "What is necessary for an enforceable contract is [only] that the person receiving the promise . . . effectively separates himself from something valuable under his control. The person making the promise need not actually take possession of it. She need only agree that this alienation of an object of material value [in this instance, a horde of 'enslaved' Africans] . . . is an acceptable consideration."[70] Apparently Wade, who aspired to secure US geopolitical might and financial resources, found this informal social compact "acceptable," as did Bush, who stood to benefit from Senegalese capital, through a spectacle staged in the crucible of national aspiration: a soccer field some miles off the country's Atlantic coast.[71]

This auspicious event avoids the question about what sort of capital a country like Senegal is positioned to produce. Might a different demographic from the undifferentiated horde produced through detention at Gorée offer insight into dynamic features of Senegalese social life?

SIX

Production of Capital

"Unemployment? Oh. Like the young men who sit and drink tea all day?" I tried to ignore the growing sense of confusion, convinced that my discomfort was an occupational hazard of the ethnographic enterprise. Whenever I talked about studying the economic stagnation that had plagued Senegal for decades, someone mentioned unemployment (*chômage* in French) and tea (*attaya* in Wolof. In speaking with friends and colleagues, I was obliged to maneuver between French, Wolof, English, and Fulani. I wondered whether this coupling of concepts was a consequence of constant code switching.

But the more I spoke with people about Senegal's labor crisis, the more I noticed that people typically associated high rates of unemployment with young men who squander their time drinking attaya. "They're *always* drinking tea" (*Ils prend le thé à tout moments*), in the words of a Centre de Bopp camp counselor named Amadou. He insisted that in Senegal young men use tea to "kill time" (*tuer le temps*). Lacking opportunities to develop the skills employers seek, young men hang around in the streets, people repeatedly told me, wasting their time in tea-making rituals.

This public discourse had little regard for statistical data on the subject. Urban youth make up more than 40 percent of the 48 percent of citizens who are unemployed. Many of them have degrees, though women outnumber men among unemployed college graduates.[1] I thus became fascinated with the widespread notion that unemployment is a problem that affects young men exclusively. I was especially curious to know how perceptions of, and participation in, making tea entailed a historical consciousness or historicity[2] bound up in the labor drought that dominated social life in Senegal.[3] How are we to understand this disparaging discourse on unindustrious male youth in the context of what has become not simply a collective form of leisure, but a way to calibrate the skill and expertise of potential laborers in the process of fashioning a postindependence urban aesthetic?

Innovative ritual practices reveal how people navigate challenges to social and economic inclusion.[4] Thus it is important to understand how attaya is made and served before considering how it is implicated in efforts to reckon with economic crisis. Popular commentary on attaya reveals a demographic that is maligned precisely because the success of that demographic is viewed as an index of the nation's future. The discourse on attaya is used to calibrate the relation between a demographic's social standing and its productivity—the relation between the forensics of capital and the production of capital.[5]

Ingredients
1 box of tea 2 in (length) × 1.5 in (width) × 4 in (height); ¼ kilogram sugar; handful of mint leaves with stems; water

Directions
1   Boil water, then add tea; or put tea in the bottom of the pot while water boils. Keep teapot covered.
2   From shot glasses, add one cup of water for every two people present; or eyeball the amount of water to be added.
3   Add two shot glasses of sugar, or sweeten to taste.
4   Boil tea in teapot until ready (no specified time).
5   When tea is almost ready, pour it from the pot into an empty shot glass. Pour tea back and forth between different glasses to create foam (*mousse* in French, *mosse* in local vernacular).
6   Pour the tea back into the pot, preserving the *mosse* in the glasses.
7   Finish boiling the tea.
8   Rinse mint leaves. Once tea boils over, add half a bundle of mint leaves—or a third, depending on the taste you aim to achieve. Cover for approximately one minute.
9   Pour a sip of tea into a separate cup to taste.
10 Serve, beginning with guests, then elders, on down to teens and preteens. (Young children are generally not allowed to drink tea.)

These directions, distilled from several years of careful observation, reveal that there is no single way to make attaya. It entails a precise calibration of creativity and context. People often make and drink attaya in the evenings after dinner. Or when folks have idle time, a family member or neighbor might make attaya for all to enjoy. The custom is to serve guests first, then the most senior members of the family, and so on down the hierarchy. In a nation that prides itself on *teranga* (Wolof for hospitality) attaya is seen as a vehicle for building and sustaining communal ties.

Soon after moving into a small apartment in a section of Dakar dubbed Hann-Mariste, I struck up a conversation with Ibou, who worked in a *cabine téléphonique* (telephone call center) across the road. First we discussed my *origine*: "Guyanese . . . No, not French Guiana, Guyane britannique. . . . Well, I was born in Canada. . . . Actually, I was raised in the United States . . . So, yeah, okay, I guess you're right—I'm 'American.'" Then he invited me to have some attaya. From a dark corner of the *cabine téléphonique*, he lugged a squat gas tank. It was the sort of thing used to fuel barbecue grills where I was from. A small burner was mounted on the top of the tank. Moments later, Ibou gave the knob attached to the burner a slight twist and held a match to the flame, igniting it. He ducked inside for an instant and returned with a kettle no bigger than my hand. Ibou used the small pitcher by his side to fill the kettle with water. He let it boil before tearing open a gaudy gold box holding a packet of pellets that he dumped into the kettle. The tea boiled. And boiled. And boiled some more. I glanced over at the pot every so often, convinced the tea was already well steeped.

Ibou sensed my consternation, "Ha-ah, hah. Here we *cook* our tea." The tea he used consisted of leaves rolled into little black seeds. Stewing the tea produced a pile of black clumps at the bottom of the kettle.

Attaya quickly became part of our regular routine. During my first few days in Hann-Mariste, before I had established a interview schedule or identified a plan for research in local archives, we would huddle next to the kettle to chat for hours. Ibou's neighborhood friends would often join us. Most were out of work. Some had briefly attended the Université de Cheikh Anta Diop or various trade schools before realizing they weren't likely to find a job after graduation even with a degree. They often did piecemeal work: whatever they could find, whenever they could find it. Construction seemed the best local option, paying 3,000 francs CFA per day (then approximately US$6—more than six times the average national wage). With so many Senegalese traders overseas someone was always building a house back home. The down side was that these projects sputtered and stalled, depending entirely on funds sent back from overseas at a rate that was anything but steady.

When I first arrived, I chatted relentlessly with Ibou and his friends. I felt like the center of attention but assumed that it was because I hailed from the United States and had unusual stories to tell. I later noticed the same trend with all newcomers. Even when a friend appeared whom they clearly knew well but hadn't seen in a while, he or she—though usually he—would become the focus of conversation.

I noticed something else. Once I had become more or less fully integrated into the circle, the conversation fell off precipitously. I observed the same phenomenon in other parts of Dakar. I would sometimes drink attaya with Moussa, who worked at an unlicensed cell phone boutique squeezed into a row of legitimate franchises in the city, near the post office. "Ça va? Oui, ça va. Tranquille. Nnenga def? Mangi. Cool. Nice."

By the time my visits had become routine, Moussa would barely lift his head from the minuscule wooden bench that had become his personal recliner, perched conveniently across the road from his boutique. Usually attaya was in medias res when I arrived. As I routinely settled down to enjoy a frothy cup, I would notice that people seldom talked at all unless a remarkable event occurred.

Perhaps because my apartment was in a relatively *calme* part of town (as my friends referred to it), the silence was even more protracted when we gathered there. Sometimes it was deafening. Typically one person kept an eye on the attaya while dangling a mint leaf from the corner of his mouth like a cigar. Another would often lounge on the lone wooden bench that marked our informal tea lodge just beyond the *cabine*'s open doorway. Someone else would occupy one of three small stools that usually occupied the farthest corner of the cabine so they could be retrieved for company but easily stored when not in use. But the most startling aspect of the attaya experience was the inertia of these gatherings. More than conversation with lulls, they consisted of silence interspersed with infrequent commentary. This was in part why the essential ingredients included stools and benches— elsewhere felled tree trunks and grassy patches—where youth could easily assemble. I say "youth," but attaya was most frequently prepared and drunk almost exclusively by men. When a young woman makes attaya, it is generally considered the exception that proves the rule. In fact, in several years of ethnographic fieldwork, I only twice saw a woman make attaya.

In the first instance, a woman who owned a shop near my apartment made attaya for me. Interestingly, she was in many ways gendered as male according to local social mores. Yacine rented a room from a family in the community and had no relatives or husband or children. For all these reasons, she was in many ways stigmatized. Ibou visited me while she sat near my stoop making attaya one day. After she had left, he warned me to stay away from her, though he never explained why.

In the second instance, one of Moussa's childhood friends, Mame, offered to make attaya for me before I returned to the United States after several years of fieldwork. All my friends made a big production of this because they had never seen Mame make attaya before (*jamais*, they told me). That Mame had never made attaya was especially intriguing because she was the proverbial "mother" of her household. Her parents had died several years before, leaving her and her older brother to raise their eight-year-old sister alone. Mame was twenty, her brother, Pape, a couple of years older. Mame did all of the household's cooking and cleaning and laundry. Pape used the barren land in front of their modest house as the site of his business. He ran a workshop where he welded iron doors (with no helmet or eye protection) and instructed younger men and boys, ages ten to twenty-five, in the craft. They were not paid but hoped to run their own welding operations one day. When I asked Pape how long apprentices usually worked for him, the time varied considerably but was always several years. Pape had apprenticed with someone, working for free, for eight years before establishing his own franchise.

It is difficult to say how many rounds of attaya are served in any given setting, because young men often spend the entire day preparing and drinking it. It might take thirty minutes to make, and there are often at least three—though there can be as many as five—rounds of tea brewed from a single pot. There is no limit to the number of pots that can be brewed in sequence.

To the extent that one demographic more than any other produces Senegal's tea aficionados, gendered and generational attitudes structure popular discourses about this beverage. Because while most adults (by local criteria, married people with children of their own and secure employment) complain frequently and flippantly about idle young men with nothing better to do than make attaya, Senegalese youth situate this trend in the immediate context of economic crisis.

"Naw, it's more recent," Souleymane replied when I asked whether young men had always been this fond of attaya. Twenty-four years old, he was one of Pape's unpaid apprentices. "Mainly in the past ten years. Or something like that." Mohktar, a twenty-seven-year-old construction worker, was equally certain that the proliferation of attaya among unemployed young men was relatively new, but he found it hard to date the trend in any precise way.

As we sat in the parlor of his older brother's home in Dakar, Baba insisted that although attaya had emerged in the past few decades as a popular social custom, it had become closely associated with young men only during the past decade. What's more, the mode of consumption had changed even more recently. As Ibrahim, a middle-aged Senegalese accountant once remarked, "Avant le devaluée, c'était trois fois. Maintenant, c'est deux fois"

(Before the devaluation, we served three rounds. Now, only two). And this was not simply his opinion. As Cheikh, Baba's older brother, once said, "C'est devaluée . . . deux fois seulement" (It's devalued . . . now, we drink only two rounds). This from the forty-something information technology specialist whose job—and that of his partner, a management consultant—supported three siblings, three children, and a three-person household staff. Cheikh's friends and colleagues, close to his age, likewise traced a shift in tea consumption to this historical transition.

Le devaluée refers to the moment when the Senegalese government devalued its currency—the franc CFA[6]—in 1994 as part of its structural adjustment program. Rather than easing the local predicament, this development intensified economic anxieties. Because Senegalese merchants had been moving overseas in earnest since the economic slump that took root during the first decade of independence, the value of foreign currencies quickly increased against the franc CFA. People repeatedly told me that although tea was previously served in three rounds, they decided to serve only two after the currency was devalued. We might infer that the declining value of Senegalese currency encouraged people to be more frugal. But tea used to make attaya costs only 100 francs CFA (a few cents on the US dollar), a sum even Senegal's lowest-income earners can afford. And people usually pool their money to buy ingredients. So it is unlikely that people drank less attaya merely to stave off rising costs. Whatever the motivation, it is intriguing that people would record economic devastation in their techniques of making and drinking attaya.

There was a particular nuance to this historicity that hinged on wealth and status. The idea that one ought to serve fewer rounds of attaya because the currency had been devalued was a joke that affluent men told more frequently than members of other demographics. In the streets, unemployed young men have evolved practices that almost felt like tournaments where they compete to see who can stomach several rounds of the strongest attaya.[7] A young man improves his status by drinking the blackest tea. Concentrated this way, it is very harsh on the stomach. Thus men like my friend Taphar, whose stomach is upset by large quantities of caffeine, cannot drink a lot of attaya. He was consequently considered frail. But then Taphar is a law student at the Université de Cheikh Anta Diop, which reads as further evidence of his delicate constitution vis-à-vis his unemployed peers who live by their wits in Dakar streets.

The idea that attaya is ideally drunk by men of fortitude finds expression in the product's symbolic coding. Senegalese youth make attaya from a tea blend that most likely entered Middle East trade circuits—and subsequently

North Africa—through conduits in Taiwan during the nineteenth century (though it was most likely first produced during China's Tang dynasty of the seventh century). The English translation for 珠茶—"gunpowder"—derives from the way the tea is packaged and stored. Rolled into shiny black seeds, it resembles the gunpowder pellets once used to load cannons. Tea connoisseurs believe that rolling the leaves into pellets helps to retain flavor and aroma while making it easier to store.

The combustible connotation of "gunpowder" tea contributes to the public perception that attaya is a resource to be handled by the most able-bodied youth. The virility summoned here marks the truly novel circumstances in which the potency of youth is gauged by different criteria than in times past. Social predecessors of the "lazy" young men who now drink attaya all day achieved notoriety for staging a series of demonstrations that took place so frequently at the height of Senegal's economic crisis that the Université de Cheikh Anta Diop suffered an *année blanche*—a suspended year—from 1988 to 1989. The Senegalese government headed by Abdou Diouf, in response, awarded overseas scholarships to several prominent student leaders. Through these techniques of incorporation, the state side-stepped a quest for revolutionary change and transformation. In these informal urban tea lodges, it seems, the desire to hold one's ground in the midst of economic turmoil was folded inward as the citizens considered most capable of shaking up the system now instead pour scalding liquid from cup to cup.

From the beginning of the 1980s, newspaper articles and electoral speeches stressed the need to crack down on increasing lawlessness. But this apparent social disorder was the partial effect of youth protest against worsening economic conditions.[8]

Government officials recognize two distinct classes of youth. The first group is made up of *encombrements humains* ("social obstructions"), young people deemed peripheral to Senegalese society, whose lives are allegedly characterized by an affinity for loitering, sexual deviance, panhandling, and criminal violence.[9] Many of these youth migrated to Dakar some years earlier in search of work but, with opportunities so scarce, frequently found themselves incarcerated when they used illicit strategies to make a living.[10]

Most remaining members of the demographic dubbed "youth" come from the student population, which is substantial, since education—in the context of this economic crisis—is no guarantee of employment.[11] A marker of class status, degrees have nevertheless become redundant in the quest for public sector employment. More than 80 percent of unemployed youth have never worked at all, and they are better educated than Senegal's current labor force.[12]

Despite the state's effort to distinguish between lawless youth and innocent victims of economic trauma, both groups registered their critique of the nation's economic and political trajectory through diverse strategies of protest in the 1980s and 1990s.[13] When Léopold Senghor abdicated the presidency in 1981 to make way for his former prime minister, Abdou Diouf, youth became more creative than ever in cultivating ways to express their discontent. Youth had, since independence in 1960, launched recurring demonstrations against state apathy and incompetence, most notably in demonstrations that coincided with the events of May 1968 in France. But public confidence in the presidency diminished dramatically with suspicion of vote tampering during what would otherwise have been Diouf's first democratic election in 1983.[14]

By the next election period in 1987, student leaders were so well organized that they forced politicians into a series of discussions about concrete steps they might take to ameliorate unemployment. Few of these interventions paid off, though it is notable that by then young people were considered so powerful they merited an audience with political officials. Youth activists had been given a new mandate by Abdoulaye Wade's *Sopi* movement, which used the Wolof word for "Change" as part of a strategy designed to transform Senegal. This idea coincided with the *Set/Setal* program, specifically concerned with remaking the moral landscape of Senegalese society.[15] Attacking sites of wealth in some of Dakar's most affluent neighborhoods, youth also opposed alcohol sales throughout the capital city. They even attacked the drug addicts, alcoholics, and homeless people who, from their perspective, fueled social degradation.

In this way, youth simultaneously personified disorder and social progress in dramatic efforts to reshape political discourse and public works from the late 1980s well into the following decade. During this time, Dakar was cleaned from top to bottom as youth embarked on a project to rid the capital city of trash heaps, polluted water, and other signs of bureaucratic neglect.[16]

There is little doubt that youth had decided to establish the public works services they believed Senegal needed because of the state's criminal negligence, or that they explicitly meant to attack what had by then become a national tradition of authoritarian democracy. Protests centered on the most prominent institutions of state power. In one spate of uprisings, "The center of the civil administration of greater Dakar was torched; eighty of the public transit company's buses and numerous telephone booths were damaged; government and administration cars were attacked and set on fire."[17] In this way young people sought to combat the forty-year stranglehold of Senghor's Parti Socialiste. The state's response revealed its fear of the possibility for radical change inherent in this moment and its totalitarian approach to democracy. "The irruption of youth into the political arena in such violent modalities . . . culminated with the declaration of a state of emergency and the deployment of police throughout Dakar." Meanwhile, political officials were careful to protect the property of the wealthy even as they sought to contain and defuse youth protest, "the goal being to isolate the Plateau [Dakar's wealthiest district]. . . . [T]he poorer neighborhoods, especially the Médina, the HLM [Habitations à Loyer Modéré] subsidized housing development district, and Colobane, were left to the young rebels and to the opposition."[18]

This logic of redirection and containment was not simply evidence of political improvisation. It reveals an organizational principle the post independence state has used to manage its primary social menace even as youth challenged and undermined directives designed to corral them. Senegalese youth have, as Mamadou Diouf skillfully discerns, "produced a precocious reading of the nationalist movement's evolution, identifying the authoritarian drift of the postcolonial powers whose neocolonial economic and political orientations they denounce. This awareness seems to have been the basis for youth's resistance to repression, *encadrement*, and cooptation through which the state handles social movements."[19] And this strategy is not restricted to political initiatives. The Senegalese state—by using sport to combat moral degradation through initiatives that provide political positions and overseas scholarships to the nation's most radical student leaders—has managed the strategic manipulation of youth through a principle Mamadou Diouf calls *encadrement*.[20] This term, incidentally, is also used to describe summer sports camps like those hosted at the Centre de Bopp.

Encadrement is difficult to translate from French to English. It invokes techniques of quartering—in two senses. First, it denotes a way of containing youth in particular districts or quarters of specific towns and cities. Then also, because this term connotes the vicious dissection of an object, it suggests the quartering of an animal sliced into parts for sale in a marketplace.

It is tempting to translate encadrement as "containment," but this concept fails to capture the deliberate state project by which it is anchored. Perhaps, then, the closest cognate is "enframement," as it speaks to the material and geographical dimensions of Senegalese statecraft.[21]

Instead of acknowledging that "youth" refers to a demographic geographically isolated (in urban areas), gendered (as young men, more socially mobile than their female peers), and classed (as economically marginal)—a demographic produced in conjunction with the economic trials of independence—the state identifies lawless and idle youth as the source of social problems.[22] In this way "youth" are estranged from civil society. Except occasionally for students, youth are not recognized as a group to which the government must be accountable, a demographic to which the state is liable. They are, instead, imagined as the origin of social unrest. And the provocative tactics of redress by which youth counter this "nationalist reading" have, instead of reversing this outlook, ruined the public perception of this demographic.

> La violente irruption de la jeunesse africaine dans les sphères publiques et domestiques semble avoir eu pour conséquence la construction de leur comportement comme menace, et semble avoir provoqué dans l'ensemble de la société une panique à la fois morale et civique.
>
> [The violent irruption of African youth into the public and domestic spheres seems to have resulted in the construction of their behavior as a threat and to have provoked, within society as a whole, a panic that is simultaneously moral and civic.][23]

And by positioning youth as the source of social "panic," the state makes the need for government intervention all the more urgent.

Encadrement, as a mode of social organization, entails a "reclassification of young people" that "is manifested in institutionalized hostility toward them"[24]—a disdain heightened by the belief that youth have abdicated their responsibility to the state. In the context of chronic economic stagnation and political ossification, youth are thought to possess key resources of social regeneration. This attitude was evident, for instance, in Wade's strategic deployment of youth activists and artists as part of the 2000 *Sopi* campaign that ultimately earned him the presidency. His strategy involved using rap music artists—condemned by previous governments for promoting licentiousness—to spread his message as he insisted on the priority of youth concerns (in this connection, it is worth noting that one of the first hit songs for Senegal's most celebrated rap group, Positive Black Soul, was named "Attaya").

Rap music, as Wade seemed to understand, had emerged in the previous decade as part of youth discontent. When student protests led to school suspensions at the Université de Cheikh Anta Diop during the late 1980s,[25] young people formed rap groups as a way of developing a social critique. By the end of 1988, there were more than three thousand rap groups in Dakar. In fact, Dakar arguably sits alongside Tokyo and Paris as the chief sites where hip-hop music and aesthetics have flourished outside the United States. In harnessing the productive potential of youth, Wade ingeniously made use of the most valuable resource they possess: their free time.[26]

Besides their own bodies—which they likewise commodify or wield as a potential economic and sexual resource—time is a source of capital close at hand. Thus much of what constitutes social activity for unemployed youth involves using these two factors—time and the improvisational body—in concert. Some young people invest their time in the pursuit of athletic careers, music production, or political protest. Elsewhere, youth strategically use their disconnectedness from the nation's primary social institutions to travel abroad.[27] Often, enterprising youth will try to enter Europe by going north through Morocco. In the process, they tread terrain identified with the birthplace of attaya.

Despite its ubiquity in Senegalese domestic spaces, attaya is not considered indigenous to Senegal; this much was clear from the first time I experienced the beverage. "Attaya comes from Morocco," Mamadou explained matter-of-factly, shaking black pellets into a weatherbeaten stainless steel kettle. Other friends pointed to origins in the same part of the continent. "I'm not sure precisely where attaya comes from," Ibou would later confess, furrowing his brow, "but somewhere in North Africa, for sure." Bineta, in private conversation some months later, expressed greater conviction, "It's definitely from Morocco. . . . [I]t's associated with royalty." Rumors of the beverage's distinguished pedigree were what, in her mind, made the case. In fact, dozens of people insisted that attaya came from North Africa, usually Morocco. Once enjoyed exclusively by Islamic "royalty,"[28] they told me, the art of making tea using this particular repertoire of techniques had spread into Senegal.[29] These narratives underscore the cosmopolitan quality of methods now used to adjudicate local forms of economic crisis.

For improvisational youth also participate in commercial routes created by the Murid trade diaspora in New York, Tokyo, Rome, Madrid, Paris, Dubai, and other global cities: "Excluded from the arenas of power, work, education, and leisure, young Africans construct places of socialization and new sociabilities whose function is to show their difference, either on the margins of society or at its heart, simultaneously as victims and active agents, and circulating in a geography that escapes the limits of the national territory."[30] Senegalese youth inhabit a space of promise, shaped by peers who successfully transitioned to overseas employment, and a place of peril, shaped by those whose attempts have failed. This paradoxical predicament parallels the reigning model of statecraft, premised on privileges assigned to members of the Murid Islamic brotherhood, who provide its young adherents access to transnational trade networks, but who have also been successful at curtailing democracy for Senegal's youngest constituents. Of the numerous adherents to Senegal's tradition of Sufi Islam—which includes more than 90 percent of Senegal's people—the Murids are the most influential. Using the hierarchy they had already established for religious leadership, Murid clerics maintained control of groundnut production from the colonial era well into the twentieth century.

Soon after achieving independence in 1960, the agricultural sector collapsed under additional financial burdens associated with an independent government. The problem was further complicated by a series of droughts in the 1960s and 1970s that led to meager groundnut yields. On the brink of economic devastation, Murids translated international trade networks steeped in existing capital into a transnational labor diaspora that positioned vendors around the world, from Dubai and Tokyo to Milan, creating a context where youth have scrambled to gain the favor of Murid leaders they hope will offer them a chance to participate in overseas commerce. Meanwhile, local youth have built a protest tradition, drawing in large measure on technologies that entered the country amid the same international flow of capital and consumer goods that Murids promoted.

If access to transnational trade networks enables some youth to evade this specific economic predicament, it leaves others, imagined as having the requisite masculine characteristics to do so, disparaged for not capitalizing on the opportunities that allegedly are available to all who seek them. The idle young man who instead of fleeing the civil sector seems shackled to it thus becomes the index of a pathologically unproductive subject. In this sense youth are subject to the state's "frame up," or criminalizing gaze.[31]

Making attaya, then, constitutes a displacement of sorts for youth who are frustrated by the persistent absence of economic progress, unable to pursue education or employment overseas, and those who are disenchanted by the diminished local prospects of a youth social movement. It has also become a method for valorizing and reinscribing masculine notions of strength several decades after formal independence.[32] At the same time, the practice of preparing and serving attaya has become a way for potential laborers to hone their skills and expertise—to cultivate aesthetic sensibilities and foster social commentary—during a protracted economic crisis.[33]

Whenever I asked unemployed youth why they made tea so frequently, they readily answered, *Ça tue le temps*—even sometimes in English, "It kills time, as we say here." But this phrase has a different valence in the United States, where "killing time" is rather more conditional and circumstantial. There it has to do with whiling away a bit of time before a meaningful social event.

The scores of unemployed youth I interviewed considered their time superfluous. "Here we have an abundance of time," Ibrahim Coulibaly once told me. "Our time has no value," in the words of Mar'ta Diagne, where "value" is diminished by excess.[34] While it certainly makes sense that someone who is unemployed might have an abundance of free time, "killing time" does not seem a reliable strategy for escaping such a scenario. Couldn't that time be put to use acquiring skills that increase one's prospects for employment?

In fact, far from being evidence of social myopia, the need to "kill time" actually springs from the observation that there are few, if any, opportunities to improve one's chances of securing a job. As such, youth search for ways to cultivate expertise and establish meaningful critiques of the world they inhabit in the broader context of an employment vacuum.

It is difficult to think about attaya as labor according to a strict definition, since attaya has no commercial value. A few modest ingredients are purchased to make it. And the finished product—attaya—is never bought or sold. It is only shared with friends and family. And yet producing attaya requires an inordinate amount of skill and expertise. It is a means through which some of the nation's most productive potential workers organize their time. So it is difficult to think of producing attaya as a form of leisure in the strictest sense.[35] How do we analyze and situate productive activity that lacks commercial value?[36]

Value is a way of thinking through different genres of capital. Its capaciousness beckons us to theorize economic relationships by beginning with the creative potential of any social practice.[37] Value provides a conceptual frame for tracing the way individual acts can be harnessed, drawn into patterns of activity and institutional arrangements.[38] Value is the meaningful consequence of human activity. It is the by-product of social practices that are drawn into a system of production. Thus, even as attaya resists a strict sense of commercial value, it illustrates the predicament of youth estrangement from formal labor markets.

I am especially interested in the way different regimes of value get congealed in objects or, more precisely, in objectified social forms, since—as with attaya—value does not merely coalesce in discrete entities: it can likewise assume the shape of a public performance. This suggests that Senegal's labor crisis frustrates youth in multiple registers: it obscures the improvisational quality of their activity even as it excludes them from opportunities to exchange their labor power.[39] Attaya is productivity without commercial value—work without labor. As such, using the forensics of capital as a critical lens provides a rather different explanation for the significance of attaya than the dubious notion that unemployed youth somehow rest idle.

The task of translating time through tea is a way of reckoning with the forensic profiles—the characteristics and character types—that people associate with success in a context of scarce resources,[40] as the themes stressed in moral discourses often resonate with prevailing forms of social recognition and prestige.[41]

My friend Baba's older brother Mar'ta was convinced that making and serving tea was one of the best ways to build character: "If you want to be generous, start with the way you distribute tea—are you fair and just, or just selfish? Are you greedy? Do you play favorites?" These were lessons he had learned from his father as a child. Now in his late thirties, Mar'ta believes that attaya provides the occasion to discern the characteristics that shape favorable social standing. While watching his younger siblings make and share tea, Mar'ta quietly observed attributes he hoped they would develop further. His father, meanwhile, took a far more instrumentalist approach, assigning different tasks required to produce attaya to different children on different occasions to see how they managed their assignments. With stories that vary in narrative detail, people routinely insist that individual styles for making attaya index personality traits—for better or worse. And yet, to the extent that attaya is a cherished activity among unemployed young men, it yields intriguing insights into how they understand other groups of people, especially women of comparable age.

Frequently, when young men gather to share attaya, they discuss young women. There is a local custom of caricaturing Senegalese women according to certain exaggerated physical characteristics and consumption patterns. The most prominent character type is the *disquette*, a woman who covets material goods: elegant but revealing clothing, fancy European shoes and handbags, and expensive jewelry.[42] The disquette is usually a woman in her late teens or twenties who manipulates men to support her expensive lifestyle, rewarding them with the promise to satisfy their sexual desires. In this way, the disquette's main weapon is the strategic deferment of sexual gratification to ensure a high standard of living.

The term *disquette*—which originated from the now defunct idea of the diskette you slide in and out of a computer as it suits your needs—does not always convey dubious morality. A young man might jokingly ask a woman if she is a disquette to discern how chic she considers herself. In and around the attaya circle, however, conversations abound about the clever disquettes who bleed men of their money, consort with their husbands' closest friends, or defer sexual pleasure indefinitely while securing regular access to a partner's finances.

A modification of this narrative features the *neufquette*. This pun relies on the homology between the *dis* sound in the term *disquette* and the French word *dix* for ten. Instead of being a perfect ten (a woman of physical perfection), the *neufquette* has only almost attained this idealized standard, since *neuf* in French means nine. This tendency to rank and order women positions male subjects as the arbiters of proper physical and social comportment. And yet the broader context is one in which the social standing and economic leverage of young men has witnessed a precipitous decline. Even as they lament the economic stagnation that has made it impossible to secure a partner in a context that is dogmatically heteronormative,[43] many unemployed youth contend that they are unmarried because the women they interact with are of objectionable moral character.

Beyond the crucial role it plays as a medium through which young men assert social leverage, attaya has provided a forum for cultivating artistic sensibilities born of crisis. In the midst of chronic unemployment, it has surfaced as an urban aesthetic.[44]

The ideological and cultural reorganization that flows from this posture of defiance [that youth readily exhibit] takes place in the spaces deserted by political power. . . . The function of these spaces, which escape the logics of public and administrative control, communitarian prescriptions, and state surveillance, is to serve as supports for acts that express within the public sphere, in a violent, artistic, or spiritual way, a desire for recognition and presence.

—Mamadou Diouf, "Engaging Postcolonial Cultures"

Whenever I watched people make attaya, I was struck by the careful effort they took to produce *mosse* through a process (*renversé*) that requires repeatedly pouring the tea back and forth between shot glasses. This occurs at a critical moment in making tea that ostensibly reveals your true expertise. In Baba's words: "*Renversé* makes it beautiful. It's like champagne. If it doesn't have the *mosse*, it won't look beautiful. People won't drink it. Anybody can just boil some tea and serve it." And *renversé*, they claim, suits this method of making tea more than any variant of the beverage that exists in another part of the world: "In different parts of Asia, and in North Africa, tea is made by infusion. Here, we cook our tea," Mohktar would frequently remind me. Each time attaya is "cooked" and served, the foam must be created anew, "We don't use the same mosse for the second round. It must be made again." Making the foam again for each fresh pot of attaya affirms one's status as an expert, since it proves that the beautiful foam was no fluke.

This suggests that attaya's overweening sociality is in part an index for the regime of expertise by which each cup is judged. In Boubacar's words, "You can drink tea by yourself, but why would you? You do this for everyone else"—not simply to prove generosity or moral worth, as Mar'ta discussed, but to demonstrate artistry. One of the most heralded makers of attaya I ever encountered was my friend Moussa who, recall, ran an unauthorized cell phone boutique. But business was always slow—Moussa was crowded into a row of stalls selling better-quality versions of the same products. So Moussa spent long days making and drinking tea with friends employed at neighboring stalls.

Close friends and family considered Moussa more proficient at making attaya than his brother Cheikh, who was active in Senegalese politics (though in a position without pay). Cheikh assisted friends with their political campaigns and participated in Senegalese Democratic Party (PDS) youth delegations. A slightly crooked frame in their parents' home showcased a picture from a rally he had attended alongside Abdoulaye Wade.

Moussa had such a high regard for his own expertise that I only once heard him concede that someone else was more proficient in the craft of making attaya. This occurred one day when a good friend and former English major at the Université de Cheikh Anta Diop visited Moussa. Pape Ndiaye had stopped through Thiès on his way to Rome, Italy. Pape had been out of school for several years—he could no longer afford to pay for books and other related fees. He had finally received an opportunity for employment from a cousin who worked in Italy as part of a trade circuit sustained through local ties to the Murid brotherhood. With no prospect for education or employment, he had spent his time practicing brushstrokes in oil paints but had secured materials infrequently and worked only when he had the chance to sell his art at boutiques and at the beachside huts foreign tourists frequented.

After Pape made tea for us one evening, Moussa suddenly asked me, "Whose tea is better, mine or Pape's?" I hesitated, not knowing whether custom dictated that I defer to the guest or to my good friend. Beyond that, I wasn't quite sure whose tea tasted better. Pape's tea was certainly a little different, but not necessarily tastier. That's when Pape interjected, matter-of-factly, "It's mine." And, to my surprise, without even waiting for my response, Moussa agreed. "Yeah, he's the only person who makes better tea than I do."

When Mouhamed, Moussa's cousin, dropped out of school, deciding to rejoin his parents in Benin rather than stay in Dakar, he had to wait two months before his family sent someone to pick him up. For the first few weeks, he did modest tasks around the home. But after nearly a month, Moussa suddenly began asking Mouhamed to make attaya every time it was desired. "Besides me, he makes the best tea in the house," was his explanation.

More than some idea of genius or natural talent, public recognition of expertise in attaya is tied to perceptions about the amount of time someone had been idle. Expertise is linked to the number of hours, it was imagined, you had available to invest in this aesthetic. Instead of simply believing that you would inevitably become better at the craft over time in some haphazard way, youth associated proficiency with the opportunity to cultivate sustained skill at the craft. The more time they had available, the more opportunity unemployed young men had to become artists in the genre of attaya.

And this art object has several dimensions by which observers assess its value. How high does the tea maker hold the cup when pouring? How substantial is the foam? How sweet is it? How dark?

Taste is an especially slippery signifier, since people do not always agree. Most unemployed young men prefer the tea as black as possible, since it is most concentrated and because it requires a vast repertoire of skills to cook the tea for such a long time without ruining it. Older and more affluent people—and women in their twenties and thirties—often prefer their tea léger, "light," cooked with fewer pellets and more water. A diluted product is an index of elite status. People who prefer attaya léger and therefore drink less tea also usually drink fewer rounds.

The art of making tea thus requires that you assess your audience. How do you calibrate the social and economic standing of your constituency? How old are the people you will be serving? What is the gender breakdown? The expert cultivates a relationship with audience members through thoughtful attention to these dynamics. And just as a critic scrutinizing a painting might study brushstrokes, point to contrasting shadows, or note the consistency of a given hue, people who appreciate the skill involved in producing attaya rank experts according to criteria consistent with its unique status as an art object.

In this sense, the distinct contours of this urban aesthetic have to do with the way time is organized in postindependence Senegal. Young men possess time in abundance not because they are so privileged that they are freed from tiresome toil, but because work is so scarce that these potential laborers have plenty of time to fashion themselves as artists—to cultivate a painstaking technique of production and mastery of the aesthetic register by which their work will be assessed.[45]

I am not suggesting that attaya can be equated with other elite art objects in any straightforward sense. Still, there is a powerful analogy between the careful and sustained attention to fulfilling aesthetic criteria that characterizes the work of the fine artist and the careful calibration of generic qualities by which attaya is distinguished. That this occurs in the context of a product designed for popular consumption makes the scenario all the more curious, but it makes this claim no less tenable. Rather, it suggests a fractured class dynamic at the heart of this particular demographic that enables one to rank experts in attaya even though there are plenty of opportunities to develop expertise in the craft they cherish. This speaks to a paradox of time at the heart of life in postindependence Senegal, which explains why there is so much ambivalence concerning the category of youth, a demographic erected at the fault lines of this contradiction.

Free time is shackled to its opposite. Indeed the oppositional relation in which it stands imbues free time with certain essential characteristics.

—Theodor Adorno, "Free Time"

Not working has implications for one's overall ability to participate in the nation's social institutions and for one's relative maturity. Yet leisure, as I have suggested, also affords those not consumed with the burden of employment a creative capacity they can use to rework social networks. It might also translate into opportunities to reconfigure the political infrastructure that governs the nation. Facing chronic unemployment, many Senegalese youth turn to sport. Others lend their energies to political participation, having more time to invest and little to lose besides their lives (which, in the context of economic desperation, they are sometimes willing to wager). Alongside creative commodity capers, Senegalese youth use attaya to establish a proficiency that undermines the widespread impression that their days are a complete waste.[46]

Using the forensics of capital as a theoretical lens suggests that public discourse on lazy tea-drinking youth has implications beyond disdain for a particular demographic. It constitutes a displaced commentary about a government apparatus that has likewise been stagnant throughout the era of independence. "All the time they just talk, talk, talk—the politicians," says one of Wade's critics in a complaint that bears an uncanny resemblance to criticism of the chronically unemployed youth who sit around all day and chat.[47]

In other African nations the youth problem likewise mirrors public commentary on the national government. The predicament of the child soldier is often considered the chief problem for Uganda, a nation historically plagued by military rule. Nigeria, Sierra Leone, and Liberia are discussed in similar terms—all three have experienced military rule of one variety or another. In Senegal, the idea that youth sit around all day discussing issues parallels the impression that, despite having a distinguished tradition of republicanism, the Senegalese government is mired in empty rhetoric and economic stagnation. The comparison is telling, since many critics of purportedly "lazy" youth believe they should take advantage of trade routes and forms of international commerce born from the government's increased emphasis on economic liberalization and the expanding repertoire of sites for relocation that the national population has pursued. This narrative elides the experiences of those who perish in Morocco and other parts of North Africa—referred to as a literal desert or a metaphorical sea by dispossessed youth who fear its perils as they attempt to cross it in the unlikely pursuit of employment in Europe.

Despite the actors and institutions now at play in Senegal, new opportunities for employment have not matched those lost by the nation's postindependence agricultural collapse. One implication is that the state's dedication to luring foreign capital and to outsourcing labor, at the expense of sustained efforts to establish local industry, has had catastrophic consequences. Senegal, for even longer than other ostensibly socialist countries in Africa, has had little investment in state-sponsored social projects designed to stretch the nation's limited wealth and has instead solicited foreign companies that usually overlook opportunities to reinvest the wealth they generate locally. Meanwhile, unemployed young men loiter in the public sphere as social obstructions who disrupt fantasies of easy access to foreign capital: citizens who soothe their troubles by drinking attaya while they await politicians capable of serving them.

Coda

Touche pas à ma terre. [Don't touch my land.]

popular *mbalax* song in Senegal, circa 2012

By the time the 2012 elections had arrived, members of human rights organizations as well as Senegalese citizens feared that Abdoulaye Wade would use political malfeasance to retain power, maybe by using the armed forces (including federal police) to reduce voter turnout and intimidate his opposition. Others feared there would be vote tampering—and not without reason. Although the claim by scores of disgruntled and dispossessed youth that Wade "stole" the 2007 vote never gained much traction, a scholarly analysis of election results later demonstrated that it was likely the results had indeed been tainted.[1] Fearing a replay of this fraught scenario, Senegalese citizens throughout the polity—as well as many prominent, well-connected members of the expansive diaspora—used their cell phones and various applications to share information about polling sites and voter complaints and to snap pictures of suspicious activity, effectively establishing a surveillance apparatus designed to ensure due process. So, even if foreign correspondents and international lending agencies subsequently preferred to cite the "character" of Senegalese people as an explanation for the triumph of what they understood to be democracy, it is crucial to note that Senegalese actors took it upon themselves to forge an elaborate mechanism for accountability in order to preserve the tradition of just governance with which the country has historically been credited.

Despite waning support from his constituency, Wade tried desperately during the last few years of his presidency to inscribe an image of success in the Senegalese political landscape. He designed Le Monument de la Renaissance Africaine (the African Renaissance Monument) and arranged to have it built by an engineering firm from North Korea. At 164 feet tall, the monument is one foot taller than the Statue of Liberty. It pays homage to the primordial first couple of Senegal, a man and woman standing side by side as the father holds their child aloft in his muscular hands.

Many Senegalese people took offense at Wade's design. Clothed in tatters as part of a likely attempt to signify a historical triumph over adversity, the couple's attire read as unseemly to a largely Muslim populace that embraces a stricter sense of modesty. Undaunted, a spokesperson for Wade insisted the statue was an "affirmation to be proud of Africa," in a self-conscious effort to glorify the African family. Bingu wa Mutharika, president of Malawi, concurred: "This monument does not belong to the Senegalese people, but to the people of Africa, wherever we are." Wade's spokeswoman had also argued that the African renaissance monument was about what it meant "to be proud to be black." Dubbing the project "a powerful idea from a powerful mind," civil rights veteran Jesse Jackson embraced this vision. Speaking before hundreds gathered to witness the unveiling of the monument, Jackson declared, "This is dedicated to the journey of our ancestors, enslaved but not slaves." Meanwhile Benno Siggil, a local social justice organization, urged Senegalese people to distance themselves from a "fraudulent scheme" that served only to enable Wade's "fantasies" of a "dynastic reign."[2]

Beyond causing great consternation among Senegalese people, the statue provoked criticism from democratic allies because, as partial compensation for the project, Wade had granted public land to the North Korean firm that built it. In the eyes of US ambassadors this was a blatant example of corruption, as they noted in private correspondence with Senegalese politicians, a critique that ultimately became public when WikiLeaks published a confidential diplomatic cable.[3] In its memo to the Senegalese government, the United States threatens that evidence concerning the rising tide of corruption might lead Senegal to be excluded from funding by the Millennium Challenge Corporation, a bilateral aid program the US Congress established in January 2004, from which Senegal had already received more than half a billion dollars. Ironically, the MCC is implicated in land acquisition through a different set of circumstances that are, if less scandalous, no less dire for Senegalese people.

The MCC stipulates that the funds it provides must be used to develop land that is made available for sale or lease for one hundred years from the time of disbursement to anyone willing to "invest" in the land. Yet foreign agribusiness firms have more capital to invest than local farmers. In practice, the Senegalese government simply takes plots of land from peasant and pastoral communities and repurposes them as commodities in line with the terms of MCC programs.

To brace itself against the coercive terms of this agreement, the Senegalese state could tax wealthier members of society, ensure that donor aid earmarked for infrastructure is actually used for that purpose, and create opportunities for Senegalese people to invest in public works projects. Yet this kind of accountability requires oversight from government officials, who often benefit from graft and sloppy accounting, as well as from IMF and World Bank protocols that, as we have seen, encourage Senegal to "reduce" the role of the state in commercial matters. The Senegalese Forum Civil has estimated that close to $1 billion was diverted from national priorities into private investments overseas and other foreign ventures during Wade's tenure alone.[4] President Macky Sall has made strides to reclaim and tax these funds, as well as to punish political officials engaged in corruption, though how steadfast he will be in this effort remains to be seen.

Donor aid packages like the MCC Fund are the most recent iteration of strategies to address chronic drought and agricultural devastation. These programs are highly coveted in places like Senegal, where the state spends very little on local industry and where decades of structural adjustment have contributed to escalating debt. In the 1970s Senegal benefited not simply from World Bank and IMF loan programs but from funds made available by the newly established Organization of the Petroleum Exporting Countries (OPEC).[5] But the terms of these agreements caused the national debt to mushroom.

In 1970 Senegal's debt to foreign lenders was 15.5 percent of gross domestic product; within fifteen years it was 99.5 percent.[6] Senegal invested more than US$1 billion in damming and irrigation projects in the Senegal River valley during this time. But from 1984, the World Bank shifted its priorities. The terms of structural adjustment loans now meant drastically reducing funds devoted to agriculture, especially in the Senegal River valley.[7] After the bank had funded all sorts of projects, agriculture went from being 30 percent of the World Bank's loan portfolio in 1980 to just 6 percent by 2006. Likewise donor nations, which collectively reserved 19 percent of their contributions for agricultural loans in 1980, contributed only 3 percent of the funds Senegal reserved for agriculture by 2003. These developments made it difficult for the government to provide adequate irrigation or to support the flood recession agriculture systems local farmers relied on.

By 2003 most farmers in the Senegal River valley had to stop growing some of their most important crops. These families decided they could generate more income by sending their sons abroad in search of work.

In the aftermath of a 2008 global crisis in food, donor aid for agriculture returned to rates higher than had been available to economically depressed countries in many years. Yet these funds carry the same exorbitant interest rates that structural adjustment programs have been resolutely criticized for. Wade responded to the 2008 crisis in global food prices by establishing the Grande Offensive Agricole pour la Nourriture et l'Abondance (Grand Agricultural Offensive for Food and Abundance). GOANA was ostensibly devised to address food shortages. Instead, it subsidized the purchase of land by cabinet members, civil servants, CEOs, and wealthy members of the diaspora. They were supposed to develop commercial farming in Senegal to benefit the national economy, but no clear mechanism of accountability was established. During the twelve years Wade was president, more than 15 percent of Senegal's land was stripped from local farmers for such initiatives.[8] The mechanism for transferring land was so coercive in part because a 1964 statute specified that only land that had not been "developed" could be repurposed by the state. Under Wade, the state seized lands from farmers and pastoralists who supposedly lacked the means to develop it in favor of wealthy caretakers understood to have the requisite resources and technologies at their disposal. In an especially egregious example of state impropriety, the government forced a rural land council to transfer so much land to political officials and wealthy elites that it exceeded the amount available in the designated region. Protests ensued, contributing to new elections for members of the Diama Rura Council. Yet when they tried to annul these rapacious land grants, Wade redivided the territory and granted the land council that had done his bidding its own jurisdiction to manage.

These developments have been so controversial that few recipients of the land have actually tried to develop it. Activist groups and nongovernmental organizations have harnessed diverse modes of protest to their cause, including viral videos. And within two months of being elected president, Macky Sall promised to nullify many of the land grants Wade had authorized. Meanwhile, Sall has likewise been accused of mismanaging Senegalese land in ways that foster critical attention to the tradition of democratic governance his election was thought to have buttressed.

Fanaye is the name given to the more than forty-five settlements along the only major expressway in the eighty-mile stretch of land that runs alongside the Senegal River. In May 2012 the Italian company Senethanol, in which Senegalese investors own 49 percent of the shares, signed a deal with the Fanaye Rural Council to purchase more than twenty thousand hectares of land at the price of $50 per hectare, besides contributing an additional $1.6 million for local investment. Senegal's minister of decentralization and local agriculture approved the purchase even before news of the agreement reached local jurists, village authorities, or any of the area's farmers or pastoralists.[9]

The conflict concerning this parcel of land ultimately turned on whether the Senegalese state recognized vernacular uses of the land. After extensive petitions and protests—and a successful communications campaign by a group calling itself the Committee for the Defense of the Fanaye—the technical director of Senethanol was prompted to tour the area. He concluded that there was widespread support for his firm's project to build on these twenty thousand hectares of "unused" land. Meanwhile, another group calling itself the Cadre de Réflexion et d'Action sur le Foncier au Sénégal (Committee for Reflection and Action on Land in Senegal), which was likewise critical of Senethanol, cataloged "forests, wetlands, and a rich flora and fauna in those 20,000 hectares." These lands were not always submitted to intensive agricultural projects, but they "were used on a daily basis by hunters, by women gathering medicinal plants, firewood, and wild foods." Perhaps most crucially, pastoralists grazed some of Senegal's healthiest cattle, sheep, goats, and horses" on this land.[10] The state ultimately persuaded Senethanol to move the project, but the new location was no less controversial, being the site of a cherished wildlife preserve in Ndiael. As I write this, groups are mobilizing with sophisticated if diverse strategies to challenge the expropriation of land from the varied constituencies who make use of it. And yet these groups have different stakes and often do not share any coherent political vision, which makes it unclear how that mobilization will unfold.

If there can be a moral to Sall's short tenure at the nation's helm, it is that democracy in Senegal will continue to be a vexed process—as it ought to be. If a single theoretical lesson can be distilled from *Forensics of Capital*, it is that any method for establishing the profile of a nation is both incomplete and contingent. No country carries just governance in its essence—justice emerges from clear and reliable methods of accountability. And in a world where democracy is adjudicated at the interface between national legislation and international standing in a regime of nations, all citizens of the world play a role in shaping the critical theories and methods required to ensure that protocols for international governance and lending are as accessible and democratic as they purport to be, and that governments—whoever they are—face critique when they are not.

ACKNOWLEDGMENTS

As readers will have discovered by now, I think of *forensics* as a mode of inquiry concerned with who owes what to whom. For this reason I can think of no better way to conclude than to tally some of the debts I accrued in the course of this project.

The person who deserves to be credited first is perhaps William Pietz, who coined the phrase "forensics of capital" in an obscure article published more than a decade ago. Pietz's enigmatic concept helped me articulate something I had been wrestling with for some time. And to be frank, I am not entirely satisfied with what I have managed to accomplish so far. I find it encouraging that I have made ambitious strides with this concept yet don't feel I am where I would ideally like to be. I appreciate the rare pleasure to be incited this way.

As a graduate student at the University of Chicago, I had the good fortune to study with Thomas Holt. The breadth and nuance of his analysis never ceased to impress me, and I like to think I have assimilated much in the way of methodology and argumentation that would impress him. That doesn't mean I am convinced he would agree with every intellectual maneuver I have executed in these pages. In our many conversations, and after feedback on countless drafts of papers I wrote for him, Tom came to find many of my arguments "brilliant" even if my unique mode of intellectual inquiry "wasn't history" as far as he was concerned.

I had a similar experience with an economist, Allen Sanderson, who mentored me in and outside the classroom, setting aside time to discuss ideas that derived from my ongoing research concerning economic crisis and political transformation in Senegal. Still, whenever I had gathered my thoughts into the one-line claim that would define a dissertation chapter—and when

I asked if the idea made good sense—his characteristic response would be "To an anthropologist, yes. To an economist, no."

There you have it. *Forensics of Capital* is perhaps best understood as a historical ethnography of economic and political transformation, written by a professional anthropologist who has conducted original archival research but does not do "history," and who draws on and conducts research on economic phenomena but is not an "economist" as such. It's my wish that the effort to integrate cross-disciplinary approaches yields scholarship that practitioners of diverse crafts can appreciate. Because I believe, as James Baldwin once carefully noted, that while "children seldom listen to their parents" they "never cease to emulate them," I hope that both Tom and Allen are pleased—even if at times haunted—by this monstrous product of their intellectual rearing.

Michel-Rolph Trouillot initiated me into the anthropological guild, though putting it that way feels like a euphemism. As his intellectual adversaries as well as his admirers know, Trouillot was a social theory ninja. I am immeasurably grateful that he bestowed his fighting style on me. As I feel his presence looking on from elsewhere, I hope he believes I have put his training to good use.

Jean Comaroff chaired my doctoral thesis committee. The careful mentorship I received for the dissertation that inspired this book could not have been more thoughtful or encouraging. Jean challenged me to seize the precious gem deep within my argument that I could buff and polish until it gleamed with conceptual innovation. I am forever grateful. John Comaroff offered critical insights that strengthened this project immensely. Stephan Palmié read this book from cover to cover. His comments on previous drafts were relentless in their critique and yet so reassuring as to be almost suspicious. He understood this project even before I did, and I am grateful for the pivotal role he played in bringing it to fruition. William Mazzarella somehow knew when I needed to be poked and prodded, which I very much appreciate. Mamadou Diouf has arguably had the greatest impact on this book. He took a chance on a precocious graduate student and joined my dissertation committee way back when. He has since been unflagging in his support and generous with his insights in a way that is utterly unparalleled.

Bachir Diagne embraced this project at the moment of its initial enunciation and showered me with support at a critical stage in its development. Thanks to Vince Brown for staying by my side in the trenches—I appreciate his careful critique as well as his constant encouragement, on this project as on others.

This book would not have been possible without the generosity and critical sensibilities of Senegalese friends and hosts, including Bineta, Baba, Mar'ta, Tima, Amadou, Ibou, Pape, Taphar, Aida, Christiane d'Almeida, and Sandy.

The book has been further enhanced by the critical engagement of friends and colleagues. Because of the generous attention I have received over the years, I reserve explicit mention for those who read the manuscript in its entirety: Laurent Dubois, Yarimar Bonilla, Brian Larkin, Greg Beckett, Chris Freeburg, Khalil Gibran Muhammad, Andrew Sartori, Kendra Field, Khary Jones, Hannah Appel, Randy Martin, Toral Gajawarala, Christien Tompkins, Yousuf Al-Bulushi, Jini Kim Watson, Naomi Schiller, Hlonipha Mokoena, Natasha Lightfoot, Natasha Gordon-Chipembere, Vanessa Perez, Carina del valle Schorske, and David Lobenstine. Family members who deserve special mention for their powerful insights and investment in this project include Chris Lawrence and Henok Melke.

I am grateful to my colleagues in the Department of Anthropology at Cornell University, who took a profound interest in my work and encouraged me to be ambitious in foregrounding the stakes of this project, most notably David Holmberg, Kath March, Steve Sangren, Terence Turner, Dominic Boyer, and Jakob Rigi.

In completing this project, I was helped by a Woodrow Wilson Career Enhancement Fellowship. I was later blessed to spend an additional fellowship year at the Institute of Advanced Study, where this project benefitted from an atmosphere of critical engagement. I am especially grateful to colleagues who provided extensive feedback on my work, including Didier Fassin, Danielle Allen, Joan Scott, Lucas Bessire, Nicola Perugini, Deva Woodley, and Eric Chaney.

My colleagues at the Department of Social and Cultural Analysis at New York University have helped me create an intellectual home in an unwieldy city. I am especially grateful to people who have read and offered feedback on this project in different stages, including Jennifer Morgan, Awam Amkpa, Carolyn Dinshaw, Mary Louise Pratt, Andrew Ross, Arlene Davila, Danny Walkowitz, Dean Saranillio, Sharon Heijin Lee, and Luisa Heredia.

T. David Brent is more than an editor—he is a friend. Few people have the benefit of being edited by a first-rate scholar and social theorist—it's a privilege I do not take lightly. At the University of Chicago Press, I am likewise appreciative to have worked with Priya Nelson, who, because of her own ingenuity, has helped my work to be far more innovative than it otherwise would have been. Alice Bennett, Ellen Kladky, Ruth Goring, and

Ryo Yamaguchi likewise deserve credit for their careful attention to every aspect of this project.

My mother has been a librarian and my father a university administrator as long as I have known them. From that perspective, my career choice was fated. Still, my parents deserve credit for all the criticism and encouragement they have delivered over the years. Their tutelage is largely responsible for what I have been able to accomplish thus far. My brother Wole has long been a sterling example of intellectual indefatigability. And I am grateful for the role that Laurence plays in holding my work to the highest possible standard, as we strive to reinvigorate each other—to hold each other accountable—in the fullest realization of our shared passion.

Semai and Sofia deserve credit for making it impossible to differentiate between work and play, a goal of mine long before they hipped me to their vision of the world. The person I cherish most is Jerusalem. You have introduced me to so much that I can no longer imagine my life without. Most of all, I am grateful to you for making me more creative—more interesting. For knowing what I mean before I can even say it. In the rare frustrating moment, you help me find precious insights. If it's true, as Darius Lovehall would have it, that "romance is about the possibility of the thing," it's no wonder you captured my heart. Thanks to you, Semai, and Sofia, every day is an adventure. I wouldn't have it any other way.

GUIDE TO ARCHIVAL SOURCES

Archives Nationales du Sénégal (ANS), Dakar

B Series—Correspondence

D Series—Military Affairs

E Series—Councils, Assemblies

13 G Series—Political Affairs, Senegal

17 G Series—Political Affairs, French West Africa

K Series—Slavery

O Series—Navigation, Naval Affairs

Q Series—Commercial Affairs

PROLOGUE

1. Based on 2013 figures, that list would be South Africa, Gabon, the Republic of Congo, Equatorial Guinea, Sudan (grouping Sudan and South Sudan together for the purpose of expedience), Egypt, Angola, Algeria, and Nigeria.

2. Jean Christophe Servant, "The New Gulf Oil States," *Le Monde Diplomatique*, January 2003.

3. James J. F. Forest and Matthew V. Sousa, *Oil and Terrorism in the New Gulf: Framing U.S. Energy and Security Policies for the Gulf of Guinea* (Lanham, MD: Lexington Books, 2006), xx.

4. Consider the case of Ken Saro-Wiwa, an outspoken environmental critic hastily executed by the government of Nigeria after a sham trial that has since been condemned by international human rights agencies. Saro-Wiwa and members of an ethnic group known as Ogoni resided on lands targeted for crude oil extraction. Their protests against this venture were strategically undercut by the state. See *Genocide in Nigeria: The Ogoni Tragedy* (London: Saros, 1992) and *A Month and a Day: A Detention Diary* (New York: Penguin Books, 1995), both by Ken Saro-Wiwa, as well as Andrew Apter, *The Pan-African Nation: Oil and the Spectacle of Culture in Nigeria* (Chicago: University of Chicago Press, 2005).

5. For an exquisite ethnography concerning petropolitics in Africa, see Hannah Appel's "Offshore Work: Oil, Modularity, and the How of Capitalism in Equatorial Guinea," *American Ethnologist* 39, no. 4 (2012): 692–709. See also Michael Watts, "Resource Curse? Governmentality, Oil and Power in the Niger Delta, Nigeria," *Geopolitics* 9, no. 1 (2004): 50–80.

6. Note the discomfiting conjuncture between this burgeoning military infrastructure and French ethnographer Marcel Griaule's colonial-era ethnographic mission, which likewise traced a path from Dakar to Djibouti. Taken by military technologies like aerial photography and possessed of a hubris that translated into entitlement to "native" African artifacts, Griaule's mission was characterized by a kind of militaristic zeal that James Clifford has thoughtfully critiqued. See Clifford, "Power and Dialogue in Ethnography: Marcel Griaule's Initiation," in *The Predicament of Culture: Twentieth-Century Ethnography, Literature, and Art* (Cambridge, MA: Harvard University Press, 1988), 55–91.

INTRODUCTION

1. In the words of one leading scholar of the period, "Leclerc indicated that he was not surprised by the failure of his intelligence-gathering efforts because he knew that Bamba was too cautious to betray his secret plans." See Cheikh Anta Babou, *Fighting the Greater Jihad: Amadu Bamba and the Founding of the Muridiyya of Senegal, 1853–1913* (Athens: Ohio University Press, 2007).

2. Technically, his title was *dammel*—Wolof for "king."

3. Babou's *Fighting the Greater Jihad.*

4. Jean Comaroff, in private conversation, first described the Murids to me as a "army of traders."

5. Joel Millman, *The Other Americans: How Immigrants Renew Our Country, Our Economy, and Our Values* (New York: Viking Penguin, 1997), 180.

6. Mark Doyle, "Senegal: Where Democracy Was a Winner," *BBC News*, March 21, 2000.

7. Tidiane Sy, "Is Senegal's Model Democracy Tarnished?" *BBC News Online*, July 25, 2005.

8. Tidiane Sy, "Senegal Ex-PM Faces Trial," *BBC News Online*, August 4, 2005.

9. Jane Labous, "Senegal Braces for Violence after Presidential Election," *LA Times*, February 26, 2012.

10. See Wikileaks cable 10DAKAR127, "Ambassador Discusses Corruption with Senegalese President," marked CONFIDENTIAL, created February 18, 2010, released September 12, 2010, originating in the US embassy in Dakar.

11. "Senegal Opposition Celebrates Election Win," *Al Jazeera*, March 25, 2012.

12. "A Turbulence-Free Election in Senegal," *New York Times* March 25, 2012. That a protracted struggle for power could later be termed "turbulence-free" speaks to just the phenomenon I theorize.

13. I have adapted the phrase "forensics of capital" from an obscure 2002 *Theory, Culture and Society* article titled "Material Considerations: On the Historical Forensics of Contract" in which Pietz outlines an interest to "contribute to the development of a forensic method of social inquiry into the concrete historical processes of monetized valuation" and then offers a specific example:

    [T]he problem of what could be called the forensics of capital first attracted my curiosity in connection to the rise of modern tort law. In 1846 the British Parliament abolished England's quasi-religious law that compensated wrongful deaths in accidents according to the money value of the lethal object. It was replaced with a Fatal Accidents Act that calculated compensation according to the projected lost future wage income of the deceased. The Fatal Accidents Act of 1846 established the modern method for determining the money value of human life that has been used ever since in Anglophone capitalist societies.

See Pietz, "Material Considerations," 36.

In drawing upon Pietz's argument, I emphasize that many of his examples are drawn from Atlantic and not merely Anglophone polities. I am also attentive to the way that forensic inquiry is used to mediate the social standing of people and polities, as I discuss in what follows.

CHAPTER ONE

1. See *Monumenta henricina*, vol. 12 (Coimbra, 1971), 72–79, for the full text of the 1455 bull.

2. Peter E. Russell, "White Kings on Black Kings: Rui de Pina and the Problem of Black African Sovereignty," in *Portugal, Spain and the African Atlantic, 1343–1490: Chivalry and Crusade from John of Gaunt to Henry the Navigator* (Aldershot, UK: Variorum, 1995), 155.

3. Rui de Pina, *Crónica de El-Rey Dom João II*, ed. Alberto Martins de Carvalho (1792; repr., Coimbra: Atlântida, 1950). Rui de Pina, whose royal duty consisted of documenting King John II's provenance as self-declared Senhor de Guiné, "Lord of Guinea," wrote the earliest account of these developments. Pina was intimate with the affairs of the Crown. The first chronicler to witness Portugal's involvement with Africa's Atlantic coast, he died before his *Crónica* was published. Still, Pina's account is instructive for what it reveals about the way governance was conceived in this medieval moment. Because this genre of historical recollection was primarily concerned with casting John II as a "moral example and inspiration for posterity," it excludes his careful attention to matters of trade in Guinea and other details about commercial and diplomatic interactions. And while it is perhaps tempting to see Pina as a historian of Portuguese affairs in Africa, he does not characterize the continent in racial or cultural terms as a discrete entity. Pina's account ranges from Portuguese efforts to establish the fort São Jorge da Mina coast in 1482 (on what ultimately became known as Ghana's Gold Coast) to Diogo Cão's "discovery" of the kingdom of the Kongo (in present-day Angola) that same year. But as a royal scribe whose chief duty was to chronicle, and exaggerate, his imperial majesty's prowess as leader, Pina frames Portuguese involvement in these disparate polities as "different rulers and states each to be dealt with in isolation as separate political entities," as Sir Peter Russell puts it. See "White Kings on Black Kings, 152.

Garcia de Resende, who likewise labored under John II, published an account in 1545 with the same title as Pina's description, cobbled together largely from Pina's notes. Resende's chronicles were not published until 1792 (for his account, see the 1902 Biblioteca de Clásicos Portugueses version published in Lisbon).

João de Barros, meanwhile, wrote his own account of Bemoim's visit to Portugal, drawing largely from the testimony of a Portuguese official familiar with the Wolof sovereign and his affairs.

My discussion of Bemoim's visit has benefited immensely from Lauren Benton's thoughtful analysis; see *A Search for Sovereignty: Law and Geography in European Empires, 1400–1900* (Cambridge: Cambridge University Press, 2011), 65.

4. This speaks to the cosmopolitan quality of this Atlantic trade zone. In fact, crucial knowledge of the Wolof sovereign's visit to Portugal comes to us from Paolo d'Olivieri,

a Florentine merchant, who witnessed the entire affair. See Zelina Zafarana, "Per la storia religiosa di Firenze nell Quattrocento," *Studi Medievali* 9 (1968): 1109–10, for the text of D'Olivieri's letter.

5. In fact it is likely that the very name Bemoim is a Portuguese twist on the Wolof *bumi*, "heir."

6. Russell, "White Kings on Black Kings," 155.

7. As Russell has noted, Pina is "always at pains to tell his readers how truly regal" was the Wolof ceddo (or king) Bemoim's "demeanor and behavior." See Russell, "White Kings on Black Kings," 15[x].

8. Political philosopher Giorgio Agamben, in his *The Kingdom and the Glory: For a Theological Genealogy of Economy and Government*, asks, "Why does power need glory? If it is essentially force and capacity for action and government, why does it assume the rigid, cumbersome and "glorious" form of ceremonies, acclamations, and protocols?" What in other words, Agamben asks us, is the relation between "economy and glory?" Here, as in his *State of Exception*, Agamben is indebted to the political philosopher Carl Schmitt, who insisted that the most important concepts of social theory involve secular versions of theological concepts. See Giorgio Agamben, *The Kingdom and the Glory: For a Theological Genealogy of Economy and Government* (Stanford, CA: Stanford University Press, 2011); Giorgio Agamben, *State of Exception* (Chicago: University of Chicago Press, 2005); Carl Schmitt, *Political Theology: Four Chapters on the Concept of Sovereignty* (1922; repr., Chicago: University of Chicago Press, 2004). As examples of Schmitt's point, consider Hobbes's definition of citizenship as the secular equivalent of religious faith, sociologist Max Weber's notion of "charisma" as the "gift of grace," and Lincoln's view of the law as a "political religion," among other examples. See Max Weber, *Economy and Society*, ed. Guenther Roth and Claus Wittich (Berkeley: University of California Press, 1978); Thomas Hobbes, *Leviathan* (1651); and Abraham Lincoln, "The Perpetuation of Our Political Institutions," in *Abraham Lincoln: His Speeches and Writings*, ed. Roy Basler (New York: De Capo Press, 1946), 81.

Of course, the emergent body of scholarship on "secularism" has queried many of these themes in powerful ways. For some of the most prolific recent work in this tradition, consider Talal Asad, *Formations of the Secular: Christianity, Islam, Modernity* (Stanford, CA: Stanford University Press, 2003), as well as the companion volume edited by Charles Hirschkind and David Scott, *Powers of the Secular Modern: Talal Asad and His Interlocutors* (Stanford, CA: Stanford University Press, 2006). See also Mayanthi Fernando's insightful arguments concerning the contradictions of secular governance in *The Republic Unsettled: Muslim French and the Contradictions of Secularism* (Durham, NC: Duke University Press, 2014). In what might be construed as his own contribution to an ongoing conversation with Schmitt, Agamben, and others, Gil Anidjar has explicitly framed secular governance as part of a trajectory owing to Christian conceptions of the world. See "Secularism," *Critical Inquiry* 33, no. 1 (Autumn 2006): 52–77. Jean Comaroff and John L. Comaroff query the premise of secular governance's purported excision of religion, sorcery, and various notions of enchantment in their "Millennial Capitalism: First Thoughts on a Second Coming," *Public Culture* 12, no. 2 (2000): 291–343.

Forensics of Capital seeks to engage this line of inquiry concerning sovereignty and secular governance, if not in the precise way that any of these theorists have proposed. For now it is enough to note that Bemoim's ritual of anointing is not merely about "force and capacity for action and government," as Agamben would have it. I will insist that such rituals are crucial to the way political and economic partnerships are institutionalized and embodied. And I prefer to use "sanction" and "anointing" to capture many of the dynamics that Agamben groups under the heading "glory." We might, for instance, think of the formal graduation ceremonies and initiation rites that police officers in different parts of the world undergo as a crucial part of the way power is conferred on neophytes and as part of the way that bonds of fraternity are established. These quotidian rituals are hardly glorious from the perspective of most participants, but that does not mean these acts of anointing do not effectively confer privileged moral standing in a Christian genealogy of sanction that retains a quasi-theological character.

9. Benton, *Search for Sovereignty*, 65.

10. See Paolo d'Olivieri's letter in Zafarana, "Per la storia religiosa di Firenze," 1109.

11. My discussion of this event has benefitted from Lauren Benton's thoughtful analysis. See *Search for Sovereignty*, 65–66.

12. Ibid., 65.

13. In this instance Bemoim's treason would be more like "the petty treason of a breach of trust to a lord" rather than "high treason committed against a sovereign," as Lauren Benton notes (*Search for Sovereignty*, 66). On the complicated question of jurisdiction in the late medieval period, also see Bradin Cormack, *A Power to Do Justice: Jurisdiction, English Literature, and the Rise of Common Law* (Chicago: University of Chicago Press, 2007).

    That the most crucial events of the Bemoim saga took place on a boat is intriguing for additional reasons. The concept of risk, which would ultimately come to embody the hazards, perils, and threats from which polities strive to protect their inhabitants, was born during the medieval period in the maritime contracts that merchants took out on the cargo they shipped. From the thirteenth-century Italian concept of *rischio*, risk migrated to land during subsequent centuries, becoming a catchall term for capitalized risk during the nineteenth century, before diffusing into vastly different social domains to capture the sense of peril that many people came to associate with industrialized society. See Ian Hacking, "Risk and Dirt," in *Risk and Morality*, ed. Richard V. Ericson and Aaron Doyle (Toronto: University of Toronto Press, 2003), 22–47; Jonathan Levy, *Freaks of Fortune: The Emerging World of Capitalism and Risk in America* (Cambridge, MA: Harvard University Press, 2012).

14. Bemoim's assassination, of course, reveals the threat of peril or injury as well as the concern to establish who is accountable for such an offense. This dynamic is a reminder that risk as a dimension of social belonging entails procedures for establishing liability—whether for cargo in the case of maritime insurance, or for persons in the context of what, over the eighteenth and nineteenth centuries, evolved into civil law. A vexing problem for jurisprudence is the way enslaved persons have historically been slotted into both categories: insured on the high seas against the loss of cargo, but also against the threat of revolt. But then, even this dynamic is a reminder that neither risk nor liability can be taken at face value. Instead, whether as quotidian concepts or legal protocols, each assumes discrete contours in the context of social interaction and through the way legal protocols and social institutions are configured.

    Michel-Rolph Trouillot uses the concept of the "savage slot" to theorize the post-Renaissance forms of alterity that structured Enlightenment philosophy and, later, the social sciences. This discussion of Bemoim is my effort to tether Trouillot's concern with the way emerging categories of race, power, and geography shaped European political aspirations to the more specific but related discourse on the characteristics associated with a worthy creditor, as well as with someone who possesses or ceases to possess the requisite criteria for formal participation in the political institutions. See Michel-Rolph Trouillot, "Anthropology and the Savage Slot: The Poetics and Politics of Otherness," in *Recapturing Anthropology: Working in the Present*, ed. Richard Fox (Santa Fe, NM: School of American Research Press, 1991), 17–44.

15. Herman Bennett, "'Sons of Adam': Text, Context, and the Early Modern African Subject," *Representations* 92, no. 1 (Fall 2005): 16–41.

16. Ibid., 19; Kenneth Baxter Wolf, "The 'Moors' of West Africa and the Beginnings of the Portuguese Slave Trade," *Journal of Medieval and Renaissance Studies* 24, no. 3 (Fall 1994): 449–69; Emily C. Bartels, "Imperialist Beginnings: Richard Hakluyt and the Construction of Africa," *Criticism* 34 (Fall 1992): 517–38.

17. Peter Hulme, *Colonial Encounters: Europe and the Native Caribbean, 1492–1797* (New York: Methuen, 1986); Bennett, "Sons of Adam," 19; Stephen Greenblatt, *Marvelous Possessions: New World Encounters* (Chicago: University of Chicago Press, 1991); Enrique Dussel, *The Invention of the Americas: Eclipse of the "Other" and the Myth of Modernity*, trans. Michael D. Barber (New York: Continuum, 1995); Anthony Pagden, *The Fall of Natural Man* (Cambridge: Cambridge University Press, 1982); Anthony Pagden, *European Encounters with the New World: From Renaissance to Romanticism* (New Haven, CT: Yale University Press, 1993); Stuart B. Schwartz, ed., *Implicit Understandings: Observing, Reporting, and Reflecting on the Encounters between Europeans and Other Peoples in the Early Modern Era* (Cambridge: Cambridge University Press, 1994); Tzvetan Todorov, *The Conquest of America* (New York: Harper and Row, 1984),

18. James Duffy, *Portuguese Africa* (Cambridge, MA: Harvard University Press, 1959), 140; Bennett, "Sons of Adam," 20.

19. Bennett, "Sons of Adam," 19; Peter Hulme, *Colonial Encounters*, .

20. Gomes Eanes de Zurara, The *Chronicle of the Discovery and Conquest of Guinea*, ed. and trans. Charles Raymond Beazley and Edgar Prestage, 2 vols. (London: 1896-99), 1:49.

21. Bennett, "Sons of Adam," 19.

22. Ibid., 17.

23. Richard Jobson, *The Golden Trade, or Discovery of the River Gambra* ([1621] 1933), 64; http://penelope.uchicago.edu/jobson/index.html, accessed May 25, 2011.

24. Presumably these protocols for authorizing agreements were modeled on rituals that North Atlantic and African traders and emissaries had previously used to affirm ties of various kinds. In theorizing the shared lifeworld that ritual sacrifice presupposes and entails, Henri Hubert and Marcel Mauss discuss compacts modeled after human relations with divine agents where "the god is related to its devotees: they are of the same flesh and blood; the object of the rite is to maintain and guarantee the common life that animates them and the association that binds them together. If necessary, it re-establishes their unity. The 'blood covenant' and the 'common meal' thus constitute the simplest means of obtaining this result." See Henri Hubert and Marcel Mauss, *Sacrifice: Its Nature and Functions* (Chicago: University of Chicago Press, 1964).

The skepticism with which North Atlantic traders regarded African modes of jurisprudence does not have any more effect on the pragmatic efficacy of these customary rituals and "fetish oaths" than latent hostility to the institution of marriage in the twenty-first-century United States disturbs its capacity to broker legal entitlements and inheritances.

25. Walter Rodney, *History of the Upper Guinea Coast, 1545–1800* (Oxford: Oxford University Press, 1970), 87.

26. Rodney, *Upper Guinea Coast*, 88.

27. Phillip Curtin, Steven Feierman, Leonard Thompson, and Jan Vansina, *African History* (London: Longman, 1978), 224.

28. William Pietz, "The Origin of Fetishism: A Contribution to the History of Theory" (PhD diss., University of California at Santa Cruz, 1988).

29. William Pietz, "The Problem of the Fetish, I," *RES: Journal of Anthropology and Aesthetics* 9 (Spring 1985): 8. See Mike McGovern on the contradictions that have defined the postindependence state of Guinea's dogged efforts to suppress ritual practices deemed "fetish," in *Unmasking the State: Making Guinea Modern* (Chicago: University of Chicago Press, 2012).

30. Alvise da Ca Da Mosto, *The Voyages of Cadamosto, and other Documents on Western Africa in the Second Half of the Fifteenth Century*, ed. G. R. Crone (London: Hakluyt Society, 1937), 68.

31. H. Neufeld, *The International Protection of Private Creditors from the Treaties of Westphalia to the Congress of Vienna, 1648–1815: A Contribution to the History of the Law of Nations* (Leiden: Sijthoff, 1971).

32. Michael David Marcson, *European-African Interaction in the Precolonial Period: Saint Louis, Senegal, 1758-1854* (Princeton, NJ: Princeton University Press, 1976), 9, 17.

33. George E. Brooks Jr., "The Signares of Saint-Louis and Gorée: Women Entrepreneurs in Eighteenth-Century Senegal," in *Women in Africa: Studies in Economic and Social Change*, ed. Nancy J. Hafkin and Edna G. Bay (Stanford, CA: Stanford University Press, 1976), 21.

34. And France was not the only site where these developments gained traction. As Mary Poovey notes in *A History of the Modern Fact: Problems of Knowledge in the Sciences of Wealth and Society* (Chicago: University of Chicago Press, 1998), 2, "The liberal form of government that emerged in England at the end of the seventeenth century encouraged private citizens and voluntary societies to initiate all kinds of knowledge-making projects, at the same time that various types of knowledge were being presented as an aid to—or even a mode of—effective state rule."

35. G. Wesley Johnson, *The Emergence of Black Politics in Senegal: The Struggle for Power in the Four Communes, 1900-1920* (Stanford, CA: Stanford University Press), 19.

36. Bernard Moitt, *Women and Slavery in the French Antilles, 1635–1835* (Bloomington: Indiana University Press, 2001); Rachel G. Fuchs, *Poor and Pregnant in Paris: Strategies for Survival in the Nineteenth Century* (New Brunswick, NJ: Rutgers University Press, 1992).

37. Antoine Edme Pruneau de Pommegorge, *Description de la nigritie* (Amsterdam, 1789), 2–7, 28–29.

38. John Lindsay, *A Voyage to the Coast of Africa in 1758* (London, 1759), 77–78.

39. Lindsay, *Voyage to the Coast of Africa*, 79.

40. Brooks, "Signares," 35; Citoyen Prélong, "Mémoire sur les îles de Gorée et du Sénégal," *Annales de Chimie* 1 (1793): 298–300; Dominique Harcourt Lamiral, *L'Affrique et le peuple affriquain* (Paris, 1789), 53–54; Pierre Labarthe, *Voyage au Sénégal, pendant les anées 1784–1785, d'après les mémoires de Lajaille* (Paris, 1802), 163–65.

41. Even for Christians, the fusion of Wolof customs and Islamic traditions that shaped courtship practices allowed for a father to arrange his daughter's marriage without her consent. The hopeful groom was to visit his future bride and her parents

regularly, furnishing them with gifts that culminated in a dowry known in Wolof as an *ndah i far*, "to drive off rivals." See Brooks, "Signares," 35.

42. Labarthe, *Voyage au Sénégal*, 164–65.

43. Hilary Jones, *The Métis of Senegal: Urban Life and Politics in French West Africa* (Bloomington: Indiana University Press, 2013, 18-20.

44. Pierre Cariou, "La rivale inconnue de Madame de Sabran dans l'île de Gorée," *Notes Africaines* 45 (1950): 15.

45. Brooks, "Signares," 35.

46. Pommegorge, *Description*, 2–7.

47. Paolo Zacchia, *Quaestiones medico-legales* (Lyon, 1661). *Quaestiones* was published in nine volumes between 1621 and 1651.

48. Seen in this light, the "parade of the sheet" helps achieve the goal that William Pietz set out in coining the phrase "forensics of capital" as one way to promote a "forensic method of social inquiry into the concrete historical processes of monetized valuation." See Pietz, "Material Considerations: On the Historical Forensics of Contract," *Theory, Culture, and Society* 19, nos. 5-6 (December 2002): 36.

49. Ibid.

50. Rodney, *Upper Guinea Coast*, 152–55; Frank Moya Pons, *History of the Caribbean* (Princeton, NJ: Markus Wiener, 2007), 87–92; Boubacar Barry, *Senegambia and the Atlantic Slave Trade* (Cambridge: Cambridge University Press, 1997), 61-80.

51. James F. Searing, *West African Slavery and Atlantic Commerce: The Senegal River Valley, 1700–1860* (New York: Cambridge University Press, 1993), 27.

52. Rodney, *Upper Guinea Coast*, 77–79; Jean-Claude Nardin, "Recherches sur les 'gourmets' d'Afrique Occidentale," *Revue d l'Histoire des Colonies Française* 53 (1966): 215–44. That the purchase price of an enslaved woman could work so well as a dowry gives one pause not merely about the exigencies of slavery but about freedom in eighteenth-century Senegambia—and elsewhere.

53. In 1764 Poncet de la Rivière, the commandant of Gorée, noted that the term signares was a literal reference to Portuguese ancestry. Madeleine Saulnier, "Une reception royale à l'île de Gorée en 1831," *Revue l'Histoire des Colonies Françaises* 6 (1918): 344n1.

54. Jean Boulègue, *Les Luso-Africains de Sénégambie, XVI–XIX siècle* (Dakar: Université de Dakar, 1972), 11–21. Rodney, *Upper Guinea Coast*, 71–94.

55. J. D. Maillard, *Mémoire pour le colonel Lasserre . . . contenant le compte rendu de sa gestion, le recit des événements de l'insurrection et la refutation des calommies que les insurges ont dirigées contre lui* (Paris, 1805), 16.

56. Louis Henri Pierre Lasserre to Minister, C[6] 21, September 23, 1801, ANF; Marcson, *European-African Interaction*, 83.

57. Léonce Jore, "Les établissements français sur la côte occidentale d'Afrique," *Revue Français d'Histoire d'Outre Mer* 52 (1965): 309; Marcson, *European-African Interaction*, 85. This dynamic is intriguing given the large numbers of "recent arrivals" from Africa among revolutionaries in Saint-Domingue (later Haiti): "Of the half million slaves in Saint-Domingue on the eve of the revolt, about 330,000 had been born and raised in Africa," notes Laurent Dubois. In fact, "most of them were quite recent arrivals" and "more than 40,000 had stepped off the slave ships just the previous year." See Laurent Dubois, *Haiti: The Aftershocks of History* (New York: Metropolitan Books, 2011), 21.

In this regard it is worth noting that the "slaves who arrived in Saint-Domingue from central Africa in the late eighteenth century came from a region torn apart by civil wars. Many were former soldiers, sold to European slavers after being captured in battle." As such, "they were well versed in the use of firearms and experienced in military tactics involving small, mobile, autonomous units," *Aftershocks*, 23. See also John K. Thornton, "African Soldiers in the Haitian Revolution," in *Journal of Caribbean History* 25, nos. 1–2 (1993): 58–80.

58. Jore, *Établissements*, 169–73.

59. Decres to Pinoteau, C[6] 22, July 15, 1808, ANF, as quoted in Marcson, *European-African Interaction*, 85.

60. Jean Boulègue, "Lat-Sukaabe Fall ou L'opiniatrété d'un roi contre les échanges inégaux au Sénégal," in *Les Africains* (Paris, 1977), 9:171–93.

61. Searing, *West African Slavery*, 24.

62. Jacob Soll, "Accounting for Government: Holland and the Rise of Political Economy in Seventeenth Century Europe," *Journal of Interdisciplinary History* 40, no. 2 (Autumn 2009): 215–38.

63. Willem Bosman, *A New and Accurate Description of the Coast of Guinea, Divided into the Slave, the Gold, and the Ivory Coasts* (1702; repr., Cambridge: Cambridge University Press, 2011).

64. Ibid. Bosman argues that African fetish worship is defined by two main characteristics: superstition and interest. From that perspective this form of society is thought to reverse the social logic of mercantilism. Instead of suppressing superstitions in order to cultivate interest in emergent forms of material exchange, self-interested priests fostered popular beliefs in mythical origins of value.

Bosman argues that fetish religion involves the capricious and irrational tendency to endow the material objects of nature and society with a causal efficacy and libidinous impulse they do not deserve. As a consequence, he opposes fetishism to any form of monotheism, which he defines by the quest to suppress libidinous desires in the service of a transcendent God concept. For Bosman, fetishism differs even from polytheistic traditions, which he viewed through the lens of idolatry: the worship of "false" gods but that still fostered a symbolic rather than consubstantial/coterminous/material engagement with divine forces animating the world around us. See William Pietz, "Problem of the Fetish," IIIa, 105–24.

65. Although the seventeenth century is often credited with having incubated the economic and political transformations that have since defined sovereign rule—including national banks and standing armies—many of the institutions we now associate with the state were institutionalized in powerful city-states from the thirteenth through fifteenth centuries.

As early as the thirteenth century, several Mediterranean and Atlantic city-states had developed protocols for extending credit to merchants and for raising funds to commission troops to defend their borders. Some had even developed procedures through which emissaries could secure and display diplomatic credentials. In short, many of the characteristics scholars now associate with the debut of formal diplomatic standing were already established by the seventeenth century. These practices and procedures show up in pragmatic rituals, even among peoples that North Atlantic traders argued were incapable of governing themselves—of establishing durable legal regimes and viable protocols for creditworthiness.

66. Pons, *History of the Caribbean*.

67. Charles Becker and Victor Martin, eds., "Recueil sur la *Vie des Damel* par Tanor Latsoukabe Fall," *Bulletin de IFAN*, 36, ser. B, no. 1 (1974): 117–18.

68. Searing, *West African Slavery*, 19, 204–5. See also Becker and Martin, "Receuil sur la *Vie des Damel*," 112.

69. For more on the relation between finance, militarism, and state formation, see John Brewer, *The Sinews of Power: War, Money and the English State, 1688–1783* (New York: Knopf, 1989); Peter L. Rousseau and Richard Sylla, "Financial Revolutions and Economic Growth: Introducing This EEH Symposium," *Explorations in Economic History* 43 (2006): 1–12; Ross Levine, "Financial Development and Economic Growth: Views and Agenda," *Journal of Economic Literature* 35 (1997): 688–726; Elvira Viches, *New World Gold: Cultural Anxiety and Monetary Disorder in Early Spain* (Chicago: University of Chicago Press, 2010).

70. Carl Wennerlind, *Casualties of Credit: The English Financial Revolution, 1620–1720* (Cambridge, MA: Harvard University Press, 2011); Margot C. Finn, *The Character of Credit: Personal Debt in English Culture, 1740–1914* (Cambridge: Cambridge University Press, 2007).

71. Rodney, *Upper Guinea Coast*, 106; my italics. In his mid-twentieth-century ethnography of people categorized under the ethnic label "Nuer," anthropologist E. Evans-Pritchard noted that the priest, as spiritual and political leader, had two chief responsibilities: to pursue inquiries into offenses from one member of the populace to another, and to adjudicate redress. For this rather specific twentieth-century articulation of the forensics of capital, see E. Evans-Pritchard, *Nuer Religion* (New York: Clarendon Press, 1956). For another especially prescient scholarly inquiry concerning the relation between African forms of inquest and legal categories born from the exigencies of Atlantic slavery, see William Pietz, "The Spirit of Civilization: Blood Sacrifice and Monetary Debt," *RES: Journal of Anthropology and Aesthetics* 28 (Autumn 1995): 23–38 (reprinted in revised form as "Fetish of Civilization: Sacrificial Blood and Monetary Debt," in *Colonial Subjects: Essays on the Practical History of Anthropology*, ed. Peter Pels and Oscar Salemink (Ann Arbor: University of Michigan Press, 2000). These themes emerge prominently in the literature on genres of enhanced efficacy (magic, sorcery, *vodou*, *obeah*) in the Atlantic world and the legal regimes in which they were adjudicated. For recent, insightful work on this topic, see Stephan Palmié, "Thinking with *Ngangas*: Reflections on Embodiment and the Limits of 'Objectively Necessary Appearances,'" *Comparative Studies in Society and History* 48, no. 4 (September 2006): 852–86; Kate Ramsey, *The Spirits and the Law: Vodou and Power in Haiti* (Chicago: University of Chicago Press, 2011); Luis Nicolas Peres and Roger Sansi-Roca, eds., *Sorcery in the Black Atlantic* (Chicago: University of Chicago Press, 2011); Diana Paton and Maarit Forde, eds., *Obeah and Other Powers: The Politics of Caribbean Religion and Healing* (Durham, NC: Duke University Press, 2012); Natalie Zemon Davis, "Judges, Masters, Diviners: Slaves' Experience of Criminal Justice in Colonial Suriname," *Law and History Review* 29, no. 4 (November 2011): 925–84; Vincent Brown, *The Reaper's Garden: Death and Power in the World of Atlantic Slavery* (Cambridge, MA: Harvard University Press, 2011), as well as Kodi Roberts's dissertation, "The Promise of Power: The Racial, Gender, and Economic Politics of Voodoo in New Orleans, 1881–1940" (PhD diss., University of Chicago, 2012).

72. Rodney, *Upper Guinea Coast*, 107.

73. Katherine Ramsland, *Beating the Devil's Game: A History of Forensic Science and Criminal Investigation* (New York: Berkley Books, 2007), 16–17.

74. See Bruno Latour, *We Have Never Been Modern* (Cambridge, MA: Harvard University Press, 1996), 29, as well as Timothy Lenoir, *The Disunity of Science: Boundaries, Contexts and Power*, ed. Peter Galison and David J. Stump (Stanford, CA: Stanford University Press, 1996).

75. Stephan Palmié, "Historicist Knowledge and Its Conditions of Impossibility," in *The Social Life of Entities*, ed. D. Espirito Santo and R. L. Blanes (Chicago: University of Chicago Press, forthcoming). Mary Douglas warned some time ago that diverse polities generate forensic protocols that they adhere to as if they were universal, even though they are historically and geographically contingent. Douglas, "The Person in an Enterprise Culture," in *Understanding the Enterprise Culture*, ed. Shaun Hargreaves Heap and Angus Ross (Edinburgh: Edinburgh University Press, 1992), 41-62. The seed for this idea is arguably found in scattered references to forensics in the English jurist and philosopher, Sir Henry Maine's acclaimed 1861 text *Ancient Law: Its Connection with Early History of Society, and Its Relation to Modern Ideas* (London: John Murray, 1861), esp. 15-16, 29, 32, 146, and 148.

76. Palmié, "Historicist Knowledge."

77. Mary Douglas, "Passive Voice Theories in Religious Sociology," *Review of Religious Research* 21 (1979): 51-61.

78. Palmié, "Historicist Knowledge."

79. Ibid.

80. John Locke, *An Essay concerning Human Understanding* (1690; repr., New York: Meridian, 1964), 210-11. See also Palmié, "Historicist Knowledge," 16-17. Of course, centuries later Antonio Gramsci would develop a critique of the Enlightenment subject that Locke takes for granted. "The starting point of critical elaboration," Gramsci insists, "is 'knowing thyself' as a product of the historical process to date which has deposited in you an infinity of traces, without leaving an inventory," weaving a notion familiar to philosophical inquiry into his own critical apparatus for grappling with the forensics of capital—the "traces" that constitute an imperfect "inventory" of the self. See Antonio Gramsci, Quintin Hoare, and Geoffrey N. Smith, eds., *Selections from the Prison Notebook* (New York: International, 1971), 324.

81. John Locke, *Two Treatises of Government* (Cambridge: Cambridge University Press, 1963); Palmié, "Historicist Knowledge," 17.

82. John Locke, "Fundamental Constitutions of Carolina, 1669," http://avalon.law.yale .edu/17th_century/nc05.asp, accessed March 16, 2011.

83. *Le Code Noir: Receuil d'édits, déclarations et arrêts concernant les esclaves nègres de l'Amérique, 1685*, published by Les Archives du français du Québec, http://www.tlfq .ulaval.ca/axl/amsudant/guyanefr1685.htm, accessed December 30, 2012. My translation. Of course, it's worth noting that enslaved persons did indeed testify in courts throughout the South Atlantic whenever planters privileged their pragmatic interests over their concern to uphold formal legal dictates.

84. In *Saltwater Slavery*, Stephanie Smallwood has discussed how African people became commodities as part of the coercive treatment and the accounting methods that defined Atlantic slavery. Her argument has a distinct geography, showing how people who established unique forms of sociality on both sides of the Atlantic were treated as commodities during the transatlantic voyage. My argument differs in that I would insist that the juridical regimes that denied people citizenship rights and through which their monetary status was inscribed happened on land as well as at sea. In like fashion, the ingenuity bonded humans could exhibit took place on boats as well as in the communities they built on land. If this point conflicts with the explicit argument Smallwood makes in *Saltwater Slavery*, it is compatible with the work she has done on African sentries used to guard enslaved persons on transatlantic voyages. See Stephanie Smallwood, *Saltwater Slavery: A Middle Passage from Africa*

to American Diaspora (Cambridge, MA: Harvard University Press, 2007), as well as Stephanie Smallwood, "African Guardians, European Slave Ships, and the Changing Dynamics of Power in the Early Modern Atlantic," *William and Mary Quarterly* 64, no. 4 (October 2007): 679–716.

85. Soll, "Accounting for Government," 217, 220, and *Information Master*, 54–57.
86. Poovey points out that "implicitly, at least, double-entry bookkeeping was both a system of writing and a mode of government, for if merchants were to benefit from the aura of credibility cast by the rectitude of the formal system, they had to obey the system's rules"; *History of the Modern Fact*, xvii.
87. Soll, "Accounting for Government," 233.
88. Ibid., 234–35.
89. Jacob Soll, *The Information Master: Jean-Baptiste Colbert's Secret State Intelligence System* (Ann Arbor: University of Michigan Press, 2009). On nineteenth-century efforts to grapple with ever more sophisticated methods of accounting and inventory that occasioned new concerns for the perils as well as the promise of enlightened governance, see Ben Kafka, *The Demon of Writing: Powers and Failures of Paperwork* (New York: Zone Books, 2012).
90. Soll, "Accounting for Government," 236–37.
91. John Merriman, *Police Stories: Building the French State, 1815–1851* (Oxford: Oxford University Press, 2006); Clifford Rosenberg, *Policing Paris: The Origins of Modern Immigration Control between the Wars* (Ithaca, NY: Cornell University Press, 2006).
92. Gustav Peebles, "Washing Away the Sins of Debt: The Nineteenth-Century Eradication of the Debtors' Prison," *Comparative Studies in Society and History* 55, no. 3 (2013): 705.
93. Searing, *West African Slavery*, 25.

CHAPTER TWO

1. Technically Lat Dior was called *dammel*, Wolof for "king."
2. My analysis of the French colonial railroad project draws extensively upon Paul Pheffer's nuanced study. See Pheffer, "Railroads and Aspects of Social Change in Senegal" (PhD diss., University of Pennsylvania, 1975).
3. Pheffer, "Railroads," 89–97.
4. Oumar Ba, ed., *La pénétration française au Cayor* (Dakar: République du Sénégal, 1976); John Chipman, *French Power in Africa* (London: Blackwell, 1989).
5. Sven Beckert, *Empire of Cotton: A Global History* (New York: Alfred A. Knopf, 2014).
6. David Eltis and David Richardson, *Routes to Slavery: Direction, Ethnicity and Mortality in the Transatlantic Slave Trade* (London: Routledge, 1997). By Senegambia, I mean the region that today encompasses Senegal and the Gambia. At the same time, it is helpful to recall that much of the economic and political activity that historically defined this region encompassed what has been termed "greater Senegambia": that is, the region that lies between the Sahel and the forests of Guinea (with the most salient region for the purpose of this study being that which lies between the Senegal and Gambia Rivers). For more on the historical significance of greater Senegambia, see Boubacar Barry, *Senegambia and the Atlantic Slave Trade* (Cambridge: Cambridge University Press, 1997).
7. James F. Searing, *"God Alone Is King": Islam and Emancipation in Senegal; The Wolof Kingdoms of Kajoor and Bawol, 1859–1914* (Portsmouth, NH: Heinemann, 2002), 10–12.
8. James Searing, *West African Slavery and Atlantic Commerce: The Senegal River Valley, 1700–1860* (New York: Cambridge University Press, 1993), 2.

9. Abbé David Boilat, *Esquisses Sénégalaises* (1853; repr., Paris: Karthala, 1984); my translation.

10. Searing, "West African Slavery," 2.

11. Groundnuts are a legume subfamily that includes peanuts.

12. Of course, Saba Mahmood's insightful study demonstrates just how much traction piety can have as a political project. See *The Politics of Piety: The Islamic Revival and the Feminist Subject* (Princeton, NJ: Princeton University Press, 2005).

13. "[M]any Africans, particularly rulers, were willing to accept the precepts of Islam only to a degree consistent with traditional fetishist ritual and practice," as one expert would have it. See Pheffer, "Railroads," 86.

14. An implicit argument of this book is that, in addition to debt and punishment, intelligence data collection is a crucial medium through which sovereign rule is constituted. For more on the crucial relation between intelligence data and governance in France, see Martin Thomas, *Empires of Intelligence: Security Services and Colonial Disorder after 1914* (Berkeley: University of California Press, 2007), and Douglas Porch, *The French Secret Services* (New York: Farrar, Straus, and Giroux, 1995).

15. It is important to stress that Demba War Sall, a royal slave, maintained a top executive position in the Wolof aristocracy. Here being a "slave" simply meant being beholden to one's owner; it did not mean someone was merely an item of commerce or a person of little political significance. In fact, as a high-ranking bureaucrat, Demba War Sall was frequently charged with mentoring and assisting the sovereign leaders of area polities. Far from merely being Lat Dior's property, Demba War Sall is the one who had helped to select and mentor the sovereign leader of the Geej dynasty from the time that Lat Dior was circumcised.

16. Searing, "*God Alone Is King*," 40.

17. Amadou Duguay-Clédor, in *La Bataille de Guîlé*, ed. Mbaye Gueye (Dakar: Agence de Cooperation Culturelle et Technique, 1985), 74–77.

18. Searing, "*God Alone Is King*," 30.

19. Mamadou Diouf, *La Kajoor au XIXe siècle: Pouvoir ceddo et conquête coloniale* (Paris: Karthala, 1990), 212–43.

20. Searing, "*God Alone Is King*," 30.

21. Paul Bourde, "La France au Soudan: Le chemin de fer du Sénégal au Niger," *Revue des Deux Mondes* 6 (December 1, 1879).

22. Malick Ghachem, *The Old Regime and the Haitian Revolution* (Cambridge: Cambridge University Press, 2012).

23. Pheffer, "Railroads and Aspects of Social Change," 50.

24. Lauren Benton, *A Search for Sovereignty: Law and Geography in European Empires, 1400–1900* (Cambridge: Cambridge University Press, 2011), 40–103.

25. Diouf, *Kajoor au XIXe siècle*.

26. Searing, *West African Slavery*.

27. Pheffer, "Railroads," 91.

28. Ibid.

29. Pheffer, "Railroads," 103.

30. J. O. *Débats Parliamentaires*, Chambre, séance, December 13, 1879, 11052. See also C. W. Newbury and A. S. Kanya-Forstner, "French Policy and the Origins of the Scramble for West Africa," *Journal of African History* 2 (1969): 261.

31. Pheffer, "Railroads," 100–105.

32. Martin Klein, *Slavery and Colonial Rule in French West Africa* (Cambridge: Cambridge University Press, 1998).

33. Ba, *Pénétration française au Cayor*; Searing, *"God Alone Is King,"* 56–57.

34. Diouf, *Kajoor au XIXe siècle*.

35. Blondelet to GS, April 10, 1884, *ANS*, 033; GS to MMC, report, December 8, 1884, *ANS*, 2B75.

36. GS to MMC, July 8, 1884, *ANS*.

37. GS to MMC, report, *ANS*, 2B75.

38. Pheffer, "Railroads," 125–29.

39. GS to MMC, October 21, 1886, *ANS*. Searing has referred to this federated system as "the first successful exercise in state building in rural Senegal." See *"God Alone Is King,"* 61.

40. Henry M. Stanley, *The Congo and the Founding of Its Free State: A Story of Work and Exploration* (London: Sampson Low, Marston, Searle and Rivington, 1885), 89–90. See also William Pietz, "The Phonograph in Africa: International Phonocentrism from Stanley to Sarnoff," in *Post-structuralism and the Question of History*, ed. Derek Attridge, Geoff Bennington, and Robert C. Young (Cambridge: Cambridge University Press, 1987), 263–85.

CHAPTER THREE

1. Véronique Campion-Vincent, "L'image du Dahomey dans la presse français (1890–1895): Les sacrifices humains," *Cahiers d'études africaines* 7, no. 25 (1967): 27–58.

2. George W. Stocking, *Victorian Anthropology* (New York: Simon and Schuster, 1987), xx.

3. Alfred J. Skertchly, *Dahomey as It Is: Being a Narrative of Eight Months Residence in That Country; with a Full Account of the Notorious Annual Customs, and the Social and Religious Institutions of the Ffons* (1871; repr., St. Louis, MO: Adamant Media, 2003), 218.

4. Ibid., 222.

5. Vincent Brown, "Spiritual Terror and Sacred Authority in Jamaican Slave Society," *Slavery and Abolition* 23, no. 1 (2003): 24–53.

6. Skertchly, *Dahomey*, xxx.

7. See William Pietz, "The Spirit of Civilization: Blood Sacrifice and Monetary Debt," *RES: Journal of Anthropology and Aesthetics* 28 (Autumn 1995): 23–38 (reprinted in revised form as "Fetish of Civilization: Sacrificial Blood and Monetary Debt," in *Colonial Subjects: Essays in the Practical History of Anthropology*, ed. Peter Pels and Oscar Salemink (Ann Arbor: University of Michigan Press, 1999).

8. Robin Law, ed., *From Slave Trade to "Legitimate" Commerce: The Commercial Transition in Nineteenth-Century West Africa* (Cambridge: Cambridge University Press, 1995).

9. Skertchly, *Dahomey*, 180–81.

10. See Pietz, "Fetish of Civilization," 56–57; and "Spirit of Civilization, 23"

11. Contemporary analogues of this specific justification for military intervention are unsettling. Consider the February 28, 2011, press briefing, held less than a month before the US-coordinated NATO military operation that resulted in the death of the sovereign leader of the Libyan Arab Jamahiriya, Colonel Muammar Qaddafi. In her address that day, Susan Rice, US ambassador to the United Nations, commented that Qaddafi "frankly" sounded "delusional" in recent speeches to his populace. In a series of defiant statements, Qaddafi had apparently dismissed the gravity of the protest movement building in Libya, suggesting that, instead of homegrown opposition to autocratic policies, demonstrators were high on drugs, spellbound by foreign detractors bent on undermining what he considered to be a prosperous state of affairs. By this juncture, it was well documented that Qaddafi had hired soldiers of

fortune—who would elsewhere be called "private security contractors" but were here characterized as "African mercenaries"—outfitted with arms they were expected to use in putting down the opposition. Rice claimed that Qaddafi had "laugh[ed] in conversations with American and international journalists, while he was slaughtering his own people," proving that he was "disconnected from reality" and thus "unfit to lead." In like fashion, US secretary of state Hillary Clinton declared that same day before a United Nations Human Rights Commission in Geneva, Switzerland, that "Qaddafi has lost the legitimacy to govern, and it is time for him to go without further violence or delay," insisting that the international community had reached consensus on the issue. What could easily be dismissed as an impassioned response to a grave situation in fact captures the moral logic of militarism that would guide the ensuing intervention. For in suggesting that Qaddafi was "erratic, unstable, irrational," Rice and Clinton were not simply registering their discontent with his recent decisions to launch an assault on "pro-democracy protestors"; they were establishing a basis for humanitarian intervention through military engagement, a mode of foreign policy with roots in the late nineteenth century.

Note that former UN secretary-general Kofi Annan devotes much of his 2012 biography, aptly titled *Interventions*, to his pioneering efforts in helping to institutionalize a diplomatic doctrine known as the "responsibility to protect." Ostensibly concerned with the well-being of innocent people facing genocide, war crimes, crimes against humanity, and various forms of ethnic cleansing, this premise takes its exact wording from the 2000 publication of a Canadian government–sponsored report by the International Commission on Intervention and State Sovereignty. That same year the UN Security Council passed Resolution 1296, designed to "enhance the protection" of innocent civilians during armed conflicts. The specific wording of this seemingly benign phrase, the "responsibility to protect," was finally approved by member states in 2005, then established in paragraphs 138 and 139 of UN Resolution 1674 the following year. Yet for all its apparent newness, this diplomatic principle reprises the same moral logic that justified the 1892 French invasion of Dahomey, as well as the 1897 British invasion of Benin City: enlightened nations have a "responsibility" to invade a polity whose innocent population is subjected to the arbitrary, despotic rule of a tyrant. I would argue that the most crucial challenge for this normative principle is not the alleged well-being of the populace (on which human rights organizations typically focus), nor the alleged mental state of the ruler (on which Susan Rice, Hillary Clinton, and others speculated), but whether the cited criteria are reliable and whether the mechanism of authority or sanction through which this principle will be defended represents some measure of deliberation by parties that are both well informed and unlikely to benefit economically or politically from a military intervention. On the British invasion of Benin City, see Sir Alan Boisragon, *The Benin Massacre* (London, 1898), as well as Pietz, "Fetish of Civilization" and "Spirit of Civilization." On Kofi Annan's theory of military intervention in the service of humanity, see his *Interventions: A Life in War and Peace* (New York: Penguin, 2012).

On March 25, 2011, *New York Times* staff writer Nicholas Kristof tweeted that the March 19, 2011, decision by the United Nations Security Council to call for a no-fly zone in Libya, with provisions for air strikes (through a military endeavor spearheaded by the United States and North Atlantic Treaty Organization forces and their allies), reprised a pattern of "humanitarian war" that "arguably" dates back to the United Nations Interim Mission and NATO bombing campaign in Kosovo from March 24 to June 11, 1999. And from all accounts this event indeed seems to mark the first use of "humanitarian war" (and the cognate "humanitarian bombing") in news publication and political analysis. Yet the basis for Kristof's judgment that this kind of military initiative is a recent development is less reliable as a historical guide than it is useful for gauging a myopia consistent with that of the broader landscape of journalism, political punditry, and even some academic scholarship on human rights and militarism. Kristof deserves credit for his tidy invocation of a concept—"humanitarian war"—that captures the dual nature of this vexing diplomatic scenario. The military mission in Libya ties in to the history of "human rights" in one important sense, and to the modern concept of the "just war" in another. At the same time, he and I differ by a hundred years or so on the origins of humanitarian warfare. For more on "armed humanitarianism," see Nathan Hodge, *Armed Humanitarianism: The Rise of Nation Builders* (New York: Bloomsbury, 2011), though Hodge, like Kristof, considers this a very recent development. For a strident critique of the relation between liberal theory and "humanitarian intervention," see Richard Seymour, *The Liberal Defence of Murder* (London: Verso, 2008). Of course, I would say "force" rather than "murder," since whether "armed humanitarianism" constitutes "murder," "violence," or "peace" is precisely what is at issue. And it has everything to do with the moral infrastructure in which these dynamics are embedded, which is to say that it is a political matter. The entities that are understood to enjoy political legitimacy in the context of war are largely responsible for shaping public opinion about these events, whether that sanction derives from the church (in the context of European "overseas exploration" and colonial conquest) or from the UN (in a post–World War II world). Seymour chastises liberal writers from Christopher Hitchens to Michael Ignatieff for endorsing militarism in the service of human rights, a position that draws support from a striking number of international relations scholars as well. Siba N. Grovogui likewise develops a meaningful critique of this trend. See "The Secret Lives of the 'Sovereign': Rethinking Sovereignty as International Morality," in *States of Sovereignty: Territories, Laws, Populations*, ed. Douglas Howland and Luise White (Bloomington: Indiana University Press, 2009), 261–76.

12. Gustav Peebles, "Washing Away the Sins of Debt: The Nineteenth-Century Eradication of the Debtors' Prison," *Comparative Studies in Society and History* 55, no 3: 701–24.

13. Thus, like Ritu Birla, I am interested in the way late nineteenth-century modes of colonial governance sought to differentiate between "legitimate forms of capitalism and local ones embedded in kinship"—displacing the latter in favor of the former—even if diverse forms of capital retained a "vernacular" quality that evaded this project of consolidation. See Ritu Birla, *Stages of Capital: Law, Culture, and Market Governance in Late Colonial India* (Durham, NC: Duke University Press, 2009).

14. "According to this logic," Gustav Peebles notes, "only barbarians are unenlightened enough to place a money value on a human life, whereas civilized people raised it to the level of the sacred." See "Washing Away the Sins of Debt," 715.

15. Ibid. See also Vivian Zelizer, *Pricing the Priceless Child: The Changing Social Value of Children* (Princeton, NJ: Princeton University Press, 1994).

16. Gustav Peebles, "Washing Away the Sins of Debt," 2.

17. Law, *Slave Trade to "Legitimate Commerce."*

18. Marc Michel, *L'appel à l'Afrique: Contributions et réactions à l'effort de guerre en AOF, 1914–1919* (Paris: Sorbonne, 1982). See also Jean-Charles Jauffret, "La Grande Guerre et l'Afrique française du nord," in *Les troupes coloniales dans la Grande Guerre*, ed. Claude Carlier and Guy Pedroncini (Paris: Economica, 1997); Yves Pourcher, *Les*

jours de guerre: La vie des français au jour le jour entre 1914 et 1918 (Paris: Plon, 1994); Tyler Stovall, "The Color Line behind the Lines: Racial Violence in France during the Great War," *American Historical Review* 103, no. 3 (June 1998): 737–69; Charles Balesi, *From Adversaries to Comrades-in-Arms: West Africans and the French Military, 1885–1918* (Waltham, MA: Crossroads Press, 1979); Leland Barrows, "The Impact of Empire on the French Armed Forces, 1830–1920," in *Double Impact: France and Africa in the Age of Imperialism*, ed. G. Wesley Johnson (Santa Barbara, CA: Praeger, 1985); and Charles Balesi, "West African Influence on the French Army of World War I," in *Double Impact: France and Africa in the Age of Imperialism*, ed. G. Wesley Johnson (Santa Barbara, CA: Praeger, 1985).

19. A brilliant formulation concerning the historical and theoretical legacy of the Four Communes appears in Mamadou Diouf, "The French Colonial Policy of Assimilation and the Civility of the Originaires of the Four Communes (Senegal): A Nineteenth Century Globalization Project," *Development and Change* 29 (1998): 671–96.

20. Sally E. Hadden, *Slave Patrols: Law and Violence in Virginia and the Carolinas* (Cambridge, MA: Harvard University Press, 2003); Bryan Wagner, *Disturbing the Peace: Black Culture and the Police Power after Slavery* (Cambridge, MA: Harvard University Press, 2009).

21. James F. Searing, *"God Alone Is King": Islam and Emancipation in Senegal; The Wolof Kingdoms of Kajoor and Bawol, 1859–1914* (Portsmouth, NH: Heinemann, 2002).

22. To the extent that "the conflicts of the civil war continued in new guises," the idea of "peace" was vexed from the outset. See Searing, *"God Alone Is King,"* xxii.

23. Pietz, "Fetish of Civilization," 63–71.

24. Pietz, "Spirit of Civilization," 28.

25. Martin Klein, *Slavery and Colonial Rule in French West Africa* (Cambridge: Cambridge University Press, 1998).

26. The French put up few barriers to slaves' leaving their masters and acquiring access to land elsewhere.

27. Searing, *"God Alone Is King,"* 144.

28. Ibid., 150.

29. Ibid., 172–94.

30. Ibid., 195–231.

31. Ibid.

32. Donal B. Cruise O'Brien, *Mourides of Senegal: The Political and Economic Organization of an Islamic Brotherhood* (Oxford: Oxford University Press, 1971); Cheikh Anta Babou, "Brotherhood Solidarity, Education and Migration: The Role of the Dahiras among the Murid Muslim Community of New York," *African Affairs* 101 (2002): 151–70; Beth Anne Buggenhagen, "Domestic Object(ion)s: The Senegalese Murid Trade Diaspora and the Politics of Marriage Payments, Love, and State Privatization," in *Producing African Futures: Ritual and Reproduction in a Neoliberal Age*, ed. Brad Weiss (Leiden: Brill, 2004); Donal B. Cruise O'Brien, "Economic Sociology of the Murids," in *Saints and Politicians: Essays in the Organization of a Senegalese Peasant Society* (Cambridge: Cambridge University Press, 1975).

33. Cheikh Anta Babou, *Fighting the Greater Jihad: Amadou Bamba and the Founding of the Muridiyya of Senegal, 1853-1913* (Athens: Ohio University Press, 2007); Mamadou Diouf, "The Senegalese Murid Trade Diaspora and the Making of Vernacular Cosmopolitanism," *Public Culture* 12, no. 3 (2000): 679–93; David Robinson, "Beyond Resistance and Collaboration: Amadu Bamba and the Murids of Senegal," *Journal of*

Religion in Africa 21, no. 2 (1991): 149–69; Searing, *"God Alone Is King,"* 231–68; Jean Copans, *Les Marabouts de l'Arachide: La Confrérie mourides et les paysans du Senegal* (Paris: Sycomore, 1980).

CHAPTER FOUR

1. This pseudonym is used to protect the privacy and safety of an interviewee.

2. This pseudonym is used to protect the privacy and safety of an interviewee.

3. From a different vantage, one could argue the "Arab Spring" began as early as November 2010, amid protests in Western Sahara concerning a Moroccan occupation construed by many residents as unlawful.

4. The website dedicated to the US embassy's Office of Defense Cooperation (ODC) in Dakar notes its unrivaled influence: "Since 1965, more than 1000 Senegalese military officers have trained in the US. Ours is one of the most robust IMET [International Military Education and Training] programs in Sub-Saharan Africa." See http://dakar .usembassy.gov/about_the_embassy/offices/departments/odc.html, accessed August 20, 2014.

5. Lydia Polgreen, "U.S., Too, Wants to Bolster Investment in a Continent's Economic Promise," *New York Times*, August 8, 2012, http://www.nytimes.com/2012/08/09 /world/africa/us-seeks-to-step-up-africa-investment.html?_r=1&pagewanted=all& pagewanted=print, accessed September 18, 2012.

6. Jeremy Scahill, "The CIA's Secret Sites in Somalia," *Nation*, July 12, 2011, http://www .thenation.com/article/161936/cias-secret-sites-somalia, accessed September 18, 2012.

7. Nick Turse, "The Increasing US Shadow Wars in Africa," *Pambazuka News*, July 18, 2012.

8. http://country.eiu.com/Eritrea, accessed December 22, 2014.

9. Leopold II delivered these remarks in September 1876 at the conference Géographique Africane in Brussels, framing his interests as scientific and humanitarian. See *La Conférence de Géographie de 1876: Recueil d'études* (Bruxelles: Académie royale des Sciences d'Outre-mer, 1976).

10. Roy Dietzman, "Forty-Two Years of Peacekeeping: A Review of Senegalese Participation in Peacekeeping Missions" (MA thesis, Department of the Air Force, 2003), 35.

11. Ibid., 73.

12. Ibid., 35.

13. Ibid., 50.

14. Frederick Cooper, *Africa since 1940* (Cambridge: Cambridge University Press, 2002).

15. John D. Kelly and Martha Kaplan, "'My Ambition Is Much Higher Than Independence': US Power, the UN World, the Nation-State, and Their Critics," in *Decolonization: Perspectives from Now and Then*, ed. Prasenjit Duara (London: Routledge, 2003), 135.

16. But this was a very particular idea of "peace," which—despite being conceived amid economic interests and exigencies—deemphasized the role of material concerns for governance. The three most powerful allied nations—the United States, Britain, and the Soviet Union—dominated efforts to shape the moral imagination of the United Nations. Moreover, First Lady Eleanor Roosevelt chaired the Commission on Human Rights, which ultimately produced the United Nations Declaration of the Rights of Man, helping to institutionalize a distinction between two sets of rights—"civil and political rights" in purported contrast to "economic, social and cultural rights,"

where the latter were all but disregarded in deference to the former, while the former remained so vague and unspecified that they were scarcely enforceable. See Roger Normand and Sarah Zaidi, *Human Rights at the UN: The Political History of Universal Justice* (Bloomington: Indiana University Press, 2008), as well as Samar Al-Bulushi, "Review of *Human Rights at the UN: The Political History of Universal Justice*," *Arab Studies Journal* (Spring 2009): 166.

17. Sebastian Rosato, "The Flawed Logic of Democratic Peace Theory," *American Political Science Review* 97, no. 4 (November 2003): 585–602.

18. Mary L. Dudziak, *Cold War Civil Rights: Race and the Image of American Democracy* (Princeton, NJ: Princeton University Press, 2011); Penny M. Von Eschen, *Satchmo Blows Up the World: Jazz Ambassadors Play the Cold War* (Cambridge, MA: Harvard University Press, 2006).

19. Heonik Kwon, *The Other Cold War* (New York: Columbia University Press, 2010); Odd A. Westad, *The Global Cold War: Third World Interventions and the Making of Our Times* (Cambridge: Cambridge University Press, 2007).

20. Dietzman, "Forty-Two Years," 27–28.

21. Ibid., 48.

22. Karin von Hippel, *Democracy by Force: US Military Intervention in the Post–Cold War World* (Cambridge: Cambridge University Press, 2000).

23. Dietzman, "Forty-Two Years," 70.

24. Here I build on the literature concerned with the crucial role that the presumed "expertise" of international governing and lending agencies has played in encouraging former colonies to adopt very specific protocols for governance and mechanisms of credit-debt, often with unfavorable outcomes for the prospect of economic growth and autonomy. See the work of Nobel Prize–winning economist Joseph Stiglitz, *Globalization and Its Discontents* (New York: W. W. Norton, 2003), as well as that of Julia Elyachar, *Markets of Dispossession: NGOs, Economic Development, and the State in Cairo* (Durham, NC: Duke University Press, 2005); Timothy Mitchell, *Rule of Experts: Egypt, Techno-politics and Modernity* (Berkeley: University of California Press, 2002); Patrick Bond, *Elite Transition: From Apartheid to Neoliberalism in South Africa* (London: Pluto Press, 2000); Adebayo Olukoshi, *The Elusive Prince of Denmark: Structural Adjustment and the Crisis of Governance in Africa* (Uppsala: Nordiska Afrikainstitutet, 1998); William Easterly, "What Did Structural Adjustment Adjust? The Association of Policies and Growth with Repeated IMF and World Bank Adjustment Loans," *Journal of Development Economics*, no. 76:1–22; Thandika Mkandawire, ed., *Our Continent, Our Future: African Perspectives on Structural Adjustment* (Dakar: CODESRIA, 1991); Matt Ferguson, *The Anti-politics Machine: "Development," Depoliticization, and Bureaucratic Power in Lesotho* (Minneapolis: University of Minnesota Press, 1994); and Sarah Vaughn, "Reconstructing the Citizen: Disaster, Citizenship, and Expertise in Racial Guyana," *Critique of Anthropology* 32, no. 4 (2012): 359–87, among others.

25. For especially penetrating analyses of these dynamics, see Donna L. Perry, "Muslim Child Disciples, Global Civil Society, and Children's Rights in Senegal: The Discourses of Strategic Structuralism," *Anthropological Quarterly* 77, no. 1 (2004): 47–86, and Xavier Audrain, "Devenir 'Baye Fall' pour être soi: Le religieux comme vecteur d'émancipation individuelle au Sénégal," *Politique Africaine* 94 (2004): 149–65.

26. See Wikileaks cable 10DAKAR127, "Ambassador Discusses Corruption with Senegalese President," marked CONFIDENTIAL, created February 18, 2010, released September 12, 2010, originating in the US embassy in Dakar.

CHAPTER FIVE

1. As Jean and John L. Comaroff remind us, postcolonial "lawlessness" thus often "turns out to be a complex north-south collaboration." See "Law and Disorder in the Postcolony: An Introduction," in *Law and Lawlessness in the African Postcolony* (Chicago: University of Chicago Press, 2006), 8.

2. See Saidiya Hartman, "Time of Slavery," *South Atlantic Quarterly* 101, no. 4 (2002): 760: "The reenactment of the event of captivity contrives an enduring, visceral, and personal memory of the unimaginable," and not simply for people from the African diaspora returning to Senegal as part of a heritage crusade, but also for this Senegalese population, many of whom acknowledged no previous link to the history of the transatlantic slave trade, despite inhabiting a region steeped in the history of its commercial transactions.

3. Laurent Dubois, *Soccer Empire: The World Cup and the Future of France* (Berkeley: University of California Press, 2011).

4. Talal Asad, *On Suicide Bombing* (New York: Columbia University Press, 2007); Mahmood Mamdani, *Good Muslim, Bad Muslim: America, the Cold War, and the Roots of Terror* (New York: Three Rivers Press, 2005).

5. I ask readers to retain this sense of forensics as a distinct way to frame perspective as I consider the relation between sports, spectatorship, and citizenship. In other words, this chapter offers a historical materialist semiotics of Senegalese soccer fandom as a way to tease out some of the discursive thematics shared by discourses on sports and on politics in Senegal.

6. Wade's determined position on the matter did not reflect the nuanced exchanges taking place among Senegalese intellectuals. Critical of the way Bush's coalition was driven by what seemed to many to be a divine right to fight, Cheikh Bamba Dioum published an article in *Le Soleil* titled "God bless the USA . . . *and* Afghanistan" (*Le Soleil*, Friday, October 12, 2001, ANS, my italics. By contrast, Malick Ndiaye, leader of the Collective Social Forces for Change, declared that he supported "neither Bush nor Ben Laden" in his *L'Info 7* piece ("Les partisans du 'Ni Bush ni Ben Laden' remittent ça aujourd'hui," *L'Info 7*, Wednesday, November 7, 2001, ANS). Meanwhile, religious theorist Ebrahim Moosa noted parallels between the two adversaries: "Both Bush and Bin Laden claim to have divine mandates, to have access to secret spiritual knowledge that obliges them to do certain things, even if those things run counter to their religions' most basic ethical teachings. Both men claim they're going to save people through their actions." Moosa contends, furthermore, that both men "believe they have messianic missions to fulfill." See Krista Bremer, "In God's Name," *Sun*, no. 236 (April 2006): 12.

7. See "Pour la création d'un Pacte africaine contre le terrorisme," *L'Info 7*, Thursday, September 20, 2001, and "Le président Wade propose un 'Pacte africaine contre le terrorisme,'" *Le Soleil*, Friday, September 21, 2001.

8. "Les chefs d'état réaffirment l'engagement sans faille de l'Afrique," *Le Soleil*, October 18, 2001, 3, ANS.

9. Ibid.

10. Ibid. "M. Bush également annonce la création d'un fonds de soutien des investissements privés dans la région . . . des garantie et une couverture du risque politique pour leurs projets en Afrique sub-saharienne."

11. Dani W. Nabudere, "NEPAD: Historical Background and Its Prospects," paper delivered at the African Forum for Envisioning Africa, Nairobi, Kenya, April 26–29, 2002.

12. Greg Mills cites the large number of paramilitary groups operating within the African continent, and the fact that NEPAD was ratified in October 2001, as evidence that African leaders share their Western counterparts' interest in fighting terrorism. It is doubtful that African heads of state would envision their struggle against militia groups and rogue soldiers in the same uncompromising way that Bush envisioned his crusade against terrorism. Mills's claim that "had there never been a September 11, 2001, President George W. Bush arguably never would have made a visit to Senegal, South Africa," and other African countries, on the other hand, is compelling as a way to think about how US foreign policy in Africa is at times structured by geopolitical strategy and not merely the humanitarian propensity for which Bush is often credited in his dealings with the continent. See Greg Mills, "Africa's New Strategic Significance," *Washington Quarterly* 27, no. 4 (2004): 158.

13. "French President Jacques Chirac holds talks with Senegal's President Abdoulaye Wade in Paris on Thursday. The meeting comes as French-Senegalese ties appear to be under pressure, largely due to the West African state's more recent friend—the United States. France, the former colonial power, remains Senegal's biggest donor and trading partner. Dakar has played down the talks, insisting that relations are very good. . . . But skeptics say the meeting is a chance for Paris to remind Senegal who pays out millions of dollars in donor assistance each year." See Lara Pawson, "France Tackles U.S. Trend," *British Broadcast News Online*, February 19, 2004, http://news.bbc.co.uk/go/pr/fr/-/2/hi/africa/3501777.stm, accessed June 10, 2006.

14. Sheldon Gellar, *Senegal: An African Nation between Islam and the West* (Boulder, CO: Westview Press, 1982), 82–83. Note that Senegal also gained favor with the United States during Ronald Reagan's presidency for its willingness to serve as a contingency landing site for space shuttle missions. During the presidency of George H. W. Bush, Senegal supported the United States by condemning the bombing of Pan Am flight 103, for which two Libyan men were convicted (although suspicions were subsequently raised about whether due process was upheld during the trial).

15. Brennan M. Kraxberger, "The United States and Africa: Shifting Geopolitics in an 'Age of Terror,'" *Africa Today* 52, no. 1 (Fall 2005): 47–68.

16. "Bush et Wade rêvent d'une finale Sénégal–USA," *Le Soleil*, Wednesday, June 19, 2002. The front-page headline translates as "Bush and Wade dream of a Senegal–USA final match." The article itself, in the newspaper's interior, carries a similar title: "Bush et Wade souhaitent USA–Sénégal" ("Bush and Wade wish for a USA–Senegal final").

17. Mamadou Diouf, "Urban Youth and Senegalese Politics, 1988–1994," *Public Culture* 19 (1996): 225–49.

18. Admittedly it is not altogether clear how this demographic label is being deployed. To the extent that "youth" as a sociological moniker often refers not simply to people of a certain age but to those who have not yet accessed well-recognized institutions of social reproduction (marriage, parenthood, and stable employment), in Senegal it encompasses people from ages associated with adolescence up through age thirty—and beyond. What is more, as the Senegalese case emphasizes, the term is typically gendered as male.

19. See statistics provided by the United States Central Intelligence Agency: www.cia worldfactbook.com/senegal.

20. "Senegal Celebrates Cup Heroics," *British Broadcasting Corporation News-Sport*, July 21, 2001.

21. "Senegal Back to Heroes Welcome," *British Broadcasting Corporation News-Sport,* July 22, 2001, 26, 27; "Lions Players Rule in France," *British Broadcasting Corporation News-Sport,* August 13, 2001.

22. "Africa's Obsession with Soccer," *British Broadcasting Corporation News-Sport,* August 18, 2001.

23. "Senegal in Fever over World Cup Debut," *British Broadcasting Corporation News-Sport,* May 14, 2002.

24. "Soccer Fever," *British Broadcasting Corporation News-Sport,* June 12, 2002.

25. "Divided Loyalties for Fadiga," *British Broadcasting Corporation News-Sport,* April 8, 2002.

26. "The Whole of the Cameroonian Squad Plays Abroad, along with 22 Senegalese, 21 Nigerians, 16 South Africans, and Nine Tunisians"; Isabelle Saussez, "Africa on the Sidelines," *Courier ACP-EU,* July–August 2002.

27. Mamadou Diouf, "The Senegalese Murid Trade Diaspora and the Making of a Vernacular Cosmopolitanism," *Public Culture* 12, no. 3 (2000): 700.

28. "Senegal's Success Story," *British Broadcasting Corporation News-Sport,* June 16, 2002.

29. Maurice Wallace refers to the "spectacle charm of charisma" in a formulation that resonates with Erica Edwards's theorizing on the same concept. See Maurice Wallace, "Our Tsunami," *Transforming Anthropology* 14, no. 1 (April 2006): 24–26, and Erica Edwards, "Contesting Charisma: Political Leadership in Contemporary African American Culture" (PhD diss., Duke University, 2006).

30. For many elites, "the watch words of the sporting canon: competition . . . 'fair-play' . . . transpose quite naturally from his [or her] individual conduct to that of a company or indeed a nation. Here they may take on fancier, more imposing titles: Free Enterprise, Competitive Trading Position . . . the National Interest, Equality before the Law, etc., but the inherent ideas are still the same." See Jean Brohm, *Sport: A Prison of Measured Time,* trans. Ian Fraser (London: Ink Links, 1978), ix. Nancy Birdsall and John Nellis, for instance, assess the impact of privatization by distinguishing between winners and losers. See Birdsall and Nellis, "Winners and Losers: Assessing the Distributional Impact of Privatization," *World Development* 31, no. 10 (2003): 1617–33.

    Using sport to track Senegalese economic and political aspirations suggests that it is likewise crucial to consider lackluster performances. In Amanda Alexander's study of the tension between World Bank practices and policies, she notes that critics have sometimes overstated the organization's claim to efficiency, "The World Bank has attained a reputation as a polished neo-colonial enterprise despite its daily actions, which look more like over-confidant games of trial-and-error—with devastatingly high stakes." See Amanda Alexander, "'A Disciplining Method for Holding Standards Down': How the World Bank Planned Africa's Slums," *Review of African Political Economy* 39, no. 134 (2012): 593.

31. Ian Taylor, *NEPAD: Towards Africa's Development or Another False Start?* (Boulder, CO: Lynne Rienner, 2005; J. Pender, "From 'Structural Adjustment' to 'Comprehensive Development Framework': Conditionality Transformed?" *Third World Quarterly* 22, no. 3 (2001): 397–411. International lending agencies, North Atlantic economists, and donor nations seem agreed that good governance correlates with economic prosperity even though Angola, the Democratic Republic of the Congo, Equatorial Guinea, Nigeria, and increasingly the Sudan have topped the list of African countries receiving foreign investment capital during the past decade despite, for different reasons, evincing some of the continent's most glaring forms of political and civil unrest.

See James Ferguson, *Global Shadows: Africa in the Neoliberal World Order* (Durham, NC: Duke University Press, 2006), 196, and William Reno, "External Relations of Weak States and Stateless Societies," in *African Foreign Policies: Power and Process*, ed. Gilber Kaldiagala and Terence Lyons (Boulder, CO: Lynne Rienner, 2001), 187. Meanwhile, development discourses insist that Côte d'Ivoire's recent political turmoil and Sierra Leone's protracted social crisis surrounding fierce competition for illicit diamonds are to blame for lackluster economic performance. See *African Development Report* (Oxford: Oxford University Press and African Development Bank, 2004).

32. Francis Owusu, "Pragmatism and the Gradual Shift from Dependency to Neoliberalism: The World Bank, African Leaders, and Development in Africa," *World Development* 31, no. 10 (2003): 1660; see also *African Development Report* (Oxford: Oxford University Press and African Development Bank, 2004), 28–29.

33. See "Pèlerinage à la Maison des Esclaves," *Le Soleil*, 1998, ANS.

34. See "Le méridien président sous haute surveillance," *L'Info 7*, July 2, 2003, ANS. The writer who chronicled the modes of surveillance Bush's security forces used found it important to emphasize that not even Clinton's 1998 visit seemed to necessitate such precautions. ("Il faut souligner que même la visite que le prédécesseur de Bush, Bill Clinton, avait effectuée au Sénégal avant l'alternance, n'avait nécessité autant de précautions.")

35. Mark Hinchman, "The Traveling Portrait: Women and Representation in Eighteenth-Century Senegal," in *Interpreting Colonialism*, ed. Byron Wells and Philip Stewart (Oxford: Voltaire Foundation, 2004), 49.

36. Mark Hinchman, "From the Maison Pépin to the *Maisons des Enclaves*," paper given as part of a panel titled "The Power of Expression: Identity, Language, and Memory in Africa and the Diaspora," African Studies Association and Canadian Association of African Studies 47th/34th Annual Meetings, November 11–14, 2004.

37. Ralph Austen, "The Slave Trade as History and Memory: Confrontations of Slaving Voyage Documents and Communal Traditions," *William and Mary Quarterly* 58, no. 1 (2001): 229–44.

38. Bayo Holsey's work on slave tourism to Ghana reveals the cleavage between the absence of historical work on the slave trade in Ghanaian educational curricula and the diasporic discourses prevalent among African Americans that encourage them to visit Cape Coast and Elmina Castle to confront a key point of departure for their ancestors who, it is believed, embarked on a transatlantic journey to the Americas from these sites. See Bayo Holsey, *Routes of Remembrance: Refashioning the Slave Trade in Ghana* (Chicago: University of Chicago Press, 2008). See also Sandra Richards, "What Is to Be Remembered? Tourism to Ghana's Slave-Castle Dungeons," *Theatre Journal* 57, no. 4 (2005): 617–37, and Salamishah Tillet, "A Race of Angels: (Trans)Nationalism, African American Tourism, and the Slave Forts," in *Sites of Slavery: Citizenship and Racial Democracy in the Civil Rights Imagination* (Durham, NC: Duke University Press, 2012), 95–132.

39. For the full transcript of this speech, see "President Bush Speaks at Gorée Island," Remarks by the President on Gorée Island, July 8, 2003, as posted on the official website of the White House, http://www.whitehouse.gov/news/releases/2003/07/20030708-1.html, accessed April 19, 2007.

40. Djibril Samb, ed., *Gorée et l'esclavage: Actes du Séminaire sur "Gorée dans la traite atlantique: Mythes et réalités"* (Dakar: IFAN, 1997). See also James F. Searing, *West African Slavery and Atlantic Commerce: The Senegal River Valley, 1700–1860* (New York: Cambridge University Press, 1993), ix.

41. Bruce Lincoln, "From Artaxerxes to Abu Ghraib: On Religion and the Pornography of Imperial Violence, Religion and Culture," Web Forum, http://marty-center.uchicago .edu/webforum/archive.shtml, accessed February 15, 2007.

42. Here Bush suggests that the United States government is using its "power and resources" to introduce "peace" and "end conflict" in ways that are especially beneficial to African people. The millennial *captiveries* at Gorée, meanwhile, tell a very different story. For productive insights on these dynamics, see Barnor Hesse, "Forgotten like a Bad Dream: Atlantic Slavery and the Ethics of Postcolonial Memory," in *Relocating Postcolonialism*, ed. David Theo Goldberg and Ato Quayson (Oxford: Blackwell, 2002), 143–73.

43. Owusu, "Pragmatism"; Taylor, *NEPAD*.

44. Frederick Cooper, *Africa since 1940* (Cambridge: Cambridge University Press, 2002).

45. Beth Buggenhagen, "At Home in the Black Atlantic: Circulation, Domesticity, and Value in the Murid Trade Diaspora" (PhD diss., University of Chicago, 2003).

46. Joel Millman, *The Other Americans: How Immigrants Renew Our Country, Our Economy, and Our Values* (New York: Viking Penguin, 1997), 180.

47. Paul Stoller, *Money Has No Smell: The Africanization of New York City* (Chicago: University of Chicago Press, 2002), 88–90.

48. Ibid.

49. See Loïc Wacquant, "Inside 'The Zone': The Social Art of the Hustler in the American Ghetto," in *The Weight of the World*, ed. Pierre Bourdieu (Stanford, CA: Stanford University Press, 1999). Also see Sudhir Venkatesh, *Off the Books: The Underground Economy of the Urban Poor* (Cambridge, MA: Harvard University Press, 2006), and Venkatesh, *American Project: The Rise and Fall of an American Ghetto* (Cambridge, MA: Harvard University Press, 2002).

50. Michael Ralph, "Prototype: In Search of the Perfect Senegalese Basketball Physique," *International Journal of the History of Sport* 24, no. 2 (August 2007): 238–63.

51. Laura Checkoway, "The Kon Artist," *Vibe*, April 2007, 92.

52. And for young actors in postcolonial and postindustrial contexts, "criminality" has provided, if not exactly "a means of production," a repertoire of techniques for achieving the "productive redistribution" of resources in sites where people are "alienated by new forms of exclusion." See Jean Comaroff and John L. Comaroff, "Criminal Obsessions, after Foucault: Postcoloniality, Policing and the Metaphysics of Disorder, in *Law and Disorder in the Postcolony*, ed. Jean Comaroff and John L. Comaroff (Chicago: University of Chicago Press, 2006), 278. See also Venkatesh, *American Project*. Ironically, this was less true for Akon than it most likely was for his peers in the underworld. The top-selling recording artist was, by his own admission, raised "middle-class," though he "gravitated toward the 'hood, running with tough crews in all the cities where his parents moved." See Checkoway, "Kon Artist," 94.

53. See Stoller, *Money Has No Smell*, 88–90. Laura Checkoway's 2007 *Vibe* magazine article quotes Akon as saying, "Bend . . . over, look back, and watch me," to former "it" girl Tara Reid, whose legs were then wrapped around his waist as the hip-hop balladeer performed "Smack That" before an audience at the 2006 Sundance Film Festival. See Checkoway, "Kon Artist," 94. Crucial to how Akon understands himself to be racialized in ways consonant with African Americans' experience is his concern with celebrating what I have elsewhere termed "hip-hop fantasy." This ideational frame hinges on performances of material excess and the insistence—at least in the public persona of many hip-hop (and, in this case, hip-hop/R&B) artists—of depicting the female body as a vehicle for sexual escapades. See Michael Ralph, "'Flirt[ing] with

Death' but 'Still Alive': The Sexual Dimension of Surplus Time in Hip Hop Fantasy," *Cultural Dynamics* 18, no. 1 (2006): 61–88.

54. Checkoway, "Kon Artist," 94–95.

55. Michael Ralph, "(At) Play in the Postcolony" (PhD diss., University of Chicago, 2007).

56. Name changed to protect the privacy of the interviewee.

57. Alexander, "Disciplining Method," 592.

58. Ibid., 594. On this point, see Eric Toussaint, *The World Bank: A Critical Primer* (London: Pluto Press, 2008), 9–10; C. L. Gilbert, A. Powell, and D. Vines, "Positioning the World Bank," in *The World Bank: Structure and Policies*, ed. C. L. Gilbert and D. Vines (Cambridge: Cambridge University Press, 2000), 600–605; Louis Galambos and David Milobsky, "Organizing and Reorganizing the World Bank, 1946-1972: A Comparative Perspective," *Business History Review* 69 (1995): 163–70.

59. Robert McNamara, "To the Board of Governors, Washington, DC, 1 September, 1975," in *The McNamara Years at the World Bank* (Baltimore: Johns Hopkins University Press, 1981), 295–334.

60. Alexander, "Disciplining Method," 598.

61. Michael Cohen, "Aid, Density, and Urban Form: Anticipating Dakar," *Built Environment* 33, no. 2 (2007): 145–56.

62. "Jackson," said one senior official, "has given us a lot of help on this, and we'll all remember him for it"; see "Clinton Opposes Slavery Apology," in *When Sorry Isn't Enough: The Controversy over Apologies and Reparations for Human Justice*, ed. Roy Brooks (New York: New York University Press, 1999), 352.

63. Recall the scene in Voltaire's 1759 novel *Candide* when a mutilated slave who has escaped from a plantation in Suriname confronts the novel's young protagonist and displays fleshy scars to remind him, "It is at this price that you eat sugar in Europe"— and that Senegal might enjoy a bigger helping of foreign capital.

If "slavery" successfully "established a measure of man and a ranking of life and worth that has yet to be undone," nineteenth-century modes of forensic calculation established what were then deemed objective criteria for determining "worth" in emergent forms of monetized value. These protocols drew on a shift in Anglo-American legal perspective that suddenly made human beings (previously considered more sacred than scientific) available for quantification based on the physiological and demographic variables planters considered in the "slave pens" where they examined prospective chattel. On this mode of legal reasoning, see William Pietz, "Death of the Deodand: Accursed Objects and the Money Value of Human Life," *RES: Anthropology and Aesthetics*, no. 31 (1997): 98. On the exigencies of pricing slaves in the marketplace, see Walter Johnson, *Soul by Soul: Life inside an Antebellum Slave Market* (Cambridge, MA: Harvard University Press, 1999), 118. On slave insurance, life insurance, and the diverse, if related, protocols involved with assessing the monetary value of a human life, see Michael Ralph, "'Life . . . in the Midst of Death': Notes on the Historical Relationship between Slave Insurance, Life Insurance and Disability," *Disability Studies Quarterly* 32, no. 3 (Summer 2012).

64. Joseph H. Drake, "Consideration vs. Causa in Roman-American Law," *Michigan Law Review* 4, no. 1 (1905): 19–41.

65. William Pietz, "Material Considerations: On the Historical Forensics of Contract," *Theory, Culture and Society* 19, nos. 5–6 (2002): 35.

66. That such a legal concept could nevertheless fit this scenario so appropriately makes one wonder whether this militaristic spectacle is evidence of the way "force 'trumps'

law" or if "the very concept of law," indeed, "juridical reason itself, includes a priori a possible recourse to constraint or coercion and thus to a certain violence," says Derrida. Of course, I would use "force" where Derrida invokes "violence," for reasons stated at the outset. See Jacques Derrida, *Rogues: Two Essays on Reason*, trans. Pascale-Anne Brault and Michael Naas (Stanford, CA: Stanford University Press, 2005), xi; cf. Pierre Bourdieu, *Outline of a Theory of Practice*, trans. Richard Nice (Cambridge: Cambridge University Press, 1997), 95. Further reason to be critical of the methodological approach Derrida undertakes is that, like Pietz, I believe legal concepts and categories are to be engaged and not dismissed as mere "ideologized obfuscations of how social life really comes about and operates . . . studied only in order to debunk them." See Pietz, "Material Considerations," 35.

67. Pietz, "Material Considerations," 39.
68. These Senegalese "slaves," then, might be considered "virtual commodit[ies]" in both senses of the term. See Michel-Rolph Trouillot, "Comment," on Virginia R. Dominguez, "A Taste for 'the Other': Intellectual Complicity in Racializing Practices," *Current Anthropology* 35, no. 4 (1994): 333–48.
69. Pietz, "Material Considerations," 38.
70. Ibid.
71. Apropos here, articles 1109 and 1117 of the Code Civil des Français (French civil code) indicate that a contract is not valid if consent derives from misapprehension (*erreur*), is achieved under duress (*violence*), or results from misrepresentation (*dol*). For the articles in question, see the Code Civil: "Il n'y a point de consentement valable, si le consentement n'a été donné que par erreur, ou s'il a été extorqué par violence ou surpris par dol" (article 1109). "La convention contractée par erreur, violence ou dol, n'est point nulle de plein droit; elle donne seulement lieu à une action en nullité ou en rescision (article 1117).

CHAPTER SIX

1. Mamadou Diouf, "Urban Youth and Senegalese Politics, 1988–1994," *Public Culture* 19 (1996): 228.
2. Michel-Rolph Trouillot, *Silencing the Past: Power and the Production of History* (New York: Beacon, 1997), 9.
3. Though writing about a rather different context, C. M. Hann likewise notes that tea clubs are the exclusive province of men. See C. M. Hann, *Tea and the Domestication of the Turkish State* (Huntingdon, UK: Eothen, 1990), 103.
4. Hylton White, "Ritual Haunts: The Timing of Estrangement in a Post-apartheid Countryside," in *Producing African Futures: Ritual and Reproduction in a Neoliberal Age*, ed. Brad Weiss (Leiden: Brill, 2005), 141—66.
5. As noted above, for the purposes of my analysis *capital* refers to a range of assets, whether an investment portfolio or a family name: both derive from economic cleavages and are available for economic projects.
6. CFA was the acronym for Colonies Françaises d'Afrique (French Colonies of Africa) between 1945 and 1958, then for Communauté Française d'Afrique (French Community of Africa) between 1958 and the independence of the African nations included under these distinctions beginning in the 1960s. Since the time of independence, CFA has referred to either Communauté Financière d'Afrique (African Financial Community) in the case of West Africa or Coopération Financière en Afrique Centrale (Financial Cooperation in Central Africa) for central African nations.

7. Nelson W. Keith, "Nonnibutibus: The Sociocultural Messages of the Jamaican Tea Meeting," *Anthropology and Humanism Quarterly* 17 (1992): 3.

8. Diouf, "Urban Youth," 231.

9. René Collignon, "La lutte des pouvoirs publics contre les encombrements humains à Dakar," *Revue Canadienne des Études Africaines* 18 (1984): 573—82.

10. Diouf, "Urban Youth," 231; Mamadou Diouf, "La jeunesse au coeur," *Le Soleil*, special edition, May 19, 1992.

11. For comparable circumstances, see Craig Jeffrey, *Timepass: Youth, Class and the Politics of Waiting in India* (Stanford, CA: Stanford University Press, 2010), and Ritty Lukose, *Liberalization's Children: Gender, Youth, and Consumer Citizenship in Globalizing India* (Durham, NC: Duke University Press, 2009).

12. P. Bocquier, "L'insertion et la mobilité professionelles à Dakar" (PhD diss., Université de Paris V, 1991), 55.

13. Abdoulaye Bathily, Mamadou Diouf, and Mohamed Mbodj, "The Senegalese Student Movement from Its Inception to 1989," in *African Studies in Social Movements and Democracy*, ed. Mahmood Mamdani and Ernest Wamba-dia-Wamba (Dakar: CODESRIA, 1995), 369–408.

14. Robert Fatton Jr., *The Making of a Liberal Democracy: Senegal's Passive Revolution, 1975–1985* (London: Lynne Rienner, 1987).

15. Enda Tiers Monde, *Set, des murs qui parlent . . . nouvelles cultures urbaines à Dakar* (Dakar: Enda, 1991); J. C. Niane, Vieux Savané, and B. Boris Diop, *Set/Setal: La seconde génération des barricades* (Dakar: Sud, 1991).

16. For insightful work on the relation between sanitation and governance in Senegal, see Rosalind C. Fredericks, "Doing the Dirty Work: The Cultural Politics of Garbage Collection in Dakar, Senegal" (PhD diss., University of California, Berkeley, 2009).

17. Diouf, "Urban Youth," 240.

18. Ibid., 241.

19. Ibid., 226.

20. Michael Ralph, "'Crimes of History': Senegalese Soccer and the Forensics of Slavery," *Souls* 9 (2007): 193–222.

21. In coming to terms with the Senegalese government's strategies of "enframement," I find it useful to note Maurice Wallace's critical insight that visual artifacts are "always subject to reproducing blind spots that tell more about the scopic criminality of the one who enframes than the enframed one." Maurice Wallace, *Constructing the Black Masculine: Identity and Ideality in African American Men's Culture, 1775–1995* (Durham, NC: Duke University Press, 2002), 29. Jacques Derrida, *Memoirs of the Blind: Self-Portrait and Other Ruins*, trans. Pascale-Ann Brault and Michael Naas (Chicago: University of Chicago Press, 1993), 29; Jacques Derrida, *The Truth in Painting*, trans. Geoff Bennington and Ian McLeod (Chicago: University of Chicago Press, 1987), 74.

22. Here as elsewhere, "punishment has replaced rehabilitation," eliding any sustained effort to identify "the root causes of crime." Harvey Molotch and Noah McClain, "Dealing with Urban Terror: Heritages of Control, Varieties of Intervention, Strategies of Research," *International Journal of Urban and Regional Research* 27 (2003): 685.

23. Mamadou Diouf, "Engaging Postcolonial Cultures: African Youth and Public Space," *African Studies Review* 46 (2003): 7.

24. Derrida, *Truth in Painting*, 5.

25. Ndiouga Adrien Benga, "Dakar et ses tempos: Significations et enjeux de la musique

urbaine (c. 1960–année 1990)," in *Le Sénégal contemporain*, ed. Momar-Coumba Diop (Paris: Karthala, 2002), 289—308.

26. Michael Ralph, "'Le Sénégal Qui Gagne': Soccer and the Stakes of Neoliberalism in a Postcolonial Port," *Soccer and Society* 7 (2006): 300–317. Mamadou Diouf's work on Senegalese youth suggests that "their demonstrations, even those whose principal idiom is violence, always have an element of playing hooky." See Diouf, "Engaging Postcolonial Cultures," 7. "Hooky," in my view, because youth self-consciously abstain from participation in formal social institutions.

27. See Jean Comaroff and John L. Comaroff, "Réflexions sur la jeunesse: Du passé à la post-colonie," *Politique Africaine* 80 (2000): 90–110, and Beth Anne Buggenhagen, "At Home in the Black Atlantic: Circulation, Domesticity and Value in the Senegalese Murid Trade Diaspora" (PhD diss., University of Chicago, 2003).

28. This narrative recalls Thorstein Veblen's discussion about the way objects mark class divisions that map onto social distinctions, though unevenly in some instances. Besides Thorstein Veblen, *The Theory of the Leisure Class* (1899; repr., New York: Kelley, 1965), see Pierre Bourdieu, *Distinction* (Cambridge, MA: Harvard University Press, 1984), and Rudolf Josef Colloredo-Mansfeld, *The Native Leisure Class: Consumption and Cultural Creativity in the Andes* (Chicago: University of Chicago Press, 1999), 199.

29. Here, it seems, as among Kenya's Samburu pastoralists, tea is both "a global commodity and an indigenized food." See John D. Holtzman, "In a Cup of Tea: Commodities and History among Samburu Pastoralists in Northern Kenya," *American Ethnologist* 30 (2003): 137.

30. Diouf, "Engaging Postcolonial Cultures," 5. Also consider Donald Martin Carter, *States of Grace: Senegalese in Italy and the New European Immigration* (Minneapolis: University of Minnesota Press, 1997).

31. Wallace, *Constructing the Black Masculine*, 30.

32. Jennifer Schirmer, "The Claiming of Space and the Body Politic within National-Security States: The Plaza de Mayo Madres and the Greenham Common Women," in *Remapping Memory: The Politics of TimeSpace*, ed. Jonathan Boyarin (Minneapolis: University of Minnesota Press, 1994), 43—44; Rosalind Shaw, *Memories of the Slave Trade: Ritual and the Historical Imagination in Sierra Leone* (Chicago: University of Chicago Press, 2002); Jennifer Cole, *Forget Colonialism? Sacrifice and the Art of Memory in Madagascar* (Berkeley: University of California Press, 2001); and Phillip Connerton, *How Societies Remember* (Cambridge: Cambridge University Press, 1989).

33. Here the work of Maurice Halbwachs is instructive; see *The Collective Memory*, trans. Francis J. Ditter Jr. and Vida Yazdi Ditter (New York: Harper and Row, 1980). Also consider two of his earlier attempts to grapple with these issues: *La topographie légendaire des Évangiles en Terre Sainte: Étude de mémoire collective* (Paris: Presses Universitaires de France, 1941), and *Les cadres sociaux de la mémoire* (Paris: Alcan, 1925). Despite Halbwachs's attention to the social components of "collective memory," I prefer the concept of "historicity," following Trouillot, *Silencing the Past*, 21. Historicity, as I've discussed elsewhere, has two dimensions: it refers to historical movement, the conditions under which people (and their environments) are transformed through social processes. Historicity likewise encourages us to consider the narratives people produce about these developments. See Michael Ralph, "'Flirt[ing] with Death' but 'Still Alive': The Sexual Dimension of Surplus Time in Hip Hop Fantasy," *Cultural Dynamics* 18 (2006): 80n6.

In the anthropological tradition, there is a tendency to emphasize culturally specific forms of time reckoning. For a classic attempt to theorize this phenomenon, see Martin P. Nilsson, *Primitive Time Reckoning* (Lund: Gleerup, 1920), though for a masterful summary of the literature one should consult Nancy Munn, "The Cultural Anthropology of Time: A Critical Essay," *Annual Review of Anthropology* 21 (1992): 93–123. Scholars have convincingly argued that distinct notions of time arise from their association with customary activities; elsewhere they are linked to seasonal cycles and ethnic attitudes. Theorizing differing notions of temporality through the lens of historicity has the advantage of locating social perceptions within the contexts that produced them without taking these ideas to be permanent features of any social landscape, as analysts sometimes inadvertently infer. See Gregory A. Beckett, "The End of Haiti: History under Conditions of Impossibility" (PhD diss., University of Chicago, 2008), and Yarimar Bonilla, "The Past Is Made by Walking: Labor Activism and Historical Production in Postcolonial Guadeloupe," *Cultural Anthropology* 26 (July 2011): 313–39, as well as Bronislaw Malinowski, "Lunar and Seasonal Calendar in the Trobriands," *Journal of the Royal Anthropological Institute* 57 (1927): 209; E. E. Evans-Pritchard, *The Nuer* (Oxford: Clarendon, 1940), and Evans-Pritchard, "Nuer Time Reckoning," *Africa* 12 (1939): 189–216; Clifford Geertz, "Person, Time, and Conduct in Bali," in *The Interpretation of Cultures* (New York: Basic Books, 1973), 360–411; Boyarin, *Remapping Memory*; Johannes Fabian, *Time and the Other: How Anthropology Makes Its Object* (New York: Columbia University Press, 1983); John S. Mbiti, *African Religions and Philosophy* (New York: Praeger, 1969).

34. This sense of "personal time" that Durkheim theorized is, as Nancy Munn suggests, "infused with collective time representations and activity rhythms." See Émile Durkheim, *The Elementary Forms of Religious Life* (London: Allen and Unwin, 1915), 441, and Munn, "Cultural Anthropology of Time," 95.

   In terms of the way people locate themselves in temporal schemes, I follow Jennifer Cole closely in that I understand "memory as simultaneously constituted by public representations and social consciousness woven together through social practice." Though I clearly prefer the notion of historicity, I find that my sense of the concept resonates with her careful attention to the way "people selectively remember and rework the historical past" (Cole, *Forget Colonialism?* 2).

35. Economists tend to believe that leisure becomes increasingly important as salaries increase. Following this logic, a worker who is paid by the hour wants to work as many hours as possible—but only up to a point. Once people reach a certain level of income, economists tend to believe, they are more willing to take a vacation. The worker trades labor for leisure, following this argument, so this principle is called the "substitution effect." See Miles S. Kimball and Matthew D. Shapiro, *Labor Supply: Are the Income and Substitution Effects Both Large and Small?* (Cambridge, MA: National Bureau of Economic Research, 2008).

36. Value is of course a notoriously troublesome concept. It has a rather specific valence in the discipline of economics, where it registers as an index and a consequence of maximizing self-interest. Anthropologists and sociologists have questioned this paradigm, however, proposing alternative "standards of value" as the basis of a more holistic inquiry. This theoretical tradition has purchase for showing how people articulate new social networks and for broadening our conception of productive activity, but it has elsewhere made the concept of "value" so vacuous that it is impossible to pin down analytically. Paul K. Eiss and David Pedersen capture the elastic quality of "value" in anthropological parlance in "Value in Circulation," special issue of *Cultural Anthropology* 17 (2002): 283–459: "The category [of value] has been used in varied ways to illuminate ethical, economic, aesthetic, logical, linguistic, and

political dimensions of human life. . . . Value is about measure or meaning; it is material or symbolic, secular or sacred, abstract or concrete, individual or collective, qualitative or quantitative, global or local." Add to this Anson Rabinbach's claim that theories of value reproduce the dubious nineteenth-century belief that civil society is simply the product of human energy, or *Arbeitskraft* (which Marx and others translated into the concept of labor power), and one might not even see the merit in using "value" as part of a critical lexicon; see Anson Rabinbach, *The Human Motor* (Berkeley: University of California Press, 1990).

See David Graeber, Toward *an Anthropological Theory of Value* (New York: Palgrave, 2001), 26; Bronislaw Malinowski, *Argonauts of the Western Pacific* (London: Routledge, 1922), 41; Marshall Sahlins, *Culture and Practical Reason* (Chicago: University of Chicago Press, 1976), 51; Ebony Coletu, "Forms of Submission: Acts of Writing in Moments of Need" (PhD diss., Stanford University, 2007), 52; P. Steven Sangren, *Chinese Sociologics: An Anthropological Account of the Role of Alienation in Social Reproduction* (London: Athlone, 2000), 17; Nancy Munn, *The Fame of Gawa: A Symbolic Study of Value Transformation in a Massim (Papua New Guinea) Society* (Cambridge: Cambridge University Press, 1986), 216; Albert C. Whitaker, *History and Criticism of the Labor Theory of Value* (New York: Columbia University Press, 1904); C. R. B. Menon, *Value Economics* (Calcutta: Oxford Book and Stationery, 1960); Jeffrey T. Young, *Classical Theories of Value: From Smith to Sraffa* (Boulder, CO: Westview Press, 1978); Arjun Appadurai, "Introduction: Commoditization and the Politics of Value," in *The Social Life of Things*, ed. Arjun Appadurai (Philadelphia: University of Pennsylvania Press, 1986), 14; Paul K. Eiss and David Pedersen, "Introduction: Values of Value," in "Value in Circulation," special issue of *Cultural Anthropology* 17 (2002): 24; and Terence Turner, "Value, Production, and Exploitation in Non-capitalist Societies," paper presented at the eighty-second annual meeting of the American Anthropological Association, Denver, Colorado, 1984.

With specific reference to postindependence Africa, these issues are thoughtfully teased out in economic anthropologist Keith Hart's dissertation fieldwork concerning what he considered to be an "informal economy" in Ghana, and in scholarship that has debated the analytic purchase of such a concept, including Hart's own later work. See Keith Hart, "Informal Income Opportunities and Urban Employment in Ghana," *Journal of Modern African Studies* 11, no. 1 (1973): 61–89; Kate Meagher, "Crisis, Informalization, and the Urban Informal Sector in Sub-Saharan Africa," *Development and Change* 26, no. 2 (April 1995): 259–84; Alejandro Portes, "The Informal Economy and Its Paradoxes," in *Handbook of Economic Sociology*, ed. Neil J. Smelser and Richard Swedberg (Princeton, NJ: Princeton University Press, 1994), 426–49; Keith Hart, "Market and State after the Cold War: The Informal Economy Reconsidered," in *Contesting Markets: Analyses of Ideology, Discourse and Practice*, ed. Roy Dilley (Edinburgh: Edinburgh University Press, 1992), 214–26.

37. The concept of value is tied to the development of nineteenth-century thermodynamics and theories about the conservation of energy developed, most prominently, by Herman von Helmholtz. For Helmholtz, energy could not be created out of nothing; it could only be transferred from one form to the next. Based on this insight, he coined the term *Arbeitskraft* for the smallest detectable unit of force. Still, that "value" has its basis in nineteenth-century mechanics need not invalidate this perspective or serve as the sole basis on which a theory of "creative action" (Graeber, *Theory of Value*) can be constituted. Productive activity always begins with actors' efforts to reorganize their

worlds. This invariably involves the expenditure of something like human energy in the transformation of existing circumstances. See Rabinbach, *Human Motor*, 55.

38. More than a "labor theory of value" (that awkward and unclear concept derived from a prevalent misreading of the argument Karl Marx outlines in *Capital*, vol. 1), I have in mind something like what Diane Elson calls "a value theory of labor"—a theory of labor that builds on moments when creative action works to articulate new social networks. See Diane Elson, "The Value Theory of Labor," in *Value: The Representation of Labour in Capitalism*, ed. Diane Elson (London: CSE, 1979), 115—80.

39. Turner, "Value, Production, and Exploitation," 17. Graeber, *Theory of Value*, 143.

40. In this regard, Senegalese attaya forms an instructive counterpoint to Piya Chatterjee's work on feminized circuits of tea cultivation and circulation involving South Asian women. Piya Chatterjee, *A Time for Tea: Women, Labor, and Post/colonial Politics on an Indian Plantation* (Durham, NC: Duke University Press, 2001).

41. Graeber, *Theory of Value*, 7–9.

42. Insightful discussions of the disquette include the work of Beth Anne Buggenhagen (originally in her dissertation, "At Home in the Black Atlantic," then in her manuscript *Muslim Families in Global Senegal: Money Takes Care of Shame* [Bloomington: Indiana University Press, 2011]), and Francis Nyamnjoh, "Madams and Maids in Southern Africa: Coping with Uncertainties, and the Art of Mutual Zombification," *Afrika Spectrum* 40 (2005): 181–96.

43. When I asked unemployed young men if they were married, they would invariably reply, "Who me? I don't have anything!"

44. Cole, *Forget Colonialism?*, 1.

45. Thus even under conditions where the "spatial form"—in this case, the geography of dispossessed youth in urban Dakar—"controls temporality [and where] an imagined geography controls the possibility of social change and history[,] not all forms of temporality are [necessarily] erased." David Harvey, *Spaces of Hope* (Berkeley: University of California Press, 2000), 160. In such a context, Harvey continues, "the time of 'eternal return,' of recurrent ritual, is preserved"—especially in local contexts where youth perfect the art of attaya. Note that by referring to attaya variously as an "art object," a "craft," and an "aesthetic," I am deliberately rejecting the distinction that obtains in many discussions of "high" versus "low" art. Instead, I am attentive to the regimes of expertise that young men develop and rely on as well as their sustained attention to work of producing attaya.

46. Zhang Zhen, "Mediating Time: 'The Rice Bowl of Youth' in Fin de Siècle Urban China," *Public Culture* 12 (2000): 99.

47. Will Ross, "Senegalese Hope Election Brings Jobs," *British Broadcast News Online*, February 24, 2007, news.bbc.co.uk/2/hi/africa/6394009.stm.

CODA

1. Bernd Beber and Alexandra Scacco, "What the Numbers Say: A Digit-Based Test for Election Fraud," *Political Analysis* 20, no. 2 (Spring 2012): 211–34.

2. See CNN Wire Staff, "Senegal Unveils Colossal Statue amidst Criticism," April 3, 2010, www.cnn.com/2010/WORLD/africa/04/03/senegal.statue/index.html, accessed January 30, 2012.

3. See WikiLeaks cable published February 18, 2010, http://wikileaks.org, accessed January 30, 2012. A representative for Wade would ultimately acknowledge that the deal was in part made possible by a land concession but insisted this transaction

was for the good of "Senegalese children," even as critics rebelled against the self-aggrandizement they attributed to this project. See CNN Wire Staff, "Senegal Unveils Colossal Statue."

4. Radio France International, "Sénégal: Le pays enquête de son argent détourné," June 9, 2012, http://fr.allafrica.com/stories/printable/201206110482.html, accessed February 12, 2013.

5. Jeanne Koopmann, "Land Grabs, Government, Peasant and Civil Society Activism in the Senegal River Valley," *Review of African Political Economy* 39, no. 134 (December 2012): 655–64.

6. Demba Moussa Dembélé, *Dette et destruction au Sénégal: Une étude sur vingt années de mise en oeuvre des politiques de la Banque Mondiale et du Fonds Monétaire International*, World Development Movement, http://www.liberationafrique.org/IMG/pdf/senegal debt.pdf, accessed February 12, 2013.

7. Koopman, "Land Grabs," 656; Phillipe Lavigne Delville, "Migration et structuration associative," in *La vallée du fleuve Sénégal: Évaluations et perspectives d'une décennie d'aménagements*, ed. Bernard Crousse, Paul Mathieu, and Sidy Mohamed Seck (Paris: Karthala, 1991), 117–39.

8. Iba Mar Fall et al., *Les acquisitions de terres à grande échelle au Sénégal: Description d'un nouveau phénomène* (Dakar: Initiative Prospective Agricole et Rurale, 2011). See also Koopman, "Land Grabs," 658.

9. Koopman, "Land Grabs," 659.

10. Ibid., 660.

INDEX